DATE DUE

Yeats
the
Playwright

A Commentary on
Character and Design
in the Major Plays

by

PETER URE

New York
Barnes & Noble, Inc.

First published in Great Britain 1963
Reprinted 1969
Published in the United States of America by
Barnes & Noble, Inc.
105 Fifth Avenue, New York, N.Y. 10003

Printed in Great Britain

Contents

Preface

SINCE my first book on Yeats was published sixteen years ago I have learnt much from many distinguished students of Yeats's poetry; but to Birgit Bjersby (*The Interpretation of the Cuchulain Legend in the Works of W. B. Yeats*), Giorgio Melchiori (articles later incorporated in his *The Whole Mystery of Art*), Thomas Parkinson (*W. B. Yeats: Self-Critic*), and F. A. C. Wilson (*W. B. Yeats and Tradition*), all of whom have written at length on the plays, I am more particularly indebted in the writing of this book. I regret that Mr. Wilson's second book, *Yeats's Iconography* appeared after the greater part of my work was done, as did an excellent brief account, with superb illustrations, by D. J. Gordon and Ian Fletcher, in *W. B. Yeats: Images of a Poet*. Some portions of this book (Chapter I in part, Chapter III, Chapter VI, and a section of Chapter VII) have appeared previously in periodicals and I am grateful to the editors and publishers of *The Modern Language Review*, *English Studies*, *The Review of English Studies*, and *The Huntington Library Quarterly* for permission to revise and reprint them. Thanks are due to the following for permission to reprint copyright material: Mrs. W. B. Yeats and Messrs. Macmillan and Co. for passages from the works of W. B. Yeats; Mrs. Yeats and Rupert Hart-Davis for passages from *The Letters of W. B. Yeats*, edited by Allan Wade; Messrs. Faber and Faber for a passage from *The Translations of Ezra Pound*.

P. U.

Introduction

Yeats's plays have not, generally speaking, been much regarded by his modern critics. They have tended to judge the earlier ones (1889–1906) as flaccid and sentimental, and the later ones (1915–38) as barbarous, remote, theatrically impractical, or merely puzzling. This commentary attempts to consider their strengths and weaknesses in plot, characterization, and the handling of morals and ideas. The unit of discussion throughout the book is the individual play. This method has been chosen because it seemed the best way of making the book a supplement to the reading of the plays themselves. No one reads through the *Collected Plays* from start to finish except at the risk of bewilderment and mental indigestion. But a reader may look at a play here and there in the volume, or study a group of like-minded plays, and he may then find it useful to test his impressions by a critical account of what he has read. What is offered here, therefore, is a critical handbook or companion to some features of the plays rather than an attempt to judge and arrange them all in the light of a dominant theory.

The arrangement adopted recognizes that the plays tend to be read in groups, although these will not necessarily be the same for every reader, or constituted on the same principles. The order of discussion is not, except in the first and shorter Part, a chronological one, but I have supplied in an Appendix a brief guide to the order in which the plays were written, performed, and printed. In the second Part the plays are grouped according to theme and subject-matter: Cuchulain, life-in-death, Christianity, the Unicorn and the 'beast' (the last collocation I borrow from Professor G. Melchiori). This method seems to avoid the risk of there being

I

too much repetition in what it is necessary to say about Yeats's philosophical mythology. It is also, of course, a risk to put together into the same chapter plays which differ from one another in form so clearly as do, for example, *Purgatory* and *The Words upon the Window-pane*; but it sometimes makes it possible to stress the formal experimentation and variety which Yeats went in for when he was writing for the theatre, and, it is hoped, to bring out important differences in construction and characterization.

I have also felt free, as a commentator, rather than a writer with any very confident prepossessions about what modern poetic drama ought to be, to consider these groups of plays with the aid of techniques and criteria which are not necessarily compatible with one another. These have been applied where they were most useful and then abandoned even when to continue to apply them would have seemed more thorough and consistent. Thus, in the first two chapters, on *The Countess Cathleen* and *The King's Threshold*, there is a great deal about the variant texts of these two heavily revised plays. Study of the revisions could have been continued on much the same scale for a number of other plays, because Yeats was a constant reviser of his plays as of his poems, but the character of his work in this kind is such that the result would have been more of a book about Yeats as a reviser than a companion to the reading of his plays. But I wanted to discuss other matters as well in the chapters that follow: the relation between dramatic theory and dramatic practice in Chapter III, Yeats as an ironist in Chapter IV, the relation (and the difference) between the philosophical mythologist and the playwright in Chapter V, between remoteness and realism in Chapter VI, between theme and image in Chapter VII. All these—and many others suggest themselves—are matters which could be used to establish a thesis which might hold good for all of the plays. Perhaps one or other of them is the ingenious tool which could force Yeats to divulge his secret. But none of them is pursued here to more than a provisional conclusion because it seems more important at the present stage of Yeats's reputation as a playwright to subordinate them to an attempt to describe one by one the organization of the plays. The naïvete and eclecticism of this manner of proceeding, together with its inevitable mass of unexamined and unconscious critical assumptions, may justly displease those who feel that the time has come for Yeats to be firmly placed in the history of the development of poetic drama. But this book is written in the conviction that Yeats's plays—even those earlier ones which are now dismissed as pseudo-Elizabethan or post-Maeterlinckian, and certainly those later ones of which the last were written only a couple of decades ago—need to be lived with a little longer as individual works of art, and more intensively than they have been, before they are fitted into any consistent scheme.

It is for similar reasons that I have not written about the poetry of the plays as such. A great deal of material lies ready to hand for such an exercise, not least those transpositions from prose into verse represented by alternative versions of *The Hour-Glass, The Golden Helmet, The King of the Great Clock Tower*, and other plays or portions of plays. But sooner or later any enquiry runs foul of current arguments about the principles, needs, and desirability of poetic drama on the modern stage. No one can deny the probable relevance of Yeats's precepts and practice to these arguments; but both are of such a kind that they will be found more often to conflict than to accord with the formulae at present dominant, nearly all of which have been contrived by Mr. Eliot, the other great poet of the century who has written poetry for the English-speaking stage. Yeats, for example, was willing to mingle verse and prose in the same play, and this directly contravenes one of Eliot's laws; he often wrote Shakespearian or Jacobean blank verse (when it is not more like Dryden's), and whether this was a fatal error or a just and natural recognition of its usefulness can hardly be discussed until the rigour which is appeased only by the employment of non-Shakespearian rhythms can be relaxed. Disagreements of this kind are so far-reaching that, although separation must, in the end, appear artificial, they are best handled independently of the attempt to describe construction, theme, and character.

The term 'major plays', although evaluative, is not intended to be taken very seriously as such, but chiefly as an indication that not all the plays are discussed here. I have left out *The Island of Statues* (1885) and *Mosada* (1886), the juvenile lyrical dramas which Yeats did not reprint in the definitive edition of his poetry. Of the other plays written before 1906, I have omitted *The Land of Heart's Desire, Cathleen ni Houlihan, The Hour-Glass, The Pot of*

Broth, and *The Shadowy Waters.* The first and the last of these seem too closely connected with the poetry of that time to be usefully discussed independently of it, and *The Shadowy Waters* has also had the advantage of a very full treatment in Professor Parkinson's *W. B. Yeats Self-Critic* (1951); the others are best thought of in relation to the full reassessment of the work of Lady Gregory that one hopes will some day be written. I have discussed at greater or less length all the plays written or finished after 1915, except *The Cat and the Moon* and the translations from Sophocles.

It is, unfortunately, the reader rather than the theatregoer who has to assume the burden of deciding whether or not they are 'major' in a grander sense. It is difficult to make bold claims for them as plays for the theatre, because the modern theatre has simply decided that they cannot be fitted in. This judgement would be more worthy of respect if it did not extend to the work of such masters of the stage and audience as Jonson, Middleton, and (on this side of the Atlantic) Shaw. It is more understandable in the case of Yeats, who created his own instrument and traditions, which were dissipated when their constituent persons went their ways.

> But actors lacking music
> Do most excite my spleen,
> They say it is more human
> To shuffle, grunt and groan,
> Not knowing what unearthly stuff
> Rounds a mighty scene,
> > *Said the man in the golden breastplate*
> > *Under the old stone Cross.*

But there is still the obligation, entailed upon those who wish to understand his art, to try to measure his plays by those criteria, infinitely slippery though they are, which are appropriate to works written for performance by actors before an audience. It is at least an important fact about this great lyric poet that he should have continued to labour so long at 'plays That have to be set up in fifty ways', and that he should have felt that he *needed* a theatre:

I believe myself to be a dramatist; I desire to show events and not merely tell of them; and two of my best friends were won for me

4

by my plays, and I seem to myself most alive at the moment when a room full of people share the one lofty emotion.

It is possible that the dramatist in Yeats was merely the stalking-horse of the symbolist poet and the philosophical mythologist. But the evidence, though it is far from clear, is also far from being all in favour of that opinion, and it is hoped that this book gives some reasons why.

If this book can serve at all as a supplement, it is intended for *The Collected Plays of W. B. Yeats*, first issued in 1934 (second enlarged edition 1952), the only collection still kept in print. For various reasons, such as the need to investigate variant texts, and Yeats's Introductions and Notes (all omitted from *Collected Plays*), my work has normally been with the earlier editions, of which the most important are *Four Plays for Dancers* (1921), *Plays . . . for an Irish Theatre* (1922), *Plays and Controversies* (1923), and *Wheels and Butterflies* (1934), all now out of print. The student will presumably need to consult these on occasions when the general reader does not. My quotations are normally from the texts in the volumes named and in others earlier still. Although, when discussing a particular play in the section or chapter devoted to it, I have always indicated which text (or texts) of it I am using, I have not usually supplied a page-reference for each successive quotation from the play under discussion. This has been done in order to avoid an excessive accumulation of such references and in the belief that, because the plays are so short, it is not difficult for readers wishing to look up the passage in its context to find it in *Collected Plays* or in one of the other volumes. References for all quotations and allusions not of this particular kind are of course supplied.

PART ONE: APPLIED ARTS

I disliked the isolation of the work of art. I wished
through the drama, through a commingling of verse
and dance, through singing that was also speech,
through what I called the applied arts of literature,
to plunge it back into social life.

*—Pages from a Diary
Written in Nineteen Hundred and Thirty*

Chapter One

A Counter-Truth

THE COUNTESS CATHLEEN

I

'YEATS was there, listening reverentially to the sound of his own verses', wrote George Moore in *Ave*, and went on to give an account of his own sensations during the famous first week of *The Countess Cathleen* in May, 1899. Writing ten years after the event, he was able to charge them with that delightful note of ironic bewilderment which became him so well and made the fortune of his masterpiece. Earlier, he had written more brutally about the defects of the performance:

The Countess Cathleen met with every disadvantage. Here is a list which must not, however, be considered exhaustive. First, the author's theory that verse should be chanted and not spoken; second, the low platform insufficiently separated from the audience; third, a set of actors and actresses unaccustomed to speak verse; fourth, harsh, ridiculous scenery; fifth, absurd costumes. . . . Many times I prayed during the last act that the curtain might come down at once.[1]

Although Moore was unimpressed by the group of professional players which Florence Farr had brought from London, including the young May Whitty in the part of the Countess, he claimed that the intense beauty of the play was not completely obscured by its representation. In the gloomy, improvised Dublin concert room it awakened in him 'just such a sense of beauty as I have

B   9

experienced in dim museums, looking at some worn and broken bas-relief'.

The police were present—twenty men and a sergeant, according to Yeats[2]—to discourage those who, stimulated by the pamphlet *Souls for Gold! Pseudo-Celtic Drama in Dublin*, were determined to suppress heresy:

The accusation made was that it was a libel on the people of Ireland to say they could under any circumstances consent to sell their souls and that it was a libel on the demons that they counted the soul of a countess more worth than those of the poor.[3]

There were other signs that the occasion was historic. The Dublin *Daily Express*, under the editorship of T. P. Gill, had during that same month of May reprinted as a booklet the contributions which John Eglinton, Yeats, and A. E. had made to its columns the previous autumn about whether or not the ancient Irish legends constituted proper material for a modern Irish poet. A. E. had closed the discussion with his argument that to use the heroic legends was to fight on behalf of Irish nationality against the cosmopolitan spirit which was rapidly obliterating all distinctions. Such an obliterator, according to A. E., was Professor Dowden. Yeats, with greater circumspection, had named Goethe, Wordsworth, and Browning as poets of utilitarianism and rhetoric, through whom poetry had given up 'the right to consider all things in the world as a dictionary of types and symbols'. 'The other path'—so ran A. E.'s appeal—the path of nationality and myth and dream,

winds spirally upwards to a mountain-top of our own, which may be in the future the Meru to which many worshippers will turn.[4]

'This was a stirring row', Yeats commented later, '. . . and we were all very angry'.[5] Nationality, *The Countess Cathleen*, and the Irish themes were at the same time making an appeal of some historic importance to two other members of the audience in the Antient Concert Rooms: the brothers William and Frank Fay were more magnanimous than George Moore:

We liked it very much and thought the company gave an excellent performance, one thing being very noticeable—the admirable delivery of Mr. Yeats's verse, which was not so speakable then as in his later plays for he had had little experience of writing for the stage. . . . It was this performance of *The Countess Cathleen* that first suggested the idea of the company that eventually became known as the Irish Players. When Frank and I left the hall we were enthusiastic about what we had just seen. We had enough personal experience to be able to allow for the loss the play suffered through having its production on a 'fit-up' stage and in a hall that was not intended for dramatic entertainment. Yet even so there seemed to be something missing. What was it? Then it suddenly flashed upon me that what was wrong with the performance was that, though the artists were most efficient, they were not Irish. To get the full value of the play one must have native actors. . . . Frank quite agreed with me, but he very pertinently asked, 'Where in Ireland could you get any company of actors that could compare with those we have just seen?' [6]

It was because the Fays, Yeats, and Lady Gregory contrived to answer this question between them that Yeats got, for a lifetime at least, access to a living theatre.

All that glory and excitement have faded now, and *The Countess Cathleen*, with its careful piety and mannered exaltation, has faded too. 'It was not, nor is it now, more than a piece of tapestry,' Yeats remarked.[7] As it lies folded in the mouth of the standard edition of the Collected Plays, dated 1892 with seriously misleading pedantry, it is a dragon without much fire left in its belly. But an examination of its genesis and history still has something to reveal about Yeats as a dramatic craftsman. An intelligible map of the first of his two phases of dramatic work, that which extends from *The Countess Cathleen* to *Deirdre*, cannot be drawn without such aid as it supplies. In the help it gives towards delineating the phase, which comprises only four other major plays (*The Shadowy Waters*, *On Baile's Strand*, *The King's Threshold*, *Deidre*), it shows how Yeats came to recognize, despite a good deal of resistance, some of the limits and bounds of his craft.

II

The reverence and intentness which Moore observed in Yeats as he listened to Florence Farr and her company arose from Yeats's determination to discover what could and could not be done in

the theatre. He wrote towards the end of his first period as playwright:

> Every one who has to interest his audience through the voice discovers
> that his success depends upon the clear, simple and varied structure of
> his thought. I have written a good many plays in verse and prose, and
> almost all those plays I have rewritten after performance, sometimes
> again and again, and every re-writing that has succeeded upon the
> stage has been an addition to the masculine element, an increase of
> strength in the bony structure.[8]

Describing Yeats's evolution as a playwright would be a simpler
business than it is if this and similar observations could be taken as
a safe guide through the labyrinth of the different versions of *The
Countess Cathleen*. All that it would then be necessary to do would
be to look for and acclaim the gradual emergence of structural
order out of the monotony and effeminacy and 'strained lyricism'
for which Yeats in the same passage censured William Morris,
contrasting *The Earthly Paradise* with *The Canterbury Tales* and
blaming Morris for being 'too continuously lyrical in his understanding of emotion and life'. And much later, Yeats described the
1889 version of *The Countess Cathleen* as 'ill-constructed, the
dialogue turning aside at the lure of word or metaphor, very
different, I hope, from the play as it is to-day after many alterations, every alteration tested by performance'.[9]

The history of *The Countess Cathleen*, so far as it can be examined by means of the printed texts, does not entirely confirm
this version of events. There were in the revisions of the play more
indirection and resistance and regression than will admit of any
very clear progress from lyrical effeminacy to masculine strength.
Sometimes, indeed, the expected process seems to go into reverse; a structure originally simple and clear might become
blurred with afterthoughts or strained out of shape by fresh in-
sights. It is a story of loss as well as gain. The gain is hardly to be
measured by any version, even the final version (if finality was
ever reached) of *The Countess Cathleen* itself, but by what Yeats
achieved when he tackled fresh themes and abandoned for the
time the Countess's singularly obdurate story.

The version which aroused such passions in the Antient Concert
Rooms was the third of five major revisions. The record of

revision,* extending over nearly thirty years, is lengthier than that of *The Shadowy Waters* or of any other play by Yeats. Only an edition which printed all the *varia* could justly show the full extent of the minor alterations, which are by no means confined to the four occasions, in 1895, 1901, 1912, and 1919, when the play underwent major revision. But I shall confine this discussion mostly to the first version and to the first text of each of its four successors. The table on pages 14–15 is a convenient, if graceless, way of providing a basis for considering how much, and how little, the alterations affected the story, shape, and construction of the play.

Its genesis was laborious, from March, 1889, until October, 1891. Various references to it in the letters show that it was from the first conceived as a stage-play, never as a purely lyrical drama. There were two other matters that influenced its design in 1889–92. The first of these was the idea of it as a counter or contrast to the recently published *Wanderings of Oisin* (1889). In 1892 Yeats wrote of the play as:

an attempt to mingle personal thought and feeling with the beliefs and customs of Christian Ireland; whereas the longest poem in my earlier book endeavoured to set forth the impress left on my imagination by the Pre-Christian cycle of legends. The Christian cycle being mainly concerned with contending moods and moral motives needed,

* Yeats planned out and began to write *The Countess Cathleen* in February/March, 1889 (*Letters*, pp. 108, 114), and it was first printed in *The Countess Kathleen and Various Legends and Lyrics* (1892). In March, 1894, *The Land of Heart's Desire* was presented in London as a curtain-raiser for *Arms and the Man*. It was the first play by Yeats to be produced on any stage. In the light of this experience Yeats revised and expanded the earlier play and printed this version in *Poems*,1895. The play was again revised for the Dublin production in 1899; this version, the third, was first printed in *Poems*, 1901. (A copy of *Poems*, 1899, in the Huntington Library preserves the autograph revisions made for the performance, and the Huntington also has the typescript of the enlarged third Act: see Parkinson, p. 188.) This version appeared in *Poems*, 1904, in *The Poetical Works of William B. Yeats* (New York, 1907), in *Poems*, 1908, and, for the last time, in volume III of the Stratford-on-Avon *Collected Works* (1908). The fourth version—which is sometimes erroneously described as the final version (for example, by Henn, p. 30)—was first printed in 1912 as Volume I of 'Dublin Plays' and in *Poems*, 1912. After this the play was revised again: the texts in *Poems* 1919, and *Plays and Controversies* (1923) represent this fifth version.

REVISION OF THE COUNTESS CATHLEEN

*A: This indicates scenes in which Aleel (Kevin in 1892) appears

1892 Countess Kathleen and Various Legends and Lyrics	1895 Poems, 1895 & 1899	1901 Poems, 1901, 1904, 1908, Poetical Works (New York), 1907, Collected Works (Stratford-on-Avon), 1908	1912 'Dublin Plays' edition and Poems, 1912	1919 Poems, 1919 Plays & Controversies, 1923 Collected Plays, 1934, &c.
SCENE I — The inn of Shemus Rua called 'The Lady's Head'; the starving family (Shemus, Mary and their son Teig); the entry of the two Demon-Merchants and their offer to buy souls.	*A ACT I — Adds entry of the Countess with Aleel; her charity; Aleel's song ('Impetuous heart, be still').	*A ACT I	*A SCENE I — Completely re-written, but with episodes as in 1895.	*A SCENE I — New song for Aleel ('Were I but crazy for love sake') replaces 'Impetuous heart, be still'.
SCENE II — The Castle Hall; the Countess and Oona; servants bring news of theft and disorder; two peasants bring news of the traffic in souls; the Countess instructs her steward to sell her lands and distribute her money to all suppliants.	ACT II [Part i]	ACT II	*A SCENE II — Completely re-written, using episodes of 1892 in shorter form. Adds new scene for Aleel, Countess of Oona in place of passages for Countess and Oona only in 1892.	*A SCENE II
SCENE III — The Castle Hall; the Demon-Merchants discuss their progress so far; they rob the	ACT II [Part ii]	*A ACT III — Adds (at beginning of the Act) the love-scene for the Countess and Aleel.	*A SCENE III — Robbery-scene re-written in shortened form.	*A SCENE III — Robbery scene cut to a few words and actions; all supernatural aides eliminated.

treasure-house and summon spirits and lost souls to aid them in carrying away the bags of treasure; the Countess enters and talks with them about the state of the land; but their identity is not recognized until the theft is discovered after they have left; the Countess gives her last directions to her servants.			SCENE IV A new scene for Demon-Merchants and Peasants on their way to the market [18 lines, excluding S.D.s].	SCENE IV *A Demon-Merchants re-placed by song for Aleel ('Impetuous heart, be still', be still').
SCENES IV & V *A SCENE IV: Merchants and Peasants traffic in souls; Kevin attempts to sell his soul but it is refused; the Countess enters and sells her soul; the scene ends with the triumphant disappearance of the Merchants ('Leap, feathered, on the air . . .').

(No scene-division.)

Completely re-written as Aleel's vision.

SCENE V: Oona's vision. | ACT III *A | ACT IV *A | SCENE V *A

[Modified for 1911 revival.] | SCENE V *A |

I thought, a dramatic vehicle. The tumultuous and heroic Pagan cycle, on the other hand, having to do with vast and shadowy activities and with the great impersonal emotions, expressed itself naturally—or so I imagined—in epic and epic-lyric measures. No epic method seemed sufficiently minute and subtle for the one, and no dramatic method elastic and all-containing enough for the other.[10]

The writing and thinking here seem clumsy, but Yeats did not lightly abandon anything having to do with *The Countess Cathleen*, a play which gave him 'more pleasure in the memory than any of my plays'.[11] The cumbrous distinctions of the 1892 Preface took fire nearly half a century later in the majestic lines of 'The Circus Animals' Desertion':

> What can I but enumerate old themes?
> First that sea-rider Oisin led by the nose
> Through three enchanted islands, allegorical dreams,
> Vain gaiety, vain battle, vain repose,
> Themes of the embittered heart, or so it seems,
> That might adorn old songs and courtly shows;
> But what cared I that set him on to ride,
> I, starved for the bosom of his faery bride?
>
> And then a counter-truth filled out its play,
> *The Countess Cathleen* was the name I gave it. . . .[12]

The play, then, at its earliest stage was to be dramatic, not epic-lyric, Christian, not Pagan, and was to deal with subtle actions and personal and moral emotions. Here a second influence on its design needs to be taken into account. 'He started', writes Mr. Henn, speaking of the year 1889, '*The Countess Cathleen* . . . the first projection of his own love and despair.'[13] Yeats in 1938 would have agreed with him, for the stanza in 'The Circus Animals' Desertion' continues:

> *The Countess Cathleen* was the name I gave it;
> She, pity-crazed, had given her soul away,
> But masterful Heaven had intervened to save it.
> I thought my dear must her own soul destroy,
> So did fanaticism and hate enslave it. . . .

Hone, too, writes, dating the incident in 1891, that Yeats read to Maud Gonne 'his unpublished *Countess Cathleen* and told her that

she had come to interpret the life of a woman who sells her soul a
a symbol of all souls that lose their peace, their fineness in politics,
serving but change'.[14] It is true that Maud Gonne, whom Yeats
met for the first time on January 30, 1889, shortly after the
publication of *The Wanderings of Oisin*, was very much present in
his mind when the play was begun in March. She was perhaps the
unnamed 'actress' to whom on May 6, 1889, as Yeats told John
O'Leary the following day, he read 'a scene' of the new work:
'She seemed to think it suitable in all ways for the stage. I think
you will like it. It is in all things Celtic and Irish. The style is
perfectly simple and I have taken great care with the construction,
made two complete prose versions before writing a line of
verse.'[15] Much later, according to Maud Gonne, he was still
hoping that she would play the part:

That evening Willie Yeats was sad and tried hard to persuade me to
act the part of Countess Kathleen. 'I wrote it for you and if you don't
act it we shall have to get an actress from London to take the part',
which eventually he did, with no marked success.[16]

The dedication of 1892 went even further: '. . . To My Friend,
Miss Maud Gonne, At whose Suggestion It was Planned out and
Begun. . . .' The statement, though, conflicts with an earlier one,
made in another letter to John O'Leary on February 1, 1889, that
he had 'long been intending to write [a poetic drama with a view
to the stage] founded on the tale of "Countess Kathleen O'Shea"
in the folk lore book'.[17]

The difficulty about accepting Henn's or Hone's or Yeats's own
interpretations (whether of 1891 or 1938) simply as they stand is
that none of the versions of *The Countess Cathleen* offers us a protagonist whose selling of her soul can possibly be interpreted as self-
destruction through fanaticism or hate; nor can the Countess's
bargain, in its context, be easily read as a symbol of the loss of
peace and fineness through political activity. Whatever the part
played by 'personal thought and feeling', as developed in Yeats's
relation to Maud Gonne, in *The Countess Cathleen*, it was much less
forthright than 'The Circus Animals' Desertion' suggests and
much more gradually infiltrated into successive versions than the
story of the play's origin between 1889 and 1891 at first sight
implies. Had the play resembled its description in the poem more

closely it might have proved a more powerful and lasting work. Had the 'personal thought and feeling' been accorded franker recognition in the text from the beginning, instead of gaining admission to it by stages, it might have been an altogether better piece of architecture. And the 'soul-making' Yeats of the later period may well have permitted his repugnance at the idea of anyone's actually giving her soul away 'under any circumstances' to blind him to what he had written.

III

A comparison of the 1892 version with its source makes some things clear. Yeats adopts most of its details with some significant changes of direction: the appearance of the demon-merchants in the poverty-stricken land, their ostentatious display of wealth, Ketty O'Donnor's decision to save the peasants by selling all her treasure, and the consequent frustration of the demons, who decide, therefore, to rob her:

Aidés par un valet infâme, ils pénétrèrent dans la retraite de la noble dame et lui dérobèrent le reste de son trésor . . . en vain lutta-t-elle de toutes ses forces pour sauver le contenu de son coffre, les larrons diaboliques furent les plus forts. Si Ketty avait eu les moyens de faire un signe de croix, ajoute la légende irlandaise, elle les eût mis en fuite, mais ses mains étaient captive—Le larcin fut effectué.[18]

The Countess has no resource left but to sell her own soul for the highest price she can get.

The powerful and self-consistent structure of this fable is present in Yeats's play but the weight of scene and incident rests only lightly upon it. Thus, the passage which has just been quoted seems to provide an obvious opportunity for a dramatist. Even if the rendering of the conflict with the demons as the physical struggle implied in the source might have appeared too external a way of treating it, the plot seems to call here for some surge of the protagonist's will against demonic outrage. Instead, the Countess remains passively in her oratory while the merchants rob her treasure-house, nor does she discover her loss and their identity until after they have fled the scene. The robbery-scene itself, as preserved through several re-writings until it is virtually eliminated after 1912, is an elaborate affair during which the water-spirits and lost souls (sheogues, tevishies, and sowlths—there are variant spellings) carry away the bags of treasure under the compulsion of the demons. That this kind of thing should be substituted for the more direct encounter with the Countess (and that that suggestive figure the 'valet infâme' should disappear altogether) is in part a concession to Yeats's desire to make his drama 'in all things Celtic and Irish'. This was undoubtedly one of the factors that influenced his treatment of his source.

But, perhaps more important, the Countess's altered role here points directly at an element in the play for which Yeats had no warrant in his source. The original story stresses conflict between the saint and the demonic powers. It was open to Yeats to dramatize this as an outward and inward struggle in and for the soul and body of his protagonist, and in particular to represent her final decision to sacrifice her soul as the outcome of a profound and agonizing προαίρεσις. This is what the critics of the play were dismayed to find largely missing from it. Yeats must have known what was said by the first man to write a book about him, who affirmed in 1904, with (presumably) the version of 1901 in mind, that there was

no obstinate struggle of opposing notions in the soul of Cathleen herself, and no stirring dramatic conflict between the forces of good and evil. . . . The dramatic knot is tied and untied in the simplest way . . . the climax scene is not made the most of dramatically.[19]

But this criticism misses the point in so far as it fails to observe how Yeats was deliberately re-shaping his material. For his Countess the interior conflict is not between the need to sacrifice and the desire to save her soul; her trouble begins at an earlier stage. It has to do with the war between dreams and responsibility, between the land of pagan images of Fergus and Adene, Usheen, young Neave and the Fenians on one side and the 'burden of the world's wrongs', the famine, and the starving peasantry on the other. It is in this sense that *The Countess Cathleen* is a 'counter-truth' to *The Wanderings of Oisin*. In that poem Oisin finally chooses the Fenians and rejects St. Patrick; in the play the Countess reverses this choice. In the 1892 version her reluctance to do this is rendered in Scene ii:

O, I am sadder than an old air, Oona,
My heart is longing for a deeper peace
Than Fergus found amid his brazen cars:
Would that like Adene my first forebear's daughter
Who followed once a twilight piercing tune,
I could go down and dwell among the Shee
In their old ever-busy honeyed land.

But her peace is interrupted three times: by the Gardener with his
news of pillaged orchards, by the Herdsman with his news of
stolen sheep, and finally by the peasants with their news of the
Mephistophelean bargaining. When once her peace has been
destroyed by this last manifest claim for succour, such 'struggle of
opposing notions' as is allowed for by the design is over. Her
charity takes a plain course and surmounts the ultimate test of it;
we hear no more about that in herself which alone could have
made it falter—the longing for, in Oona's words in the 1895
version, 'a soft cradle of old tales, And songs, and music'. The
dramatist interprets his task, after her first and last renunciation
has been made, as simply to render as veraciously and spiritedly as
possible the tale of the demon-merchants and how they are finally
cheated of the Countess's soul.

This is unexpected, but it has a pace and logic of its own. It is
the element in the play which is most easily to be identified with the
'personal thought and feeling' mentioned in the 1892 Preface.
Flight into the artifice of dream 'under quiet boughs apart' is a
constant theme of the lyrics in the volumes of 1889 and 1892.
There is little reason to suppose that the first version of Cathleen
would have been any different had Yeats and Maud Gonne never
met. For what the Countess there embodies is thematic material
which had already found expression in the lyrics. If she is to be
identified with anyone it is with those fictive voices rather than
with a living woman.

But with later versions it is another matter. Yeats had begun by
introducing an emphasis alien to his source and by refusing sug-
gestions that might have appealed to a dramatist less concerned
with the personal and the subtle. It was this re-making of the
'conflict between the forces of good and evil' into a hinted
choice between dreams and responsibility that was to grow progressively into a much more elaborate structure. It changed and

expanded until it can fairly be said that some symbolic adumbration of Yeats's notions about Maud Gonne and about beautiful women who betray themselves by climbing on wagonettes to scream can, by the eye of faith, be discerned in it. It can at least be said that the Countess, who began as a *persona*, in some degree, of Yeats himself, began to look much more like a heroic mask modelled from Maud Gonne's noble lineaments. But for the critic of the play this is not the primary issue: his task is rather to decide whether the new growth didn't mortally injure the old tale. Its roots begin to split the old foundation, like those of a tree growing upon a ruin. Did the foundations, already rendered dramatically less robust than they might have been, simply crack, and bring themselves and their parasite down in mutual disorder?

IV

The new element, as it expanded, did not mean that Yeats simply yielded to an appetite for what bore upon 'personal thought and feeling' without regard for his structure as a whole and for the needs of the theatre as he came to understand them better. The changes in 1895, indeed, attempt chiefly to devise a better final scene and a more efficient narrative.

The entry of the Countess, Aleel, and the Musicians in Act I was written into the 1895 version. This episode was retained in all subsequent versions, although it was entirely re-drafted along with the rest of the Act in 1912. While it does not tell us very much about the new characters, and while the necessity which it imposes upon the Countess to call on one of her cottagers in order to find the way to her own Castle is a trifle grotesque, the episode can be justified in two ways. The difference between them provides an insight into the curious economies practised by Yeats in the work of revising. On one level, the entry of the Countess and her crowd of 'fantastically dressed musicians' into the hunger-bitten cottage, her charity (ineffective), and Aleel's lyrical insouciance, as well as the whole pictorial stage-contrast between real rags and gorgeous livery, foreshadow what is later to be the Countess's choice: retreat into the artifice of fable or acknowledgement of a land where people die of hunger, their mouths 'green with dock and dandelion'. Here is an early example of the handling of counter-truths of which Yeats never wearied. On another level, it must have seemed an advantage to introduce the Countess at an earlier stage than the opening of the second Act. This risked breaking up the action that, in the 1892 version, leads straight from starvation-induced despair to the entry of the demon-merchants; a parable, complete in itself, about the irruption of supernatural evil into the heart and hearth. But Yeats apparently preferred to interweave his first and second Acts more efficiently at the cost of losing some sharpness of effect within the first Act itself. This cannot have been his only motive for the alteration. For this new episode is also related to the new ending of the 1895 version of the play.

Scene v in 1892 concludes with Oona's vision of the angelic spirits. In 1895 this was transformed into the far more elaborate war-in-heaven and apotheosis, and these are mediated to us not by Oona but by Aleel. As the 1895 version stands, the only previous appearance of Aleel before the last Act was in the new episode of the first Act. His place there is justified because it would never have done for Aleel to be introduced to us for the first time at the end of the play, since curiosity about this new personage would have deflected our attention from the visionary scenes of which he is the agent and interpreter. As, in versions after 1895, the part of Aleel is expanded still further and he appears in more and more scenes, this argument in defence of the new episode in Act I becomes much less cogent. By 1901 we have already seen quite enough of Aleel in the earlier part of the play to accept him as the visionary of the last Act without wondering how he comes to be there at all or who he is. Yeats could have afforded, so far as the coherence of his narrative was in question, to eliminate in later versions the new episode in Act I and give back to the Act the driving unity and sinister logic that make the 1892 version of it structurally better than any of the later ones. This is an example of a feature which seems at one stage of the revision to be acceptable and necessary, but at another to become, in the course of the play's evolution, something that we could do without.

The new ending of 1895 was, apart from a few minor changes, retained in all subsequent versions. In so far as it gratifies expectation by giving the Countess a death-bed and not just a funeral, it is undoubtedly more effective than the final scene was in 1892.

But in lyrical elaboration, mythological allusions, and scenic effects it far surpasses anything in the earliest version, and moves away from simplicity and 'masculinity'. Just as does the new episode in Act I, with its pictorial contrast between rags and splendour, so this scene, with its knightly angels 'as impossibly tall as one of those figures at Chartres Cathedral',[20] reminds us of Arthur Symons's belief, shared by Yeats,[21] that

> If we take drama with any seriousness, as an art as well as an improvisation, we shall realize that one of its main requirements is that it should make pictures.[22]

All this proved too much for the stage at Yeats's disposal. For the revival of 1911 he was forced to produce something less elaborate.[23] And although Lennox Robinson thought well of it,[24] the result seems timid and constrained, simplified rather than simple, and marked by concessions of which John O'Leary would have disapproved, such as the substitution of Belial for Balor. Yeats did not print this more practical solution in his text, but relegated it to an appendix. Why did he not go back, at least for theatrical purposes, to the version of 1892? It has certain virtues, even though the speeches of the Angel about the Countess's acceptance into heaven have not yet attained their classic form. There is much to be said, so far as dramatic suggestion goes, for the way Oona finds the owl-feathers of the demons scattered upon the steps of the oratory:

> some bird,
> Some hawk or kestrel, chased its prey to this.

This conveys, with suggestive brevity, the war between demon and angel upon which, in the later versions, Aleel's speeches insist with something of the 'strained lyricism' that Yeats found so objectionable in Morris. But in 1911 Yeats could not go back to the 1892 version and to Oona's vision because by then Aleel had become too important in the body of the play for him not to have his place at the end of it. Here again the expansion of one element in the course of the revisions has to some extent tied Yeats's hands as a theatrical craftsman and forced him to write for the stage something he could not bring himself to print in the received text. The writing of a 'stage version' and a 'reading version' was a solution Yeats adopted on other occasions as well; but in this case it is an admission of failure as a dramatic poet.

The continuous enlargement of Aleel's role is of course the most striking feature of all the revised versions. In 1892 he makes (under the name Kevin) a momentary appearance in Scene iv, and tries to sell his soul to the merchants, and, a little later in the scene, he tries to prevent the Countess selling hers:

> You shall yet know the love of some great chief,
> And children gathering round your knees. Leave you
> The peasants to the builder of the heavens.

Out of these hints Yeats gradually developed the part. He added his entry with Cathleen in Act I and his vision in Act III (1895), the love-scene with Cathleen in Act III (1901), another similar scene in Scene iii (1912), until eventually in the final version there is no single scene of the five in which he does not appear. The impulse behind this enlargement was certainly autobiographical. Aleel now speaks for Yeats himself and is the chief means by which the element of 'personal thought and feeling' achieves progressively fuller expression. What was, in the versions of 1892 and 1895, simply the Countess's vain longing for a peace breathed forth by Oona's tales of 'the Danaan nations in their raths' becomes in the third version objectified in the relation with Aleel. As poet, dreamer, and lover, urging her retirement to the Druid forest, to the subjective life of peaceful beauty away from the objective life of self-sacrifice and war, Aleel has many links with Yeats's later verse. The invention and development of Aleel's and Cathleen's duologue is also Yeats's way of contriving a more theatrical and more deeply personal method for representing the old quarrel between St. Patrick and the Fenians, or 'dreaming' and 'grey Truth'.

In expanding this element Yeats was doing no more than submit to the logical consequences of his first departure from his source. Already, when the Countess listens to Oona's tales and songs, the possibility of a choice between dream and action, self-absorption and self-sacrifice, her own 'good' and her own 'evil', is hinted at. The scheme of the play, which shows her final sacrifice as an act of uncomplicated exaltation, seems to suggest that once she has made the sacrifice of the self entailed upon her by taking action at all, all other sacrifices, even the surrender of her soul, unresistedly ensue. In the revisions of 1901 and 1912 Yeats was moving nearer and nearer to a pattern of this kind.

Thus it is significant that nowhere in the revision does he attempt to lay any greater emphasis than he had in 1892 on what in the source is the natural dramatic climax of the fable: Cathleen's offer of her soul. And Aleel himself finally becomes, in the last version, a complete and successful symbol of the subjective life, messenger of Aedh and Aengus, bearer of the 'unchristened heart'. From the moment when he is first heard of, wandering and singing on the border of the woods 'wrapped up in dreams of terrors to come', until his last vision of Cathleen's transfiguration 'smitten of God' he serves to convey more richly than anything in the 1892 and 1895 versions what was written in the Yeatsian 'books of numberless dreams': he foreshadows Paul Ruttledge in *Where There is Nothing*, Septimus in *The Player Queen*, the author of 'The Second Coming' and even perhaps Ribh himself. The Aleel scenes, also, by the kind of contrast they make with the rest of the play, help to outline this pattern. The love scene in Act III (added in 1901) and the episode before the Castle in Scene ii (added in 1912), like the passages for Oona and Cathleen which it replaces, are slow-paced, lyrical, and evocatively full of pagan imagery. They do indeed turn aside 'at the lure of word and metaphor' because such turning-aside is appropriate to Aleel's role as the poet who repudiates the 'day's war' with the demons and 'all things uncomely and broken'.[25] The scenes strive to be timeless moments of suspended action:

> I thought to have kept her from remembering
> The evil of the times for full ten minutes.

Each is deliberately juxtaposed to other scenes that rapidly forward the perturbations of the play as it advances towards the demonic bargain: the arrival of Teig and Shemus with their gold, which moves the Countess to expend her treasure for the salvation of her people; and the robbery, leading to the Countess's 'stern resolve' and farewell to her hope of heaven. Christian images are plentifully scattered here. These contrasts of time's speed with time's suspension, of lyrical meditation with dramatic event, and of mythology with piety, actualize Cathleen's two worlds and underline in a substantially theatrical way the opposition between them.

Yeats thus gradually makes us alive to his pattern of counter-truths. In the original fable the stress was all on the Countess's desperate, physical struggle; in the first version this struggle, translated into the war between dreams and responsibility, still took place, so far as it is recognized at all, chiefly in Cathleen's soul. In later versions the divergent truths achieve greater theatrical life, but it is embodied in the antithesis between Cathleen and Aleel, two dramatic characters. The difference shows Yeats's movement towards a theatrical strategy and away from dependence upon a protagonist too close to the speaker of his lyrics, who does not really need for the expression of his nature the relationships with other people for which drama asks. It is true, however, that no struggle between self and soul, objective and subjective, in the single personality of Cathleen occurs. In the scenes with Aleel the Countess has little to do except to bring out *his* symbolic status. His is a story and a sorrow which does not touch her except with pity. It is never admitted to her imagination as a temptation which, by awakening a response in the depth of her own nature, can weaken her resolve or make her actions in other episodes appear as the issue of the soul's triumph over the self. We do not see in her what Yeats called 'the two halves of the soul separate and face to face'.[26] This is because Yeats is trying to show, in Cathleen and Aleel, what he was later to call Artist and Saint confronting each other upon the stage. We may prefer to think (as Yeats often did) of Self and Soul, or Artist and Saint, as more finely conceived when they are rendered as two contradictory elements in the same personality; and so we may criticize *The Countess Cathleen* for being too pale a version of a struggle that, partly because it is confined within the bounds of a single lyric life, seems so much more intense in such poems as 'The Choice' or 'Vacillation' or 'A Dialogue of Self and Soul'. Or we may prefer to argue that the fable which Yeats had chosen was not well adapted to the increasingly autobiographical use to which he put it; that the story of Ketty O'Donnor cannot really be made to fit what grew, as the play evolved, into the portrait of the artist as the rejected lover of Maud Gonne. These would, indeed, be valid criticisms, and there may underlie them the deeper recognition that both Cathleen and Aleel demonstrate an ever simpler and more schematic method of characterization—each the 'half' rather than the whole of a personality. But these criticisms ought not to obscure the extent to which Yeats's use of autobiography—the recognition that two persons are involved—actually supported the theatrical strategy—the recognition that a play is not a single lyric voice.

Elsewhere in the last two revisions Yeats's object was to tighten rather than to expand his construction. The most striking example of this is what happens to the robbery-scene from the going-out of the Countess until her re-entry to discourse with the merchants. In the first three versions this is very elaborately rendered and filled with Celtic colour and local pieties, such as the story of how the demons killed the good priest but could not entrap his soul. It dwells much also upon the nature and ambience of the demons themselves. In 1912 the scene, which had constantly attracted a good deal of minor tinkering, was completely re-written in a much compressed form, with only one set of servant-spirits. They are now supplied with lyric chants of a vapidity astonishing at this stage of Yeats's development. In the final version this re-writing was scrapped, leaving only half a dozen lines and a few stage directions.

Yeats judged soundly in other ways too. The complete re-vision of Scenes i and ii, accomplished in 1912, while it scarcely alters a single one of the old incidents and retains (with the exception of the new scene for Cathleen and Aleel in Scene ii) the episodes in their old order, makes both Scenes much tougher and faster. Scene ii, for example, had remained virtually unaltered since 1892, except for minor adjustments and the re-writing of two or three lines here and there. When he re-wrote it Yeats made the incidents seem much more urgent, economized on characters, and improved narrative articulation. Thus it is Teig and Shemus, characters already introduced in the first Act, and not a couple of anonymous peasants who convince Cathleen of the true nature of the evil that is abroad by showing her their infernal gold. An anxious steward brings news of the thieving and disorder in the demesne, whereas in the previous versions a Gardener and a Herdsman occupy two long passages by somewhat repetitiously conveying the same point. Similar adjustments, on a smaller scale, are found elsewhere, such as the passage added in 1912 preceding the Countess's entry in Scene v, when the peasants are panicked by the old woman's scream of hellish pain and try to revoke their bargains. This adds spirit and movement to the moment of Cathleen's arrival, which is slack and undramatic in earlier versions.

Throughout the revision Yeats sedulously watches out for the worst archaisms in modes of address and speech, gradually eliminates the more self-conscious spots of local colour and the weaker and more automatic lapses into Jacobean rhythms. Much of this work, in those parts of the play which were not completely re-written in the last two versions, had already been done by 1895. Especially in the last scene the more famous speeches had by then attained a form with which Yeats was apparently reluctant to meddle. Yet he did sometimes do so, and in making them swifter and sparer eliminated some beauty as well as some nonsense. This is the first form of a well-known passage:

> *First Merchant.* Five hundred thousand crowns—we give the price,
> The gold is here—the spirits, while you speak,
> Begin to labour upward, for your face
> Sheds a great light on them and fills their hearts
> With those unveilings of the fickle light,
> Whereby our heavy labours have been marred
> Since first His spirit moved upon the deeps
> And stole them from us. Even before this day
> The souls were but half ours, for your bright eyes
> Had pierced them through and robbed them of content.
> But you must sign, for we do all in order
> In buying such a soul—sign with this quill;
> It was a feather growing on the cock
> That crowed when Peter had denied his Master;
> 'Tis a great honour thus to write with it.[27]

In 1895 the end of this speech, which was otherwise untouched, attained the classic form which caused such concern to Dublin defenders of the papal honour:

> But you must sign, for we omit no form
> In buying a soul like yours; sign with this quill;
> It was a feather growing on the cock
> That crowed when Peter dared deny his Master,
> And all who use it have great honour in hell.

28

But the last version of all reads:

> *First Merchant.* Five hundred thousand crowns; we give the price.
> The gold is here; the souls even while you speak
> Have slipped out of our bond, because your face
> Has shed a light on them and filled their hearts.
> But you must sign, for we omit no form
> In buying a soul like yours. Sign with this quill.
> *Second Merchant.* It was a feather growing on the cock
> That crowed when Peter dared deny his Master,
> And all who use it have great honour in Hell.

The Fay brothers would have found the last version easier to speak on the stage. A preference for the intermediate version would have to meet the objections that the metaphors about 'light' seem irrelated and that a damned soul could hardly become less damned through being discontented.

These alterations are not of the sort that affect construction or change the kind of play *The Countess Cathleen* is. Throughout the thirty years' history of revision Yeats remained substantially faithful to the design which he had described to John O'Leary. If the play does not quite give us the sense of being 'laboriously constructed scene by scene', it is devised episode by episode. Yeats continued to work with these small units in all his revisions, re-handling them, or intercalating them with fresh ones on the same scale. But these new episodes—especially the two Aleel scenes of 1901 and 1912—are not out of quite the same box as the old ones. They hint at another kind of play, one which consists not of episodes linked together but of a single episode explored in depths. The story of Aleel and Cathleen moves towards such a design, but, because it is rooted in a play conceived as a cumulative succession of episodes, does not achieve it.

Amongst the plays of the Abbey Theatre period there are two which develop these contrasting principles in a specially instructive way. *The King's Threshold* is once more fashioned out of many units but they 'grow, or are wrought, together', in Ben Jonson's phrase, much better. *Deirdre*, on the other hand, is a more perfect example than *The Shadowy Waters* of a play of the other kind, a single episode more deeply explored. *Deirdre*, of all the earlier plays, has most bearing on Yeats's future as a playwright. But the curious history of *The Countess Cathleen* perhaps permitted him to observe that there were, at the least, two kinds of play for him to write, and even, as *The King's Threshold* suggests, that he could have another try at writing both kinds at once.

Chapter Two

The Man that Dies

THE KING'S THRESHOLD

I

THE difference between Aleel, the dreamer of the Pre-Raphaelite Twilight, and Seanchan, the obdurate professional of *The King's Threshold*, signalizes a well-attested shift in Yeats's interpretation of his own role as a poet in society. But *The King's Threshold* is, in the best sense, an amateur play, and almost the last play by Yeats of which this could properly be said. Unexacting in its staging and lucid in the development of its theme, it has many small parts which need only to be played with vigour and conviction to be brought to life. Yeats was later to group it with *Deirdre* and *On Baile's Strand*. Each, he thought, wanted 'one player of genius and that is out of reach probably henceforth for ever'.[1] But the difference between Seanchan and Deirdre is more justly apprehended if we remember that Frank Fay played the one part, and Mrs. Patrick Campbell the other. Earlier, Yeats had coupled the play with *The Countess Cathleen* as

easier to play effectively than my later plays, depending less upon the players and more upon the producer, both having been imagined more for variety of stage-picture than variety of mood in the player.[2]

The stage-pictures are composed by the entries of such contrasting figures as the pupils, the Mayor of Kinvara, the cripples, the monk,

31

the princesses. The construction, 'rather like a Greek play',[3] is controlled by their mutual purpose, which is to persuade Seanchan the Chief Poet to abandon his fast against the indignity that Guaire, King of Gort, has inflicted upon poetry by dismissing him from his place at the council-table. An action which consists of a series of short episodes, or temptations, is unified in place and time. The play dramatizes the last hour of the dying poet and the shame or glory which his triumph or death bestow upon Guaire's threshold; the threshold where Seanchan lies is the emblem of that in the royal condition which is capable of knowing honour and dishonour.

This element of variety within unity in the design of the play will influence a critical judgement upon it. It is an advance on *The Countess Cathleen*, where the episodes tend to fall apart and string themselves out among distracting counter-movements. The sources, too, reveal something about how the play was made: the *Immtheacht na Tromdáimhe*[4] is a good deal less important than Edwin Ellis's obscure and rubbishy verse-play *Sancan the Bard* (1895), to which Yeats acknowledged his indebtedness for 'arrangements' when the first version of *The King's Threshold* was printed in 1904.[5]

Edwin Ellis was not interested in making a play that could be put on the stage, but hankers after that continuous lyricism for which some of Yeats's earlier critics pleaded, in their dismay at the buffoonery in *The King's Threshold* and *On Baile's Strand* and at the baldness of the language of *Deirdre*.[6] Because his hero was a poet, Ellis crammed his play, which is written in rhyming couplets, with bad poems, specimens of the art that Sancan is upholding; Yeats was too skilful to endanger our belief in the Chief Poet in that way. Perhaps the most marked difference in method between Ellis and Yeats was Yeats's care to localize his drama. The principle, which is hardly operative in *The Countess Cathleen*, and is necessarily absent from the other-worldly ocean of *The Shadowy Waters*, had been determinedly applied in *On Baile's Strand* and was enunciated a few years before that play was written:

Our legends are always associated with places, and not merely every mountain and valley, but every strange stone and little coppice, has its legend, preserved in written or unwritten tradition. Our Irish romantic movement has arisen out of this tradition, and should always, even when it makes new legends about traditional people and things, be haunted by places.[7]

Once established, the principle was never forgotten; it was its sense of place that counted as one of the attractions of the Noh. In *The King's Threshold*, whereas Ellis was content to leave everything vague, Yeats sets his scene in Gort, of which Guaire is King, Seanchan is a citizen of Kinvara, and there are abounding references to the Clare-Galway landscape, as well as to hurley, salt fish, cranes, cripples, stony meadows and crooked thorn-trees.

Yet, despite these differences, the play owes much to *Sancan the Bard*. Ellis, like Yeats, devised a series of episodes in which various persons try to divert the martyr's purpose; they include the King, a Courtier, a Princess (and her attendant), and one of Sancan's pupils. Yeats added the Mayor of Kinvara, Seanchan's faithful servant (in the first version there are two of them), a Monk, and a Soldier. Seanchan's betrothed Fedelm in Yeats's play is, however, a radically different character from the Girl in Ellis's, who is a 'tribal maid' captured in battle and ordered by the King to persuade Sancan to eat under penalty of being burnt at the stake if she fails. *Sancan the Bard* ends with the mysterious love which Sancan and the Girl discover for each other: as singer and lover, each actualizes the other's ideal. Their determination to perish together causes the King to relent, while a Chorus of Bards proclaims a general reconciliation. Yeats, who had temporarily exhausted this *Axël*-like theme in *The Shadowy Waters* put nothing of it into *The King's Threshold*, but, apart from the general debt which his construction owes to Ellis, he borrowed other details from his work. An example is Seanchan's speech about the leprous beggar, which so horrifies the Princess, and which derives from a passage in Scene iv of *Sancan the Bard*:

> Long years ago I saw thy granddam, girl:
> She sat upon a bank one summer's day,
> Then came three lepers asking her the way.
> She told them, and her hand she waved and showed;
> The lepers saw, and passed upon the road.
> Your hand has still some evil taint of this.

It will be seen that *Sancan the Bard* ends not with the death of the poet but with the repeal of the ordinance that had banished him from his place amongst the makers of the law at the king's table. In the received text of *The King's Threshold*, of course, this is not so. At the end of the play Seanchan dies and is carried to his mountain-tomb far from the 'worsening world'. Yeats's sense that 'the man that dies has the chief part in the story' did not become clear until the play had undergone two revisions. In both the versions which precede the final one (which was done in 1922 and first printed in *Plays in Prose and Verse Written for an Irish Theatre*) the play ends with the happy restoration of the poet's right, as Guaire kneels before him and accepts his crown from his hands.

The revisions of *The King's Threshold* tell a simpler story than those of *The Countess Cathleen*, but the two stories have some common features. The first version, printed in 1904, did not last very long before about two-thirds of it were thoroughly rewritten as printed in *Poems 1899-1905* (1906).* A comparison of these two versions of 1904 and 1906—for they may be spoken of as two, although there are a great number of minor differences between the various printings of the second version—shows how skilful Yeats had become, once he had seen a play of his performed, in making better theatre out of it. A few examples are enough, for the operations are of the same kind as those carried out for those parts of *The Countess Cathleen* where the introduction of new thematic material is not in question.

It is plainly less tiresome for the audience to listen to Guaire's expository speech near the beginning of the play in its new form—broken up by interruptions from the Pupil—than in its

* The 1904 version was printed privately at New York (Wade No. 55) and in Volume III of *Plays for an Irish Theatre*; identical with this is a Dublin edition of 1905 (Volume V of the 'Abbey Theatre Series'). The 1906 version is substantially that found in all reprintings before 1922, but there are slight differences between these reprintings as they appear successively in *Poems 1899-1905*, *The Poetical Works of William B. Yeats* Volume II (New York, 1907), *Collected Works* Volume II (Stratford-on-Avon, 1908), and *Plays for an Irish Theatre* (London and Stratford-on-Avon, 1911). This last edition restores to the text the long prose-prologue which furnished forth the play in the editions of 1904 and 1905, but the prologue disappeared again in the final (third) version in *Plays in Prose and Verse Written for an Irish Theatre* (1922). The author's note on performance and revision, misleadingly dated 1911, in the 1922 edition is a shortened form of a similar note which first appeared in *Poems 1899-1905* (1906).

first form, where it continues without change of direction for nearly fifty lines. There is far more interplay between the subsidiary characters, as in the new passage where the Chamberlain fails, but the girls with their blandishments succeed in persuading the reluctant Soldier to tempt Seanchan with the food. The Monk is handled in much the same way, and given more satirical vitality by a speech against the music and dancing that the court-ladies have been deprived of by Seanchan's strike. The Fedelm episode towards the end of the play bites deeper because the cross-purposes in which the lovers are entangled break, in the second version, into a bitter quarrel. This sharpening of the relations between the characters has the general effect of clarifying the issue between Seanchan as the transcendent poet and all the other personages, who stand by Church, by State, by pleasure, or by love. The episode most radically affected by this process is the visit of the Mayor of Kinvara. He, of course, is deplorably bourgeois and low in the first version, but comically so in the second, and a renegade as well; he is the true voice of the 'blind and ignorant town', of the greedy and sycophantic philistinism which Yeats attacked in the poems in *Responsibilities*. Indeed, in the second version he becomes almost too complex a figure, for we may suspect Lady Gregory's hand in the cosy comedy of his half-remembered speech,* and Yeats's in the fresh virulence with which the Cripples now rhyme him from the door and the Chamberlain pushes him, a turncoat and flatterer, off the stage.

All such changes light up more effectively those 'stage-pictures' which, as they are revealed in successive episodes, compose the outward theatrical 'busyness' of the play; they also underline the theme of the society which mistakes just pride for arrogant assertion. As Yeats himself observed, the play was not changed 'in the radical structure' [8] in 1906, and the revision simply brings to fuller life what was already there. He found Ellis's original

---

* We can only speculate about how much Lady Gregory helped. The play's debt to *Sancan the Bard* makes it probable that the original plan was Yeats's, since he would have been the first to get to know of the work of a friend and co-editor. Lady Gregory writes: 'For *The Pot of Broth* I wrote dialogue and I worked as well at the plot and construction of some of the poetic plays, especially *The King's Threshold* and *Deirdre*; for I had learned by this time a good deal about playwriting to which I had never given a thought before' (*Our Irish Theatre*, New York, 1914, pp. 82–3).

structure adequate for embodying a vision of Seanchan and his martyrdom which was much nearer to Swift and Shaw than to Ellis's rhapsodies about love and fate.

The sharper colour, because it is new, has called attention to itself; but it ought not to be overstressed when the play as a whole is thought about. What Una Ellis-Fermor described as 'the apocalyptic vision of the function of poetry' [9] is brilliant in the first version and undiminished in the second and third. It was to be some time before the more sardonic eye that he was now in 1906 turning upon the poet's town took in the poet himself and transformed *him* into an 'old scarecrow'.[10] But this, too, was to happen, and it is Yeats himself who has made it difficult for us to accept sentiment or idiom in such a speech as

> O silver trumpets be you lifted up
> And cry to the great race that is to come. . . .

The quieter and less exalted passages carry more conviction, such as the Pupil's image of a world without art as

> like a woman
> That looking on the cloven lips of a hare
> Brings forth a hare-lipped child

or Seanchan's reply to the Soldier's 'Eat this, old hedge-hog'. This is a fine example of dramatic speech, tied to its context, and conveying the movement of the speaker as his mind turns away in self-contemplation from his interlocutor and then back again in vivid indignation as the angry pride rises:

> You have rightly named me.
> I lie rolled up under the ragged thorns
> That are upon the edge of those great waters
> Where all things vanish away, and I have heard
> Murmurs that are the ending of all sound.
> I am out of life, I am rolled up, and yet
> Hedgehog although I am, I'll not unroll
> For you, King's dog. Go to the King, your master. . .

But these excellent inventions of the first version are all the better for the more generally efficient context which the second provides for them.

Yet even this version must always have been regarded by Yeats as an unsatisfying compromise. It was not until the third and final version that Yeats gave the play the 'tragic end I would have given it at the first, had not a friend advised me to "write comedy and have a few happy moments in the theatre" '.[11] The earlier part of the 1922 text differs here and there only in minor ways from the 1906 version; but the play has a quite new ending, a passage of some sixty lines (incorporating the old 'O silver trumpets' speech which Yeats could not bear to abandon); it begins after the Youngest Pupil's 'Die, Seanchan . . .' with Seanchan's dying speech ('Come nearer me . . .').[12]

This type of alteration is one that is bound to arouse suspicion about the integrity of any of the versions. If the last episode in a play made up of a series of episodes can be so utterly transformed, could not the celebrated objection that Dr. Johnson brought against that other 'Greek' play, *Samson Agonistes*, be brought against the construction of this one, that 'the intermediate parts have neither cause nor consequence, neither hasten nor retard the catastrophe'?

I think it can be shown that the violence was done to the two earlier versions rather than to the last, and that it is they which bear the scars. Nothing in the various episodes enforces a happy ending. Each, even the climactic one of the temptation by Fedelm, terminates in Seanchan's remaining irremovably staunch. This lays it down plainly enough that, if anyone is to yield, Guaire must do so. Yet everything we are told about Guaire's dilemma suggests that it has been carefully contrived to prevent his escape from it by any mere change of heart. If Seanchan dies, Guaire's house will be shamed; but if he restores the poet's right, his throne will be in danger. Apart from this dilemma and his masterful impatience at being faced with it, we are told very little about Guaire. This does not help us to believe in his final reversal of his decision. We cannot explain his change, since the pressures upon him have not apparently been in any way modified in the course of the play's action, nor are we vouchsafed any explanation of it in terms of movements in Guaire's own mind. In the first version Yeats, with some dexterity, succeeds in keeping these worries mostly dormant by bringing the curtain down before we have had time to think about them, and bringing it down on a scene of melodrama—the Pupils with halters round their necks, their last-ditch defiance in defence of the ancient right, and Guaire's sudden collapse.

If this is true, can it therefore be said that when Yeats reverts to his original tragic purpose in the final version, the episodes appear to re-order themselves and point forward to the new ending? The new ending has at least the virtue of not implicating Guaire at all; he is now no longer required to act in a way which appears to be justified only by the dramatist's desire to solve his own problem as a narrator. But in order to describe in a more positive way the quality of the new version, we must look not at that structural feature—the chain of episodes—on which attention has so far been fixed, but consider also another element in the construction. This could be labelled 'the character of Seanchan', or, more accurately, the story of his death: 'the man that dies has the chief part in the story'.

Linking the various episodes, the beads on the string, there is the thread itself, the fasting Seanchan. He is the element in the play which was represented in *The Countess Cathleen* by the scenes between Aleel and Cathleen. In that play it was to some extent at odds with the original fable. In *The King's Threshold* it is co-terminous with the play itself, in one sense *is* all the play, or the 'chief part' in it, fully present from the beginning, not growing into it during the revision. And what the final revision did was simply to allow it to run its natural course to its predestined end. Yeats had his own set of metaphors for an element of this kind when he wrote in the Preface to *Poems 1899–1905*:

After I had learned to hold an audience for an act in prose I found that I had everything to learn over again in verse, for in dramatic prose one has to prepare principally for actions, and for the thoughts or emotions that bring them about or arise out of them; but in verse one has to do all this and to follow as well a more subtle sequence of cause and effect, that moves through vast sentiments and intricate thoughts that accompany action, but are not necessary to it. It is not very difficult to construct a fairly vigorous prose play, and then . . . to decorate it and encumber it with poetry. But a play of that kind will never move us poetically, because it does not uncover, as it were, that high, intellectual, delicately organized soul of men and of an action, that may not speak aloud if it do not speak in verse.[13]

Not all the terms and implications of this passage, in particular the contrast between verse and prose, are relevant. But the 'more subtle sequence', the intricate thoughts that accompany action and uncover its soul—these can be found in the play and do belong to its chief character.

II

The dying Seanchan, like the dying Samson, has been criticized for being too passive a protagonist. But he is rendered with a good deal of varied life. We hear about his family and his neighbours and his singing-school, so that his character acquires a solidity of specification matching the sense of place that was so lacking in *Sancan the Bard*. But the most vital element is Seanchan's struggle between vision and delirium. This is the inner story of his dying and has a progressive movement of its own, one that is cheated of its resolution in the earlier versions. It 'speaks aloud' in the imagery of his verse, which is destructive, joyful, 'apocalyptic', visionary— or mournful, diseased, delirious. The antithesis is established early in the play. The Oldest Pupil (called Senias in the first version) says, using a similitude that was to recur in Yeats's studies of the subjective man:

> for your hunger I could weep;
> And yet the hunger of the crane that starves
> Because the moonlight glittering on the pool
> And flinging a pale shadow has made it shy,
> Seems to me little more fantastical
> Than this that's blown into so great a trouble.[14]

Seanchan answers:

> There is much truth in that, for all things change
> At times, as if the moonlight altered them,
> And my mind alters as if it were the crane's;
> For when the heavy body has grown weak
> There's nothing that can tether the wild mind
> That being moonstruck and fantastical
> Goes where it fancies.

The Pupil's betrayal of his poetic faith is next associated by Seanchan with the changing moon. Later in the same episode with the Pupils comes the Nietzschean joy:

Have I not opened school on these bare steps,
And are not you the youngest of my scholars?
And I would have all know that when all falls
In ruin, poetry calls out in joy,
Being the scattering hand, the bursting pod,
The victim's joy among the holy flame,
God's laughter at the shattering of the world,
And now that joy laughs out and weeps and burns
On these bare steps.

This theme, too, of Dionysan art, has a long future history in Yeats's work, culminating in 'The Gyres' and 'Lapis Lazuli'.*

In the central portion of the play Seanchan is the Dionysan poet, and is therefore both benign and comminatory. The powers that oppose poetry, particularly the Mayor, the Monk, and the Soldier, are cursed as king's dogs, fools, and hypocrites, who require a tame song-bird for their god; but the girls who want to dance and make love are blessed in the speech beginning 'Yes, yes, go to the hurley'. This speech is placed close to one which shows the progressive movement towards weakness, delirium, and disease. Seanchan outrages beauty and charity by cursing the Princess and telling the story of the leper that blessed her mother:

Hold out your hands,
I will find out if they are contaminated . . .

and

There are no sound hands among you. No sound hands.
Away with you, away with all of you,
You are all lepers. There is leprosy
Among the plates and dishes that you have brought me.
I would know why you have brought me leper's wine?
[*He flings the wine in their faces.*

* Compare Nietzsche, *Birth of Tragedy*: 'We are to perceive how all that comes into being must be ready for a sorrowful end . . . We are really for brief moments Primordial Being itself, and feel its indomitable desire for being and joy in existence; the struggle, the pain, the destruction of phenomena, now appear to us as something necessary. We are pierced by the maddening sting of these pains at the very moment when we have become, as it were, one with the immeasurable primordial joy in existence, and when we anticipate, in Dionysan ecstasy, the indestructibility and eternity of this joy' (*Works*, tr. Levy, I. 128–9).

The moon-image recurs, infected. Seanchan's wavering mind sees everything as 'blessed' by its leprous hand:

> Where did I say the leprosy came from?
> I said it came out of a leper's hand
> And that he walked the highway; but that's folly,
> For he was walking up there in the sky
> And there he is even now with his white hand
> Thrust out of the blue air and blessing them
> With leprosy.
> *A Cripple.*   He's pointing at the moon
> That's coming out up yonder, and he calls it
> Leprous, because the daylight whitens it.

In the episode with Fedelm, Seanchan's images are again those of the joyful visionary, foreseeing the 'immeasurable primordial joy' of the future race:

> I lay awake,
> There had come a frenzy into the light of the stars
> And they were coming nearer and I knew
> All in a minute they were about to marry
> Clods out upon the plough-lands, to beget
> A mightier race than any that has been;

and

> The stars had come so near me that I caught
> Their singing; it was praise of that great race
> That would be haughty, mirthful, and white-bodied
> With a high head, and open hand, and how
> Laughing, it would take the mastery of the world.

The images of the infected moon, whose blessing is a curse, and the joyful, procreative stars, compose an antithesis mediating the 'more subtle sequence' that speaks aloud in verse. His ordeal, as it sharpens in intensity, has brought Seanchan to a vision of the contraries.

It is this issue and this way of stating it as what Seanchan, Chief Poet, sees, that fail to achieve resolution in the earlier versions. 'They breathe truth that breathe their words in pain.' [15] Seanchan's double vision becomes merely a pointless theatrical exercise in the psychopathology of hunger if it is not to be shown as expressing the truth about present and future worlds. The dead, infected world cannot so easily put itself to rights if it is, in this truth, a land of king's dogs and beauty poisoned at its source.

The earlier ending is wrong for a second and more positive reason. Seanchan's vision and his power to curse and prophesy are rooted in the gradual process of bodily derangement. This is depicted as of a kind which allows spiritual insight, images of good and evil, to become cruel and joyful and specific. Flesh is refined into knowledge. Where bodily weakness and mental vision are so intimately related, it is right that each should attain their natural goal, the grave which is also a watch-tower, the death that finishes the body but frees the spirit. But in the earlier versions we have to believe that bodily disorder ends in one way, with the recovery of life, and vision in another, with the acceptance of death—for it is essentially a vision of life through death, of the future race that supplants the one that is dying. Seanchan's gaze reaches beyond the dead world to the new life revealed to him by his suffering; but his story turns away, to Fedelm and Kinvara and the king's table again. 'The man that dies' to Guaire's world should die in the story, too, because the story is what he shares with Guaire and Guaire's well-meaning and high-principled allies, whom Seanchan in satire, prophecy and delirium has despoiled of fallacies. Only the Pupils, themselves finally ready for death, and the cripples, with their unfantastical hunger and superstitious awe of the poetic office, are cast out from Guaire's kingdom: all the story has gone to show that Guaire's place is with them, on the confines.

Yeats's last version of *The King's Threshold* is the best because it does not break the 'more subtle sequence', whereas in *The Countess Cathleen* it was the attempt to introduce such a sequence into a vigorous and self-consistent fable that caused some confusion to the design. *The King's Threshold*, although a much less ambitious piece, succeeds in being the kind of play that *The Countess Cathleen* failed to become through its long history of stitching and unstitching. Meanwhile, in *Deirdre*, Yeats tried his hand at constructing a play in which the episodes themselves have been transformed into the movements within 'the high, intellectual, delicately organized soul' of the chief character.

Chapter Three

Deirdre

I

ABOUT *Deirdre* the commentators disagree even more than usual. It is described as 'poetry written round the central crisis . . . not an expression of it'; 'a shadow-play, although sometimes the shadows perform an exquisite movement'.[1] It is 'pseudo-Elizabethan',[2] 'a charade', 'elegant and two-dimensional, the characters never come out at the audience'.[3] On the other side, we find that 'Yeats has travelled far from *The Land of Heart's Desire* and *Countess Cathleen*. There is no more remoteness from common experience, but, instead, an immediacy as terrible as that of Middleton, severest of Jacobean tragic poets.'[4] Deirdre's affirmation of love reflects a permanent reality of the human situation;[5] and Lennox Robinson testifies that 'Every part in the play is roundly written, every part has its variety, and of the one-act verse-plays it is the most supremely satisfactory.'[6]

Differing critical assumptions lead to these contrary conclusions, and it would not be hard to discover a Law of Parsimony which would permit one opinion or the other to be discarded. Taken in their variety, they do indicate the staginess (in both the bad and good senses) of *Deirdre*. A play which appears either austere or decorative, which admits or exiles reality, might stand as an emblem of the theatrical art, where at every point, in the author's brain as on the playhouse-stage, artificer and realist so habitually frustrate one another.

This staginess, in a narrower sense, enters into the first records of the play. The problem was, who was to perform the vast, central role, a virtuoso display-piece for an actress, on a scale that Yeats had not attempted before. Mrs. Patrick Campbell had her eye on it, but, according to Yeats, had had the wrong training in 'plays like *Mrs. Tanqueray*, where everything is done by a kind of magnificent hysteria';

This school reduces everything to an emotional least common denominator. It finds the scullion in the queen, because there are scullions in the audience but no queens. . . . A new school of acting is now growing up under the influence of the various attempts to create an intellectual drama, and of changes deeper than that. The new school seizes upon what is distinguished, solitary, proud even. One always got a little of this in Mrs. Emery when she was good, and one gets a great deal of it in Miss Darragh.[7]

It was not hysteria that Yeats sought in the creation and presentation of his central character, but energy: 'intensity of personal life, intonations that show . . . the strength, the essential moment of a man'.[8]

Of all Yeats's plays, *Deirdre* is the one where it is easiest—although still far from easy—to decipher some correspondence between play and the jumble of self-criticism, propaganda, and oracular sayings which constitute Yeats's reflections on the needs of the theatre at the time when *Deirdre* was being written and performed. *Energy* is a key-word, a masterful fullness of life, 'energy of soul'. It corresponds to or is transmuted into abundant personality; it is expressed (on the stage and in life) in the extravagant, personal, reckless gesture:

We, who are believers, cannot see reality anywhere but in the soul itself, and seeing it there we cannot do other than rejoice in every energy, whether of gesture, or of action, or of speech, coming out of the personality, the soul's image.[9]

This was a comparatively new complex of ideas. It was connected, as Thomas Parkinson has shown, with the poet's growing willingness to submit to the playwright's obligation to dramatize personalities, and with an increasing distaste for the unmoving and the silent, for the 'still life' and impersonality that had characterized figure and landscape in the earlier poetry of 'essences and states of mind'.[10]

There were several different ways of justifying the concern with heroic and personal energies. There was the patriotic way:

an imaginative delight in energetic characters and extreme types, enlarges the energy of a people by the spectacle of energy.[11]

There was the psychological way:

The creative energy of men depends upon their believing that they have, within themselves, something immortal and imperishable, and that all else is but as an image in a looking-glass. So long as that belief is not a formal thing, a man will create out of a joyful energy, seeking little for any external test of an impulse that may be sacred, and looking for no foundation outside life itself.[12]

And there was the dramaturgical way. The stress on heroic energy supported the campaign against naturalism in the theatre and helped to shape its strategy. The 'more important' kind of drama, which is 'an activity of the souls of the characters' is 'an energy, an eddy of life, purified from everything but itself'.[13] Yeats's doctrine here shows an interesting affinity with the practice of Chapman or Dryden, who sought to fill their plays with heroic energies and to empty them of Shakespearian particularity, continually contriving exemplars of passionate virtue and Herculean strength and flame. For Yeats, Shakespeare appeared 'mixed with the whole spectacle of the world', but the characters in heroic drama live with an intensity that burns up their links with the world. It is this intensity, according to Yeats, that is the proper subject of drama:

If the subject of drama or any other art, were a man himself, an eddy of momentary breath, we might desire the contemplation of perfect characters; but the subject of all art is passion, and a passion can only be contemplated when separated by itself, purified of all but itself, and aroused into a perfect intensity by opposition with some other passion, or it may be with the law.[14]

It was the process of separation, purification, avoidance of distractions that counted when it came to establishing principles for the drama, and this process ran counter to the assumptions of the naturalistic drama as Yeats understood them. He argued, for example, that the dramatist must invent not the typical but the

exceptional personage. The 'typical' character as defined by the
naturalistic school meant that a writer must create 'personifications
of averages, of statistics, or even personified opinions, or men and
women so faintly imagined that there is nothing about them to
separate them from the crowd'.[15] But such characters are falsely
fathered upon the poets by the propagandists. For the poets meant
by the 'typical' character 'the character who must be typical of
something which exists in all men because the writer has found it
in his own mind'; they meant personages 'which startle us by
being at once bizarre and an image of our own secret thoughts'.[16]
'A poet creates tragedy from his own soul, that soul which is
alike in all men' [17]—the *anima mundi* itself. The exceptional, the
heroic, the solitary, the Fool or the Queen, command response at
the level where the poet's vision and experience as incarnate in his
inventions speak to and awaken their simulacra in the spectator's
heart. The spectator, like the magus Zoroaster, continually meets
his own image, but walking upon the stage:

The greatest art symbolizes not those things that we have observed
so much as those things that we have experienced, and when the
imaginary saint or lover or hero moves us most deeply, it is the moment
when he awakens within us for an instant our own heroism, our own
sanctity, our own desire.[18]

It is the anti-naturalist who is most concerned with reality,
because in this way he touches the 'intimate life' of the spectator,
instead of presenting him, as the naturalist does, with personages
in whom the inner life beats faintly because all their energy is
taken up with the accurate imitation of life's surfaces. And the
power of a theatre which acknowledges and encourages this deep
and intimate communion of playwright and spectator is thauma-
turgical indeed:

All creation requires one mind to make and one mind of enjoyment.
The theatre can at rare moments create this one mind of enjoyment,
and once created, it is like the mind of an individual in solitude,
immeasurably bold—all is possible to it.[19]

Backed by arguments of this kind Yeats advocated a drama
which bestowed primacy on speech. Speech is the only medium
capable of developing the subtlety of expression needed to lay bare
'that which hides itself continually' in the depths of the soul.[20]

By the same token, the natural energy and subtle precision of this speech and the spectacle of the personage scrutinizing what is within him by the discipline of sincerity and logic will only be spoilt and diverted by the 'hysteria' that Yeats suspected in Mrs. Patrick Campbell, by elocutionary expertise or constantly varying attitudes:

When one requires the full attention of the mind, one must not weary it with any but the most needful changes of pitch and note, or by an irrelevant or obtrusive gesture.[21]

Let actors rehearse in barrels that they may be free to think of speech![22] Like Arthur Symons and Gordon Craig, Yeats stressed the theatrical value of immobility and silence. Scenery, too, full of possible distractions, must be austere and suggestive only. It must not compete with 'the illusion created by the actor, who belongs to a world with depth as well as height and breadth'.[23] The modern naturalist thinks continually about how his audience is going to behave, and is continually working to impress and manipulate it; instead of thinking about his own subject, he seeks 'external aids, remembered situations, tricks of the theatre',[24] but:

If we understand our own minds, and the things that are striving to utter themselves through our minds, we move others, not because we have understood or thought about those others, but because all life has the same root . . . the following of art is little different from the following of religion in the intense preoccupation that it demands. Somebody has said 'God asks nothing of the highest soul but attention'.[25]

An energy flowing from the depths of personality and expressed in a medium of subtlety, austerity, and restraint—this is what Yeats sought in the writing of *Deirdre* and expected the player of his principal part to understand. If it is true that the consolidation of the Abbey and its audience by 1906 allowed Yeats to be bolder than he had been before in aligning dramatic theory with dramatic practice, then *Deirdre* is, in some respects at least, recognizable as the kind of play that might have been expected to result from the conjunction. In *Deirdre* everything concentrates on the way the single heroic individual confronts her destiny. Our contemplation of this encounter is as little disturbed as possible by other elements, even by the presence, obligatory though it is, of the other characters in her story. Unlike Synge, Yeats cuts the intrigue to the bone, subordinates Naoise very deliberately, and does the same with Conchubar.* They must not be permitted to diminish Deirdre's personal, heightened, exceptional existence. Yeats was striving to create a memorable character of the 'kind that follows us into our intimate life' because of the level at which it commands response, as do Odysseus, Don Quixote, or Hamlet, who are 'with us always'.[26] Yet, because the dramatist was obliged by his experience to acknowledge that certain kinds of artifice are unavoidable, this ideal had a year later to be discriminated more carefully. Homer and Cervantes were, after all, freer than Sophocles or Shakespeare, and their freedom was the measure of their greater access to energy and intimacy and personality:

> I met an old man out fishing a year ago, who said to me, 'Don Quixote and Odysseus are always near to me'; and that is true for me also, for even Hamlet and Lear and Oedipus are more cloudy. No playwright ever has made or ever will make a character that will follow us out of the book as Don Quixote follows us out of the book, for no playwright can be wholly episodical, and when one constructs, bringing one's characters into complicated relations with one another, something impersonal comes into the story. Society, fate, 'tendency', something not quite human, begins to arrange the characters and to excite into action only so much of their humanity as they find it necessary to show one another.[27]

An irony of a more local but perhaps equally unavoidable kind attended the first performances of *Deirdre*. The choice of Miss Darragh rather than of Mrs. Campbell to play the part was another attempt to prevent depths and intimacy being disturbed more than could be helped by the glitter of artifice. But it seems to have had the contrary effect, according to W. G. Fay. Miss Darragh's sophisticated, professional style contrasted too much with the very different manner of the Abbey players: 'It

---

* Yeats would, I think, have been disappointed and surprised, even if unable to deny the connexion, at the way this play is related to *On Baile's Strand* and *The King's Threshold* by Parkinson (see below, p. 65), whom Ellmann follows: 'Deirdre and Naisi, Cuchulain, and Seanchan represent the reckless ideal and the kings with whom they war the inglorious reality (*Identity of Yeats* [London, 1954], p. 106).'

was like putting a Rolls-Royce to run a race with a lot of hill ponies.' *

II

Despite the frustrations that threatened it, the life of Deirdre herself, conceived—at any rate in some measure—as a practical expression of a complex of ideas about what the theatre ought to be and do, is the chief thing in the play, and dominates its design as neither Seanchan nor the Countess Cathleen dominate in their plays. The single episode which constitutes the plot is shaped to produce this effect, and everything the other characters do or say is intended to give us the measure of Deirdre and her situation.†

During the protasis, before the entry of Deirdre and Naoise, the audience is invited to ask, 'What kind of story is this?' This

---

* W. G. Fay and Catherine Carswell, *The Fays and the Abbey Theatre* (London, 1935), p. 208. Miss Darragh's appointment also offended the other players. Miss Darragh, whose real name was Letitia Marion Dallas, was later one of the founders of the Liverpool Repertory Theatre. She died in 1917. Mrs. Campbell eventually played *Deirdre* in Dublin and London in the last months of 1908. Yeats, who genuinely admired her art (see *Letters*, p. 360), began to compose what much later became *The Player Queen* with Mrs. Campbell in mind for the part of Decima.

† *Deirdre* was revised much less than *The Countess Cathleen* or *The King's Threshold*. The general effect of the revisions is to make Deirdre more prominent and central. (1) First version, 1907: in *Plays for an Irish Theatre*, Volume V., *The Poetical Works of William B. Yeats* (New York, 1907, Volume II), and, slightly revised, in *Collected Works* (Stratford-on-Avon, 1908, Volume II). (2) 'Alterations in "Deirdre",' November, 1908. Yeats wrote, in this four-page leaflet printed for insertion in *Plays for an Irish Theatre*, Volume V (see Wade, p. 79): 'There are two passages in the play which I always knew to be mere logic, mere bones, and yet, after many attempts, I thought it impossible to alter them. When, however, Mrs. Campbell offered to play the part, my imagination began to work again.' The two passages concern the first entrance of Deirdre and her later attempt to pretend to arouse Naoise's jealousy. The new version of the entrance had already been printed in the Appendix to Volume II of *Collected Works*. Both the new passages, with some further alterations, were incorporated in the text for the first time in *Deirdre*, 1911 (Wade, No. 86) and in *Plays for an Irish Theatre* (Stratford-on-Avon, 1911). (3) *Plays in Prose and Verse*, 1922. Yeats's note, dated 1922, is misleading: 'I have revised it a good deal of recent years, especially this last year.' The changes are not very considerable, but include one cut of about 25 lines. There are a few more small changes in the text in *Collected Plays* (1934). My quotations are from this edition.

element is stressed by the intentionally emphatic use which Yeats has made of the expository material forced upon him by his decision to plunge *in medias res*, and so is the feeling that there is somewhere hidden a pattern, or archetype, to which, if it can be found out, the story will be seen to conform. 'We are in a story,' says the First Musician in the opening lines, 'such a story as we sing':

> I have a story right, my wanderers,
> That has so mixed with fable in our songs
> That all seemed fabulous.

But the tale of Deirdre, Naoise, and Conchubar, which she now relates, in order to perfect its nature as a story asks for an ending, and then only will it win complete, professional approval:

> The tale were well enough
> Had it a finish.

Audience and tale-teller would then know what kind of story it is, whether happy or sad, and be able to judge it. They are about to be told:

> But gather close about that I may whisper
> The secrets of a king . . .
> I have been to Conchubar's house and followed up
> A crowd of servants going out and in . . .
> and came at length
> To a great room.

On this forboding note the Musician is interrupted by the entry of Fergus, who proceeds to offer his version of the story's end. It is to be reconciliation.

> *First Musician.* Are Deirdre and her lover tired of life?
> *Fergus.* You are not of this country or you'd know
> That they are in my charge and all forgiven.
> *First Musician.* We have no country but the roads of the world.

The 'roads of the world' tell them that 'an old man's love . . . is hard to cure', that 'old men are jealous': it is *that* kind of story, so their experience of stories tells them. They admit none of Fergus's attempts to qualify the pattern upon which the story seems to

them to be insisting, and they finally lead him back to the point
that had been reached just before his entrance:

There is a room in Conchubar's house, and there—

The sinister re-iteration of this note carries unimpeachable
authority for the audience, and makes Fergus's cheerful babble
convey the truth even while he denies it:

> I know myself, and him, and your wild thought
> Fed on extravagant poetry, and lit
> By such a dazzle of old fabulous tales
> That common things are lost, and all that's strange
> Is true because 'twere pity if it were not.

This is another way of indicating that the professional storyteller recognizes an analogue when she sees one, and the next
moment Fergus's own tongue unwillingly stumbles across one
too when he urges the Musicians to begin an appropriate song for
the entrance of Deirdre and Naoise:

> Begin, begin, of some old king and queen,
> Of Lugaid Redstripe or another; no, not him,
> He and his lady perished wretchedly.

The audience now knows that it is the Musicians rather than
Fergus who must be believed, and knows as well the kind of
story it is. The opening phase of the play is a device for subordinat-
ing interest in plot to interest in character. When Deirdre enters,
we know that her tale is about to end in tragedy, although we do
not know how she will confront this destiny, or when she herself
will learn the nature of the story she is in. In the next phase the
question is asked not by the spectator but by the *dramatis persona*
('What kind of story am I in?'), and, set against the key which the
spectator already holds to the answer, can be rephrased by him as
'What kind of person is this?'

From the moment of her entrance Deirdre is preparing herself
for the role that she considers appropriate to her story as she
understands it so far. Throughout the rest of the play there is a
similar bond between her choice of role and her diagnosis of
story. At this point, she puts on her jewellery and her paint:

> These women have the raddle that they use
> To make them brave and confident . . .
> You'll help me, women.

She is ready to 'dress for the part', her share in the feast of forgiveness. But the role she has chosen contravenes her instinctive feeling that the story which it is designed to fit is not the true story:

> My husband took these rubies from a king
> Of Surracha that was so murderous
> He seemed all glittering dragon. Now wearing them
> Myself wars on myself, for I myself—
> That do my husband's will, yet fear to do it—
> Grow dragonish to myself.*

Further omens—the chess-board of Lugaid, and the absence of a messenger from Conchubar to greet them—hint that the story is other than it seems. The fact that Fergus and Naoise refuse to attend to these hints, while Deirdre does, distinguishes her. Naoise reproaches her in words like those spoken by Fergus earlier: 'You have muddled yourself with old tales, seeing story-analogues where none exists':

> We must not speak or think as women do,
> That when the house is all a-bed sit up
> Marking among the ashes with a stick
> Till they are terrified.

But when Fergus and Naoise go out to see if any welcoming messenger is on his way, Deirdre turns to the Musicians with her question, 'What kind of story is this?' From them she gradually learns the true answer. They lay open to her the analogies that are crying out for recognition, and affirm that there are rules about the way people behave that will apply in her case as in any other. These they know about from their elder experience of love and 'the roads of the world'. But at first Deirdre misreads their hints and analogues:

> *First Musician.* I have heard he loved you
> As some old miser loves the dragon-stone
> He hides among the cobwebs near the roof.
> *Deirdre.* You mean that when a man who has loved like that
> Is after crossed, love drowns in its own flood,

---

* The episode of the jewellery was added in 1908 (*Plays for an Irish Theatre*, 1911, pp. 11–12) and makes Deirdre's entrance more full of lustre and decision than it is in the earlier version. See note on p. 49 above.

And that love drowned and floating is but hate;
And that a king who hates sleeps ill at night
Till he has killed; and that, though the day laughs,
We shall be dead at cock-crow.
First Musician.   You've not my thought.
When I lost one I loved distractedly,
I blamed my crafty rival and not him,
And fancied, till my passion had run out,
That could I carry him away with me,
And tell him all my love, I'd keep him yet.
Deirdre. Ah! now I catch your meaning, that this king
Will murder Naoise and keep me alive.

For Deirdre, this is much the worse of two bad stories. Proof that
it is the one that is being told is given her when the Musician
reveals to her the secret of the room in Conchubar's palace that
she had twice tried to speak about before. It is a bridal chamber,
adorned with magical stones that transform hate to love.

Deirdre's actions during the rest of the play can be summed up
as a series of attempts to alter this story, as it were from inside the
story itself. She can endeavour to control events only by influenc-
ing Naoise or Conchubar, and to this end she desperately plays
one part after another in the hope of persuading them to change
the story, or of persuading herself to endure it. The 'staginess'
of the play is at its most incontrovertible in the character of
its protagonist, who has to be a versatile 'actress'. The audience,
using her breakdowns and failures to measure the effort that this
costs her, is brought into the intimate life of the character by
observing her struggle to disguise herself or to discover in herself
a self that can outface the worst. We are continually reminded by
Deirdre's own awareness of it that this is a tale in which the long-
remembering harpers will find 'matter for their song'.[28]

Deirdre tries to persuade Naoise to escape by pretending that
her jewels and adornments are intended to wake Conchubar's
desire, but, when Fergus sees through her stratagem, she abandons
this hastily assumed role of fickle woman and wants to destroy
the beauty that has caused so much harm. Naoise tells her that
they must conform to the story as it works out:

> Leave the gods' handiwork unblotched, and wait
> For their decision, our decision is past.

When the messenger from Conchubar finally reveals what is in his mind, Deirdre and Naoise plan a suitable end for their tale, an end different from the one designed by the king. They will behave like the characters in the old story of Lugaid Redstripe and his Queen:

> What do they say?
> That Lugaid Redstripe and that wife of his
> Sat at this chess-board, waiting for their end.
> They knew that there was nothing that could save them,
> And so played chess as they had any night
> For years, and waited for the stroke of sword.

And so they proceed to act out the analogue. But Deirdre, although she tries her best, finds that she cannot after all conform to her archetype:

> I cannot go on playing like that woman
> That had but the cold blood of the sea in her veins.

Passionate memories intervene between her and the due performance of the chosen role, which is abandoned before Conchubar makes his momentary appearance at the door to spy upon them. Naoise, twice mistaking the story, supposing first that Conchubar is honest and then that he is a coward, rushes out to fight him. Alone, Deirdre has thought the ending out again and begs the knife from the Musician, reminding her that the Musicians' part is to remember and record the tale:

> Women, if I die,
> If Naoise die this night, how will you praise?
> What words seek out? for that will stand to you;
> Being but dead we shall have many friends.
> All through your wanderings, the doors of kings
> Shall be thrown wider open, the poor man's hearth
> Heaped with new turf, because you are wearing this
> .   [*Gives Musician a bracelet.*
> To show that you have Deirdre's story right.

But when Naoise is trapped, her pleas, undisguisedly desperate, are powerless to change the ends which each has chosen. Naoise is determined to die rather than to assent to Conchubar's bargain; Conchubar is resolved to have Deirdre, if needs be at the price of a life. When this has been exacted and Naoise is dead, Deirdre

immediately assumes her last role. This is her final means of controlling her fate and shaping it to the ends she desires. When she
adopts the semblance of a half-reluctant mistress, attracted by the
new lover yet preserving sufficient personal dignity to insist first
on paying her debt to the old one, assuring Conchubar that this
will make a good start to their new life together, and flaring up for
a moment into a wifely termagant admonishing him for the lack
of manliness he displays by his reluctance to grant her the favour,
she plays her most testing role. Its sustained complexity is the
measure of her determination, of the 'white-heat' at the heart of
it.* For all her previous disguisings had broken down; since
Naoise is dead, there are no analogues left, and no hopes either.
To finish the story in her way, and not Conchubar's, is her
sufficient inspiration. Her role here is in the same mode as her
other disguisings, but is a kind of imaginative triumph, because
distinguished by success as they were by failure.

III

The Countess Cathleen is a play essentially episodical. In *The King's
Threshold* the successive stage-pictures are threaded through by
the gradual exaltation of Seanchan towards his double vision. But
in *Deirdre* variety of episode and variety of stage-picture are both
subordinated to the central figure and her paradigm of roles. The
crises in the play are in Deirdre's personality: in the way she
comes to interpret her fate, and in the struggle to re-shape it by
playing a part. It is on this level that the audience is expected to
pay attention, and in this sense that the action of *Deirdre* may be
described as 'an activity of the soul of the character'. Whether it
is such an activity in a more specifically Yeatsian sense is another
question. Is the activity so purified that Deirdre seems to move to
the centre where 'all life has the same root' so that we see ourselves in her? The bond between the play and Yeats's notions of
drama appears, when it is further examined, to be of an extremely
paradoxical nature.

Yeats argued, in his theory of tragedy and tragic character, that

---

* 'Yeats used to say about Deirdre's performance—"Red-heat up to Naisi's
death, white-heat after he is dead"' (Lennox Robinson, in *Scattering Branches*,
p. 96).

character—the 'discrimination and definition of individuality' as Una Ellis-Fermor defined it in this connexion[29]—is 'continuously present in comedy alone'. In tragic art 'one distinguishes devices to exclude or lessen character'. 'Tragedy must always be a drowning and breaking of the dykes that separate man from man':

amid the great moments, when Timon orders his tomb, when Hamlet cries to Horatio 'absent thee from felicity awhile', when Antony names 'Of many thousand kisses the poor last,' all is lyricism, unmixed passion, 'the integrity of fire.' Nor does character ever attain to complete definition in these lamps ready for the taper.[30]

The definition of individuality, like assertive scenery and over-emphatic gestures, will ruin the spectator's trance-like absorption in those supreme moments, for the 'reverie' they induce—a state of sharing 'at the root of life' in the tragic personage's activity of soul—is exceedingly fragile:

Tragic art, passionate art, the drowner of dykes, the confounder of understanding, moves us by setting us to reverie, by alluring us almost to the intensity of trance. The persons upon the stage, let us say, greaten till they are humanity itself. We feel our minds expand convulsively or spread out slowly. . . . It was only by watching my own plays that I came to understand that this reverie, this twilight between sleep and waking, this bout of fencing, alike on the stage and in the mind, between man and phantom, this perilous path as on the edge of a sword, is the condition of tragic pleasure. If an actor becomes over emphatic . . . or even if an electric lamp that should have cast a reflected light from sky to sea, shows from behind the post of a door, I discover at once the proud fragility of dreams.[31]

In addition to his examples from Shakespeare, Yeats cited two other passages that induced the tragic reverie. One is the third Act of Synge's *Deirdre of the Sorrows*—'a reverie of passion that mounts and mounts till grief itself has carried [Deirdre] beyond grief into pure contemplation'.[32] The other is from his own *Deirdre*:

I am content with the players and myself, if I am moved for a while not by the contrasted sorrows of Deirdre and Naisi, but because the words have called up before me the image of a sea-born woman so distinctly that Deirdre seems by contrast to those unshaken eyelids that had but the sea's cold blood what I had wished her to seem, a wild bird in a cage.[33]

If my account of *Deirdre* is admissible, the question is not one of deciding whether Yeats succeeded in writing a tragedy which reached to the height of his theory, but whether the theory, or this aspect of it, can usefully be applied to it at all. Although Deirdre has her moments of beautiful, mindless desperation—a wild bird in a cage—she is surely more full of character and artifice than the theory admits. Her last phase, the phase of 'white-heat' after the death of Naoise, is certainly not a phase of pure and almost depersonalized grief, like that of Synge's heroine. With controlled artifice, the staginess of the accomplished actress, she presents to Conchubar a mask of deceit, which depends for its success on its resourceful detail and on the verisimilitude with which it appears to answer his wish while gaining her own end. It is a battle of wit and will, resourceful wit balanced against the old man's jealous will. Deirdre is not helpless in the grip of circumstance, as Lady Gregory had laid it down that the tragic character ought to be,[34] but overcomes it by an act of the imagination, a role played out to the end. Her last, ambiguous words assert her consciousness of triumph while holding out a false promise to Conchubar. As for the spectator, trance or reverie seems out of the question during the scene. 'We catch our breath,' as Lennox Robinson remarked.

It was after he had written *Deirdre* that Yeats wrote:

The masks of tragedy contain neither character nor personal energy. They are allied to decoration and to the abstract figures of Egyptian temples. Before the mind can look out of their eyes the active will perishes, hence their sorrowful calm. Joy is of the will which labours, which overcomes obstacles, which knows triumph. The soul knows its changes of state alone, and I think the motives of tragedy are not related to action but to changes of state.[35]

The passage could be taken point by point as presenting the opposite of what is actually the case with *Deirdre*. The state of Deirdre's soul—if by that is meant the deepest level of her personality, the fundamental passion of her nature which motivates her behaviour—changes not at all in the course of the play, but remains always her passionate love for Naoise. Her active will never rests, but is pitted turn by turn against her own weakness, against the Musicians, against Naoise; and finally against Conchubar; and the 'masks' which she adopts, her roles, are directly the instruments of this will, and gradually strengthen in both the definition of individuality and in the personal energy with which they are played out. She knows at last joyful triumph, which, according to Yeats, is the reward of comedy:

Comedy is joyous because all assumption of a part, of a personal mask, whether of the individualized face or of the grotesque face of farce, is a display of energy, and all energy is joyous.[36]

Here *energy* (and this might reasonably have remained unguessed from many of his other uses of the word) is the sign of comedy alone. In effect, *Deirdre* is nearer to what Yeats defined as comedy than to what he held tragedy to be. The irrelation between practice and theory has beome almost grotesque.

If Yeats suspected that his own version of the great tragic tale of the 'Irish Helen', the theme hallowed for him by the pen of the dying Synge, was queerly inapposite to his own thoughts about tragedy, he might well have been confused and disappointed by the difference between what he had done in the theatre and what he wanted to do. This was perhaps one cardinal reason, amongst many lesser ones, for the moratorium of ten years on play-writing. It is broken only by *The Green Helmet*, a comedy full of 'joyous energy' but a trifle none the less, and by the abortive attempt to start *The Player Queen*.* Apart from these, only the continuing process of revision of the plays already written, the endless concern with what he described, in the essay on 'The Tragic Theatre', as 'the wheels and pulleys necessary to the effect, but in themselves nothing', show that a second attempt, after so many at most precarious, and now faded, successes, was the recognition of a need.

* The date 1914 attached to *The Hour-Glass* in *Collected Plays* (1934) is misleading. The first prose-version of this play was first printed in 1903 (slightly revised in 1908 and 1911). A poetic version was being planned as early as June, 1903 (*Letters*, p. 393); the version in *Collected Plays*, partly in prose and partly in verse, was first printed in Gordon Craig's periodical *The Mask* in 1913 (Wade, No. 108, No. 110, No. 115).

PART TWO:
THE MYSTERY
TO COME

I wanted a theatre where the greatest passions and all the permanent interests of men might be displayed that we might find them not alone over a book but, as I said again and again, lover by lover, friend by friend. All I wanted was impossible, and I wore out my youth in its pursuit, but now I know it is the mystery to come.

—Pages from a Diary
Written in Nineteen Hundred and Thirty

Chapter Four

The Cuchulain Plays

---

*Even though he represent no man of worth in his art, the worth
of his own mind becomes the inheritance of his people.*

I

IN one of the papers from *Samhain* (1905) in 'The Irish
Dramatic Movement' Yeats writes of his rejection of the
'white phantoms' of the falsely idealized dramatic character, and criticizes *Caste* as an example of the conventional
idealism of the English theatre:

the central persons, the man and woman that created the dramatic
excitement, such as it was, had not characters of any kind, being vague
ideals, perfection as it is imagined by a commonplace mind. The
audience could give them its sympathy without the labour that comes
from awakening knowledge. If the dramatist had put into his play
whatever man or woman of his acquaintance seemed to come closest
to perfection, he would have had to make it a study, among other
things, of the little petty faults and perverted desires that arise out of
the nature or its surroundings. He would have troubled that admiring
audience by making a self-indulgent sympathy more difficult.[1]

When Yeats chose the life and death of Cuchulain as the subject
of five plays (which he came to think of as a coherent series), this
'antiquated romantic stuff', as the Old Man calls it in *The Death
of Cuchulain*,[2] did not tempt him to romantic idealization of
character and theme. He laboured to awaken knowledge in his
audience by giving them the oblique view and engendering his

61

conflicts from a continuous interplay of ironic meanings. It was not simply that Yeats had a sceptical or reserved attitude towards the antique story. His point of view entails a generous recognition of the value of heroic revolt, courage, and love; but they are placed in a context which proves tragic because of some element which is thwarting and contradictory in the nature of the heroic acts, the man who performs them, the spirit which inspires them, or the world in which they are done. This element does not take the form of a commentary, something outside the business of the plays; it is a part of their construction, and helps to create the tensions which make them dramatic.

The first of these plays is *On Baile's Strand*. The version of 1903 differs a good deal from the version of 1906.* The source is the story called 'The Only Son of Aoife' in Lady Gregory's *Cuchulain of Muirthemne*.[3] This relates how Conlaoch, the son of Aoife and Cuchulain, had been brought up by his mother in ignorance of his father's identity because of the jealous loathing she had conceived for Cuchulain, who defeated her in battle, became her lover, and then, unaware that she had borne a son, abandoned her for marriage to Emer. Conlaoch, now grown to manhood, arrives at Baile's Strand where the High King Conchubar is holding court with his counsellors and warriors. Aoife has caused her son to take an oath to challenge the greatest champion of Ireland without revealing whose son he is. Cuchulain accepts the challenge, but learns too late, when the boy is mortally wounded, whom he has killed. Madness descends upon the hero and he fights the sea.

Of all the Abbey plays, *On Baile's Strand*, which has been called one of 'the best poetic plays of this century'[4] and which generated several spurts of creative excitement in Yeats himself,[5] seems most at home with the material of the elder world in which it is set. In it, as well as in *The Green Helmet*, we can most clearly trace what it was that Lady Gregory's two volumes of paraphrased legend contributed to the dramatist's imagination. Lady Gregory's work enabled him to see the legendary world as a whole, to hold it in

* The 1903 version was printed in *In the Seven Woods* (Cuala Press, Dublin, 1903) and Volume III of *Plays for an Irish Theatre* (1904); the revised version first appeared in *Poems 1899–1905* (London and Dublin, 1906). My quotations are from this text except where otherwise stated.

the hollow of his imagination, and to vitalize it with habits, customs, and manners. The trappings of Cuchulain in *On Baile's Strand*, the witches, warriors, hunt, and camp, and the allusions with which the speakers amplify passion and argument, are remotely clear and strange because they derive from a single vision of a past world; they are not distant from us because they are muzzy or arbitrary but because they are defined. The outlines of the story itself Yeats could and did get from elsewhere. Although Yeats made the story which I have just summarized from *Cuchulain of Muirthemne* into the climax of his play, even in the first version he added many invented incidents. There is, first, the framing underplot of the Blind Man and the Fool. They are not only expositors, but are needed for the most theatrically effective moment in the play, which several commentators have praised,[6] the moment of agony when Cuchulain learns whom he has killed. It has also been remarked that their roles parody and change places with those of Cuchulain and Conchubar:

> the blind man
> Has need of the fool's eyesight and strong body,
> While the poor fool has need of the other's wit,
> And night and day is up to his ears in mischief
> That the blind man imagines.[7]

This too is how warrior and ruler serve each other. Yeats brings the relationship to life first by stressing the differences between Cuchulain's band of young and yeasty fighters and Conchubar's group of grave, ancient counsellors. He is also departing from his source in a point vital to his reading of the story when his Cuchulain accepts Conlaoch's challenge not unhesitatingly (as he does in the source) but because he is commanded to do so by the King, and because his understanding has been corrupted by the persuasion that his strange fondness for the young man has been engendered by witchcraft.

This new material, bearing on the relation between king and hero, is faintly handled in the first version, but very greatly expanded in the second version. Yeats substitutes for the discussion of Conchubar's plan for building his city (in the first version) a prolonged debate between the two men (in the second). It culminates in a ceremony at which Cuchulain swears an oath of obedience to Conchubar and his heirs. Not until this has been done does the story, in Lady Gregory's sense, begin.

Such an arrangement of the tale, with so much emphasis on preliminaries (for Conlaoch does not enter until a good half of the play is done), might have had a strangely muffling and delaying effect upon the culminating, brutal irony of the father's fight with the son. But Yeats uses his plot, made up of two episodes instead of one, to tangle and thicken the ironies and to organize within and around his hero the perturbations proper to a protagonist of stature. We share in Cuchulain's 'intimate life' and 'activity of soul'.

Cuchulain has been troubling the kingdom. Without children himself, he will not acknowledge those of his master. The quarrel is designed to bring out the contrast between the hero's turbulence and the ruler's responsibilities. For the play, in both its versions, is about how the building of a city and a kingdom destroys another kind of life. The High King complains that:

> every day my children come and say
> 'This man is growing harder to endure.
> How can we be at safety with this man,
> That nobody can buy or bid or bind?
> We shall be at his mercy when you are gone.
> He burns the earth as if it were a fire,
> And time can never touch him.'

' I do not like your children', says Cuchulain:

> They have no pith,
> No marrow in their bones, and will lie soft
> Where you and I lie hard.

Conchubar's heirs seem ghostly and insignificant to the hero, who is unbiddable because he has no son to care for and constrain him. Instead, he has only a fantastic and overweening notion of what a child of his might be—a man that would face 'Even myself in battle'. 'Now as ever', declares Conchubar,

> You mock at every measurable hope,
> And would have nothing or impossible things.
> What eye has ever looked upon the child
> Would satisfy a mind like that!

But although Cuchulain dreams of a new generation able to challenge the splendour of his own, the dream itself only compensates for the sense of present wanting:

> I know you to the bone.
> I have heard you cry—aye, in your very sleep—
> 'I have no son!' and with such bitterness
> That I have gone upon my knees and prayed
> That it might be amended.

This ominous play upon the theme of fatherhood deepens the narrative. The debate is linked in other ways with the coming of Conlaoch. His finding the shore insufficiently guarded has brought the issue of Cuchulain's irresponsibility to a head; and the dramatic excitement is greater because Conlaoch's entrance follows immediately upon the taking of the oath, whereas in the first version his arrival merely interrupts the mild, though not inconsequential, discussion of Conchubar's plan to rebuild his capital city. Parkinson has also drawn attention to the wider field of reference, from this play to other plays, of which the completer design of the second version makes us aware:

the major subject of Yeats' Abbey dramas was the conflict between the fixed palpable world of human affairs (Guaire, Conchubar) and the world of passion and aspiration, which is beyond reason, system, or office (Seanchan, Cuchulain). The basic split in the plays is that between the institutional world—limited, tame, calculating, interested in the virtue of fixed character—and the personal world—exuberant, carefree, wild, affirming the values of intense personality.[8]

But the greatest interest of the new episode is the way in which it affects our view of Cuchulain's tragedy in the second half of the play. Variations on the subjects that are talked about during the debate and oath-taking are played through during the meeting with Conlaoch, where the attitudes of king and hero are put to the test of Conlaoch and emerge passionately disordered and ironically interchangeable. This is because the links that have been mentioned are more than merely narrative connexions. They are often vital antitheses, and hence lead to the lively interaction of the two episodes.

When even his own troopers wish Cuchulain to take the oath and become 'as biddable as a house-dog', he submits:

> You've wives and children now,
> And for that reason cannot follow one
> That lives like a bird's flight from tree to tree.

He agrees to offer up his uncaged existence through a protective ritual which is designed to ward off the temptations of the shape-changers as they are practised upon the nameless and houseless man. From henceforth his sword will, in the words of the oath,

> have for master none
> But the threshold and hearthstone.

The stability seemingly achieved through this submission next breaks down into the tragedy in which the hero is destroyed. Conchubar's paramount authority, strengthened by the oath, is once more the agent responsible.

When the Young Man from Aoife's country arrives, Conchubar commands Cuchulain to accept the challenge, while Cuchulain, touched by his half-familiar beauty, seeks peace and order in Conlaoch's friendship.[9] For the second time in the play the king requires the hero to thwart his 'energy of soul' by obeying him. Cuchulain is seen complete when he is seen trapped in this dilemma. It is created by the blindness of authority to whatever force it is that keeps the heroic spindle whirling round. But, on this second occasion, the issue has shifted, as the armed stranger begins to take on the aspect of a son. When Conchubar orders Cuchulain to fight the Young Man who will not tell his name, he is demanding the subversion in Cuchulain of that calm life of the threshold and the hearthstone, the instinctive yearning for naming instead of namelessness, which the king himself had earlier in the play bound him with, first by his reproaches and then by the oath. The authority of the Blind Man, which appears consistent in its continual demand for obedience, really asks that Cuchulain strain both ways, from turbulence into peace, and then, when that is being achieved, into houseless turbulence once more.

Thus Yeats makes a double knot out of his singly knotted source. The two central episodes are interlocked by means of certain thematic links, so that the second episode draws meaning from the first. These links serve not only to make the tale more exciting; they also tighten by twisting, making the inward life of Cuchulain tenser by pulling it in different directions. Thus to Conchubar in the first episode the childlessness and faithlessness of the hero had been the reasons for his turbulence and a cause for pride with Cuchulain himself:

> I'll not be bound.
> I'll dance or hunt, or quarrel or make love,
> Wherever and whenever I've a mind to.

In the second episode Cuchulain instinctively reaches towards alliance and fatherhood; it seems that the fantastic and impossible wish for a son that will match up to Cuchulain's dream of a son— which in the first episode was an index of his heroic excess—is about to be realized:

> Boy, I would meet them all in arms
> If I'd a son like you. He would avenge me . . .
> But I'd need no avenger. You and I
> Would scatter them like water from a dish.

Conlaoch is the man whom Conchubar believed could not exist and now cannot discern, although Cuchulain is just beginning to see him.

There is, too, the theme of Queen Aoife, whose love turned to hatred. When, during the debate, Cuchulain had argued for heroic wildness he had justified his contempt for ordinary women and his rejection of all that is settled in love by recalling the fierce beauties of Aoife.[10] When Conchubar had reminded him that Aoife now hated him, he had answered by defining heroical love as the paradoxical conjunction of love and hate:

> I never have known love but as a kiss
> In the mid-battle, and a difficult truce
> Of oil and water, candles and dark night,
> Hillside and hollow, the hot-footed sun,
> And the cold sliding, slippery-footed moon—
> A brief forgiveness between opposites
> That have been hatreds for three times the age
> Of this long-'stablished ground.

This heroical love that denies the threshold and the hearthstone

67

had been repudiated in the oath's chant against the witches, who

> will give him kiss for kiss
> While they murmur, 'After this
> Hatred may be sweet to the taste';
> Those wild hands that have embraced
> All his body can but shove
> At the burning wheel of love
> Till the side of hate comes up.

And when Aoife's son faces him, the likeness to his mother wakens in Cuchulain a love which seeks not a brief forgiveness but a life of friendly play. Not opposite meets opposite, but likeness likeness. The likeness is charged with irony: these are two sons whose fathers would, or could, kill them:

> Boy,
> If I had fought my father, he'd have killed me
> As certainly as if I had a son,
> And fought with him I should be deadly to him.

It is Conchubar's endeavour to stir up the dreadful implications of a likeness such as that. By reminding Cuchulain that Conlaoch is the emissary of Aoife he seeks to bring about that transformation of love into hatred which Cuchulain in his turbulence had acknowledged and affirmed, but which the oath had repudiated. Thus Conchubar seeks to bring back the tumult which he had earlier tried to allay and so unknowingly subjects them all to Aoife's evil will. The tragic authority, since it wants his sword in battle, wishes Cuchulain to re-assume the heroic antinomies which the hero, at the ruler's own behest, had shed.

These opposites are finely organized in the act of Cuchulain's striking the High King. It is the moment of almost wordless action when the antinomies blaze forth.

During the course of the second episode the play has taken another turn. The warriors, backed by Conchubar, challenge Conlaoch, and Cuchulain moves into his old place, fronting and defying the ruler, not on behalf of the heroic freedom, but for the new love. But he is appalled at his own deed when he strikes at the High King in the passion of revolt. Formerly, even the defence of his own freedom had concluded in submission, and it is right that the Cuchulain who took the oath should now see the

68

blow at Conchubar as the corruption of his own nature by witch-craft having its source in the Young Man who has bewitched him into friendship. Conchubar has now got the Cuchulain he wanted: the oath-taker who respects his sacred authority and goes out to fight his enemy. The irony is that this Cuchulain is also the one who, in the act of doing so, rejects and regards as corrupted the 'energy of soul', aroused by Conlaoch's significant likeness, which moves him towards peace and fatherhood and towards the threshold and the hearthstone—those very things which had been the substance and rationale of the oath that Conchubar had made him take. It is Aoife's will, the 'will of woman at her wildest',[11] that is now being fulfilled. In the hero, both the old heroic and the new anti-heroic unities of being have been manipulated to destroy each other. Confusion has fallen upon his thought.

The father who kills his son butchers his own image. Yeats has transformed this simple horror into a tangled drama of self-destruction by using his two episodes to 'arrange much compli-cated life into a single action'.[12] Fate and Conchubar combine to transform heroic energy into madness, and the Fool and the Blind Man are left as the masters of the scene.

II

In *The Golden Helmet*, re-written as *The Green Helmet* (1908 and 1910), Yeats has again worked by juxtaposing two episodes: the quarrel of the chieftains, and the test for the championship of Ulster. As Birgit Bjersby has pointed out, Yeats has put the episodes together into a single action by departing from his sources and combining Bricriu, the maker of discord, and CuRoi, the tester, into the single figure of the Red Man.[13] The knot woven from the two subjects is untied with a single move-ment when Cuchulain offers his head to the Red Man. So he pays the debt imposed by the Red Man as his condition for the ending of the strife, and gains the championship not as 'the strongest' (the claim that has led to irresolvable strife amongst the warriors) but as the one who is 'without fear',[14] the gay hero, proper to the 'gay animated stage not too far from the mood of the world' which Yeats wanted in the play.[15] Thus the play concludes with a comic irony: the champion turns out not to be the mightiest but the most comely-hearted, the one who had earlier attempted to resolve discord into harmony by turning the coveted prize, the golden helmet, into a drinking-cup to be shared by all; and it is he who is greeted by the Red Man as one who 'shall win many battles with laughing lips and endure wounding and betrayal without bitterness of heart'.[16] In this Cuchulain there is no tragic dichotomy between what he is and what he is made to do.

But the tragedy of heroic circumstance is revived once more in the third of the Cuchulain plays, *At the Hawk's Well* (finished in 1916). It is about the courage without which there can be no heroic desire, but which is made the means to thwart it. The Old Man has been waiting by the well for fifty years for a chance to drink the mysteriously flowing water, but each time the water has bubbled out he has been cheated of it by the 'deceivers', the dancers who guard the well in the form of hawks. Into their 'unfaltering, unmoistened eyes' he dares not look; although he has the desire, he lacks the courage, and whenever the water gushes their dance lulls him into a strengthless sleep. Cuchulain enters and learns this story. Then the silent Guardian of the Well becomes possessed by the hawk, the terrible life of the deity slides through her veins and reveals itself to Cuchulain in the gaze of the hawk's eyes. He stares into them, and so becomes subjected to the curse predicted by the Old Man:

> There falls a curse
> On all who have gazed in her unmoistened eyes . . .
> That curse may be
> Never to win a woman's love and keep it;
> Or always to mix hatred in the love;
> Or it may be that she will kill your children,
> That you will find them, their throats torn and bloody,
> Or that you will be so maddened that you kill them
> With your own hand.[17]

Then Cuchulain is lured from the flowing water by her dance, and at the same moment the Old Man, who has covered his head from the hawk's gaze, falls into his helpless sleep. The hero comes back to find that the well is dry again, and to learn that the warrior-women of the hills are roused against him. Shouldering his spear, he leaves the sacred mountain to confront with courage the bitter life of war.

The symbolic referents of the water and the hawk have been worked out by many commentators, but their general meaning in the play is plain, and sufficiently full to subserve the purposes of dramatic action. The water represents wisdom or immortality (either or both) or love unmixed with hatred (but surely not, as T. R. Henn seems to suggest, sexual virility).[18] But it is truer to what is in the play to see it as simply the one precious and mysterious gift that will release Cuchulain and the Old Man, the one from the toils of old age and the other from the bitter entanglements of the heroic fate, from the divided and thwarted life of the hero of *On Baile's Strand*. The guardian hawk that lulls and lures is deceit and illusion that destroy Cuchulain's unity of being, or confound his search for it. She is the 'inhuman, bitter glory', 'the persecution of the abstract'. She resembles Fand the Woman of the Sidhe in *The Only Jealousy of Emer* and Aoife in *The Death of Cuchulain*,[19] with whom in *At the Hawk's Well* she is in some sort of league (but not, I think, in this play to be identified with her, as Birgit Bjersby and Donald R. Pearce suppose).[20]

The courage of the hero is the theme which ties together the play's two episodes. They function in the design like protasis and catastrophe. It is courage which manifests itself as the major antinomy in the moment when fate is rendered through dramatic action—Cuchulain's behaviour as the hawk reveals itself and dances. The protasis is, as it was in *On Baile's Strand*, more than a mere exposition, but Yeats uses it with much greater economy and effect than he had in the earlier Cuchulain plays. The timidity and withered condition of the Old Man, the expositor, result from his long years of failure to face the demon. He is all, in respect of courage, that Cuchulain is not:

YOUNG MAN

My luck is strong,
It will not leave me waiting, nor will they
That dance among the stones put me asleep;
If I grow drowsy I can pierce my foot.

OLD MAN

No, do not pierce it, for the foot is tender,
It feels pain much.

The Old Man has never dared to gaze into the hawk's eyes; he has not risked the curse, and now is cursed with vain senescence. Dramatically, he is Cuchulain's foil.

This preparation gives full weight of meaning to the moment when the hawk manifests itself. As the Old Man hides from the terrifying eyes, heroic courage gazes into them. Ironically, his act betrays Cuchulain. His courage robs him of what the courage was for—its prize, the sacred water; it commits him to the curse, and to the dance which leads him away from undivided being. We can understand why Yeats wrote of spitting upon the dancers painted by Degas,[21] when we see this dancer 'moving like a hawk'; she must both attract and destroy; she mimics the bird whose cruelty is inseparable from its beauty and herself has something of 'the supreme beauty which is accursed'.[22] What makes *At the Hawk's Well* a play and not a symbolist poem is the way in which the contradictory nature of heroic courage is prepared for and acted out through the deed and character of the hero. Cuchulain's movement of courage expresses his nature, but it also transforms him into a victim. What he is betrays him in its acting-out.

At the same time the other character, the Old Man, makes it plain that for Cuchulain to be less than himself is no escape either. To gaze into the hawk's eyes earns Cuchulain only the curse of self-division, the unhoused condition, the mixing of hatred and impermanence with love. But the failure to dare gets no reward either, only withering and self-despite. The curse is on Cuchulain's betraying courage; it now wears the colours of doom and of the death of Conlaoch. But the play ends, as do *Deirdre* and *The Herne's Egg*, in an assertion of identity and of the heroic Name, as Cuchulain leaves the stage shouldering his spear:

He comes! Cuchulain, son of Sualtam, comes![23]

III

The Only Jealousy of Emer is perhaps the most intricately plotted of the Yeatsian Noh plays.* Despite its relatively complicated

---

* There are three versions. The first was finished in 1918, the second is a rewriting in prose, *Fighting the Waves* (written in 1928 and printed in *Wheels*

story, the ironic meanings are at their clearest, as though practice was bringing Yeats nearer to perfection. They attend upon the theme of love.

Cuchulain, after fighting the sea, lies in death watched over by his wife Emer and his mistress Eithne Inguba. When the body wakens to life at Eithne's kiss, it is seen to be possessed by the god Bricriu, the maker of discord. He offers to restore the hero's life on condition that Emer renounces her hope that Cuchulain's love will return at long last to her. He shows her the Ghost of Cuchulain being tempted by Fand, the Woman of the Sidhe, Bricriu's enemy; she is drawing the Ghost away to a life of immortal and inhuman love, and is resisted only by the Ghost's memories of Emer's earthly love. The Ghost is upon the point of yielding when Emer saves him by her renunciation, passionately withheld until this moment. But Cuchulain's first words as he wakes to life are a cry for Eithne Inguba.

The final episode is differently managed in the first and in the last versions. In the first, the renunciation breaks into the colloquy between the Ghost and Fand, and is followed by speeches from the Ghost which show his final realization of the folly of a deathless love which cannot experience suffering or memory:

> How could you know
> That man is held to those whom he has loved
> By pain they gave, or pain that he has given,
> Intricacies of pain.[24]

Fand rejects him as a man 'knotted in impurity', and there follows

---

and Butterflies, 1934), and the third is the version in Collected Plays. I use the last version, but refer also to the first as it is found in Four Plays for Dancers (1921). Yeats first heard about the Japanese Noh plays from Ezra Pound in the winter of 1913–14 (see the essay 'Swedenborg, Mediums, and the Desolate Places' in Lady Gregory's Visions and Beliefs, II. 333). At the Hawk's Well, The Only Jealousy of Emer, The Dreaming of the Bones, Calvary, and The Death of Cuchulain are the plays which most clearly show deliberate imitation of Noh techniques in their use of a 'unifying image', a dance, masks, and a chorus detached from the action. To a lesser degree the influence of the Noh can be detected in Purgatory and even in the prose-plays The Resurrection and The Words upon the Window-pane. For a useful study, see Earl Miner's The Japanese Tradition in British and American Literature (Princeton, 1958), pp. 251–65.

a quarrel between Fand and Bricriu. The last version omits all this, and places Emer's renunciation almost at the end of the play when Fand and the Ghost are just about to take horse for the Country-under-Wave. By these changes Yeats has greatly tightened the dramatic rhythm, but at the cost of making the themes slightly less clear and the interpenetration of natural and supernatural less intimate.

The major irony of the play is clear enough, though, especially when it is read in the light of the gradually sharpening ironies of the previous Cuchulain plays. Emer's renunciation of Cuchulain's love is her greatest act of love towards him. This is the same technique for the climactic moment of action as had been used in *At the Hawk's Well*. The loving wife must act so, for that is the ground of her being, but the act itself cancels out all hope of fulfilment for the loving nature from which it sprang, just as the hero's courage put out of reach for ever the prize which courage was designed to win. Her deed is solitary, 'self-delighting and self-affrighting', and by definition cannot be known to or recognized by the man whom Emer saves. A passage in the Preface to *Fighting the Waves* is relevant:

Here in Ireland we have come to think of self-sacrifice, when worthy of public honour, as the act of some man at the moment when he is least himself, most completely the crowd. The heroic act, as it descends through tradition, is an act done because a man is himself, because, being himself, he can ask nothing of other men but room amid re-membered tragedies; a sacrifice of himself to himself, almost, so little may he bargain, of the moment to the moment.[25]

Emer's heroic deed, like Cuchulain's in *At the Hawk's Well*, is an assertion of her identity, of her name as loving wife, and her only reward, like Deirdre's, is that the long-remembering harpers shall have matter for their song.

But Emer here has a dimension which is absent from the Cuchu-lain of *At the Hawk's Well*. Her act is of such a character that it knows its consequence, and this is necessitated by the conditions under which it is performed. She does not find, after she has asserted her nature, that her destiny is in consequence to suffer its frustration; she chooses this destiny. She does not, as Cuchulain in the previous play does, dare the curse as part of the adventure, but chooses to be cursed. For she is fulfilling her side of the bargain with Bricriu and knows what is bound to follow:

> He'll never sit beside you at the hearth
> Or make old bones, but die of wounds and toil
> On some far shore or mountain, a strange woman
> Beside his mattress.[26]

Her assent to the bargain is deliberate, and the nature of the bargain, as not in *The Golden Helmet,* is that neither side is pretending, so that the bargain cannot be comically evaded. Nothing Emer does is founded on a mistaking. She is more the heroine of the moral choice than any of Yeats's earlier protagonists, much more so than the Countess Cathleen, who, as we have seen, was never really given a chance to 'choose', and whose bargain is eventually annulled by heavenly justice. The difference shows Yeats's progression in the bleaker ironies.

Much more could, and has, been said about *The Only Jealousy,* in particular about 'those little known convictions about the nature and history of a woman's beauty', which Robartes found in the *Speculum* of Gyraldus and with which Yeats declared that he had filled the play.[27] But, although they are in the play, it is not, properly speaking, about them, but about the acting-out of Emer's dilemma. It was possible for W. Y. Tindall to claim that at first sight he found Emer's action unintelligible,[28] but the interpretation which he finally offers us ('man's victory over flux' and Fand as the Machine) almost suggests that he was not looking for a drama at all but for an enemy code which he could break. And Birgit Bjersby, who was interested in the correspondences between the play and the philosophical mythology, gives an account of them that seems to ignore all that makes *The Only Jealousy* an intelligible theatrical structure.[29] Yeats, although he enjoyed bringing into the play numerous echoes of the System, had not much desire that they should seriously distract the audience from the business of his stage. The descriptions of Woman's or Fand's beauty in the terminology of the phases of the moon, which we find in the Musicians' songs, help to create the chill, lofty, and allusive tone, which is a thing in itself, carried alive into the heart without need for glossing. The songs are, furthermore, detached from the play, in accordance with the principles of the Noh drama as Yeats understood them. They are a frame for the tragic struggle; they modulate towards it and away from it, but they do not enter into it. The notion of the Ghost lingering by its abode is a commonplace of tradition, and Yeats does not attempt to bestow upon it more than a hint of the elaborate schematizations that he was working out for the 'Soul in Judgement' sections of *A Vision*. The allusions to the phases of the moon in Fand's speeches work similarly to those in the musicians' songs. They sound the note of a remote, ordered, and inhuman world proper to the speech of a supernatural personage; to track them down to their lair in 'Gyraldus' and elsewhere does not seem to shed a great deal of light on the function in the drama of the character who speaks them.

What does need placing more firmly in an account of the play itself is the whole episode of Fand and the Ghost. As a dramatic device it does, I should guess, three things. It actualizes more vividly than anything merely related could have done the interpenetration of natural and supernatural which is the world of the play. It builds up tension as Emer watches it (like some dreadful sight seen in Friar Bacon's prospective glass); she resists up to and beyond the moment when the Ghost yields, and by this means the untying of the knot by her renunciation is delayed enough to point the desperate pain of her decision, and sudden and climactic enough to dismiss the demons from the play and break the interlocking of natural and supernatural worlds. Lastly, in depicting the character of the Ghost's resistance, it strengthens the ironies in the theme of love, because that resistance is compounded of his memories of Emer as bride and wife, whom when he was alive he deserted and when he is restored to life he puts by.

Yet a difficulty remains, a difficulty about the kind of temptation that Fand offers and represents. It is true that an assumption of the play must be that it is better to have Cuchulain alive than dead, whatever death may be, and that Fand, as the creature from the sea that has drowned Cuchulain, is substantially just Death itself. But Fand's characterization as a temptress cuts across her role as 'that which is not life', and what she offers is an immortal, if inhuman, love, where 'nothing but beauty can remain'. This Oisin-like state seems appropriate enough as the fate after death of the mythological hero. The feeling muddles our view of Emer's condition: from what, after all, is she saving him? It even suggests that Yeats's desire to put some of his 'little-known convictions' into his latest portrait of a Woman of the Sidhe, to plant in Ireland what he plucked in Byzantium, may have disordered his sense of the theatre—that Fand is what she is and offers what she does offer because Michael Robartes grasped at the pen. It might have been better if the Ghost's condition had been represented more neutrally, as a drawing away into some underworld of strengthless shades. It is probably significant that, when he re-wrote the play in prose 'to free it from abstraction and con-fusion',[30] Yeats reduced or evaded the problem by cutting out all the words set down for Fand and the Ghost and leaving her only her dance.

IV

The Death of Cuchulain is based upon the version of the story con-tained in the last two chapters of Lady Gregory's *Cuchulain of Muirthemne*. It makes special use of three key-incidents in it: the war-goddess's device of a treacherous message, delivered by Cuchulain's mistress, to the beleaguered hero; the death itself against the 'pillar-stone west of the lake' on the plain of Muir-themne; and the lamentation of Emer who 'took the head of Cuchulain in her hands, and she washed it clean, and put a silk cloth about it, and she held it to her breast; and she began to cry heavily over it'.[31]

Yeats wrote to Ethel Mannin in October, 1938:

Goethe said that the poet needs all philosophy but must keep it out of his work. I am writing a play on the death of Cuchulain, an episode or two from the old epic. My 'private philosophy' is there but there must be no sign of it; all must be like an old faery tale. It guided me to certain conclusions but I do not write it.[32]

I would draw a different inference from this passage than does F. A. C. Wilson who in his *W. B. Yeats and Tradition* has written at greater length on this play than any other scholar. It clearly affirms the continuing primacy, so far as the Cuchulain plays are concerned, of a theatrical rather than a symbolist strategy. Yeats still desires to 'show events' and still needs that roomful of people sharing one lofty emotion,[33] not puzzled by being presented with a chart they cannot decipher. He is ready, as in the closing song of *The Only Jealousy*, to weight his style and give strength to his imagery with obscure intimations of the philosophy. He does so, though, only when this is theatrically appropriate, as it is in this play for the song of the harlot and the beggar-man. This is detached from the play in the manner of the Noh choruses. It leads away from the event and generalizes the emotion so that the curtain is folded upon a distancing echo, the stage empty and ready to fade into silence. But the song is not the key to the play, which remains stubbornly a matter of interlocked character and plot dramatically realized, and Mr. Wilson, for all his efforts, cannot make it look as if it were. It is only by means of a formidably selective treatment of it that he is able to reach his verdict that 'the play, a play of rejoicing, centres about [Cuchulain's] transfiguration'.[34] This misrepresents the structure of a play in which I see not transfiguration, and certainly not rejoicing—though there is a kind of grim joy in it—but the death of the hero seen as the final irony of his fate.

When Eithne Inguba enters (playing the role assigned to Niamh in Lady Gregory's version) she tells him that she has been charged by Emer to urge him to go forth at once and do battle with the troops of Maeve. Cuchulain is ready, but he notices that Eithne carries a letter in her hand. It is from Emer, and when he reads it he finds that she has written something quite different:

> I am not to move
> Until to-morrow morning, for, if now,
> I must face odds no man can face and live.[35]

In the morning Conall will come to his aid. The discrepancy is explained a few moments later when the Morrigu, goddess of war, appears and stands silently between the pair. Eithne realizes that when she spoke she had been bewitched into acting as the mouthpiece of the goddess, who wishes to destroy Cuchulain. Out of this situation the first episode develops.

Eithne, restored to her faithful self after the trance of deception, cannot save Cuchulain, who is blind to his fate. Although he has Emer's true message, his heart is set upon the grand, heroical gesture, the fight in the face of treachery and against great odds.

This, indeed, is the only right way for a hero of his kind to die, unless he is caught up to heaven by the gods:

> I much prefer
> Your own unwritten words. I am for the fight,
> I and my handful are set upon the fight;
> We have faced great odds before, a straw decided.

Although, by describing Maeve and the Morrigu, Eithne gives him the unmistakable clue that magic is at work, he does not see it, but ascribes the false message to what he thinks is her natural desire to get rid of a lover of whom she is tired. He exclaims in scorn:

> A woman that has an eye in the middle of her forehead!
> A woman that is headed like a crow!

All this, he implies, is fabulous nonsense. But had he not chosen to be blind, he would have recognized the baleful stigmata of the goddess. Despite his conviction that Eithne has sought to betray him, he adopts a role of heroic magnanimity towards her, pointing out how natural her behaviour is in a mistress who longs for a younger man, and how unsurprising, since she failed him in another great crisis, when it was his wife who saved him from the sea. The irony is intensified by his failure to understand that that is precisely what Eithne is trying to do now. Eithne, in despair, accuses him of wanting to die:

> You're not the man I loved,
> That violent man forgave no treachery.
> If, thinking what you think, you can forgive,
> It is because you are about to die.

But he mistakes her horror for exultation at the prospect:

> Spoken too loudly and too near the door;
> Speak low if you would speak about my death,
> Or not in that strange voice exulting in it.
> Who knows what ears listen behind the door?

Eithne cries that, if the servants are listening, at least they won't indulge in this disgusting charade of forgiveness; they have what Cuchulain seems to have lost, 'the passion necessary to life'. When he is dead she will denounce herself for treachery to the 'cooks, scullions, armourers, bed-makers, and messengers'. They are not heroes blinded by their own stories; they will put her to death

> So that my shade can stand among the shades
> And greet your shade and prove it is no traitor.

Cuchulain, unconvinced, answers 'Women have spoken so, plotting a man's death', and his last act before he goes to battle is to ensure that Eithne is drugged in order to prevent her condemning herself, and to charge a servant to 'protect her life As if it were your own'.

It has been necessary to follow the scene in this detailed way in order to show why I cannot see in the episode any sign of a Cuchulain who goes to his last battle in bitterness of heart at Eithne's defection and 'because the death-wish has come upon him'.[36] We have, instead, a dramatization of the reckless energy of the hero, seeking glory in a fight against the odds and behaving with generous forbearance to the woman whom he thinks has tried to bring about his death. Cuchulain of course acknowledges that he may perish in the battle, but he is not, like Lady Gregory's hero, ready to say: 'there is no reason for me to care for my life from this out, for my time is at an end'.[37] That is not the feeling of the scene at all. The 'pardon' granted to Eithne—indeed, the whole elaborate and intimate scene with her—are amongst the material that Yeats did not find in his source and are intended to enhance his portrait of the great-souled man.

The irony, plain to be seen by the audience, derives from the tangle of misunderstandings that is netted about these fine attitudes and drags the hero down. Because his eyes are dazzled by the vision of heroic strife, he cannot recognize the goddess of death standing before him, who makes a doom out of the adventure. Nor can he recognize the faithfulness of Eithne, who has to suffer the worst of horrors in being forgiven for a crime which she has not committed. Cuchulain's end is being determined by his own desire and by his fixed interpretation of his hero's role. The Morrigu is the presiding deity of the play (she claims later to have 'arranged the dance', the dance of death that the drama is, and Emer's dance of mourning that follows it); but, although she presides over the sequences of mortality, she does not directly implement them. Her false message is quickly seen for what it is, even by Cuchulain, who is otherwise incapable of distinguishing the false from the true. Yet plainly, Yeats seems to imply, the hero blinded by the vision of his story, tangled in error and giving those who love him bitter pain, still astonishes us with his majesty.

What is done to this majesty when Cuchulain comes to the moment of dying? The second part of the play is constructed of two antithetical episodes, and the second of these continually looks back towards the first. Cuchulain re-enters, wounded to death. He is followed by Aoife, who has come to kill him, and who helps him to bind himself to the standing-stone so that he may die, like Vespasian and Bussy d'Ambois, upon his feet. The intensely moving dialogue between the masterful, aged Aoife, whose cruelty is full of reminiscent wonder, and Cuchulain, whose voice and rhythms have stilled and melted into the weakness and confusion of the dying, slowly shapes a pattern in which the tragedies of Baile's strand and the hawk's well are remembered. The old story of love mixed with hatred, frustration and tragic error builds up towards what is plainly its one right ending—that Aoife should at last revenge upon his father the death of Conlaoch. Cuchulain admits that she has 'the right to kill me'. 'You have the right', he repeats, and her purpose remains unaltered despite all that they remember of their common history.

But this mounting tension is suddenly diverted; the pattern, just as it is about to become complete, is suddenly abandoned and rubbed out. Aoife's leaving the stage is contrived, awkward, and feebly explained. This is a master-stroke which draws attention to what is being done by the dramatist. It reminds us, with some boldness, as does Shakespeare's occasional use of the technical terms of dramaturgy, that we are in the theatre:

> Somebody comes,
> Some countryman, and when he finds you here,
> And none to protect him, will be terrified.
> I will keep out of his sight, for I have things
> That I must ask questions on before I kill you.

A fine reason for a fine queen to give for the suspension of so vital —or so mortal—a pattern! The Blind Man, who enters now, belongs to that part of the Cuchulain story that owns to ironic commentary on the doings of these great ones:

> Somebody said that I was in Maeve's tent,
> And somebody else, a big man by his voice,
> That if I brought Cuchulain's head in a bag
> I would be given twelve pennies; I had the bag
> To carry what I get at kitchen doors,
> Somebody told me how to find the place;
> I thought it would have taken till the night,
> But this has been my lucky day.

The clown's 'lucky day' is the day on which the hero dies. This, like the final episode in *On Baile's Strand*, is a deliberate trailing of the story in the refuse-dump of 'The Circus Animals' Desertion', the foul rag-and-bone shop of the heart. Cuchulain's own comment is almost his last comment on the heroic adventure, and a total denial of all its glorious rationale:

> Twelve pennies! What better reason for killing a man?

This is an acceptance, but it is not a transfiguration, and Aoife who had all the reason in the heroic world for killing Cuchulain is cheated. The story in which revenge would have meaningfully completed work, life, and death is carefully built up but does not resolve into its climax; the actual ending runs against it. Such is the construction of the play's second part, and it embodies a resounding irony. This is heard again in Cuchulain's vision of his soul after death ('a soft feathery shape . . . a strange shape for the soul / Of a great fighting man'), and in the juxtaposition of our last glimpse of the heroic woman (Emer, as she dances before the severed heads—an episode very dependent upon Lady Gregory's account) with that of the harlot-musician from the street fair.

The Death of Cuchulain is the most majestically designed and the most perfect of the five plays. Yeats has moved a long way from the altogether more obscurely rendered antinomies of *On Baile's Strand*. In the last play he contrived more explicitly than ever before, and with a bold disregard for the timider realisms which it is not absurd to compare with the methods of Shakespeare's last plays, the acting out of the ironies attendant upon the hero's nature and fate. This is done by the characteristic Yeatsian method, which has operated in all the plays, of building up episode against episode and character against character so that the antitheses they form permit the ironic inference to be drawn, or culminate in a moment of revealingly double-natured action: the heroic decision that is also a mistaking (*On Baile's Strand, The Death of Cuchulain*), the love or courage whose expression in action unties the knot one way only to tighten it in another (*The Only Jealousy, At the Hawk's Well*). Yeats's strategy for putting the mythological hero on to the modern stage was cautious and full of ironic reserve in this series of plays. This saved his subject from the Pre-Raphaelite and rhapsodic air that dates the earlier Abbey plays, and from other perishable simplicities, Ossianic or patriotic. But he is never mean or malicious to his hero. and did not permit his audiences to look upon him with a levelling or a rancorous eye or 'pull established honour down'.

Chapter Five

From Grave to Cradle

When all works that have
From cradle run to grave
From grave to cradle run instead.

I

As his discoveries multiplied and his confidence strengthened, Yeats described the condition of the dead with ever greater *ordonnance* and precision. But, although he gradually piled up technical jargon and esoteric detail, this process does not characterize the three plays I am going to discuss in this chapter. They are *The Dreaming of the Bones*, finished in August, 1917, *The Words upon the Window-pane*, finished in October, 1930, and *Purgatory*, begun in March, 1938, and performed at the Abbey in August of the same year.

These plays, written at intervals of about ten years, are at first sight very different from one another, and perhaps they are not commonly thought of together. Of all the Yeatsian Noh plays, *The Dreaming of the Bones* is the one whose form most resembles the traditional Noh of the Ghosts as Yeats read them in the versions of Dr. Stopes, Pound and Fenollosa. *The Words upon the Window-pane*, on the other hand, is a prose one-act play of, for Yeats, a remarkably naturalistic kind, while in *Purgatory* Yeats has invented a form that is largely new. But all three plays set Yeats a similar problem: the intelligible representation of the life of the dead. This was a subject about which he had been speculating

84

with renewed concentration since about 1914. The plays demonstrate Yeats's growing mastery over methods of staging the subject, until he achieves, in *Purgatory*, a success of the first order. It is perhaps his greatest play, and certainly his most profoundly human treatment of this subject.

The plays can mostly be discussed independently of the various discourses in which Yeats worked out his philosophy of death. These discourses belong to a genre different from the theatrical one. Yeats himself was careful not to confuse the two modes; there is nothing in the three plays which is not intelligible even to the uninstructed theatrical spectator, although he may not be aware, if each play is presented to him separately, that each is a fresh attempt at an old theme. The plays do not appear to keep pace with the increasingly elaborate forms taken by the philosophy, though there would be no sense in denying what Yeats himself affirmed: the benefit which his art derived from the growing precision of his thought. 'I find', he wrote to his father at the time when he was composing *The Dreaming of the Bones*, 'the setting of it [the "System"] all in order has helped my verse, has given me a new frame-work and new patterns.'

One goes on year after year gradually getting the disorder of one's mind in order and this is the real impulse to create. Till one has expressed a thing it is like an untidy, unswept, undusted corner of a room.[1]

It would be strange, and would run counter to his own claims for it, if the philosophical mythology had not helped him to practise all his crafts with more elegance and clarity. Sometimes there was muddle which can be attributed to the intrusion of the speculative into the dramatic mode: I have discussed in the previous chapter what seems to be a muddle of this kind in *The Only Jealousy of Emer*.[2] But, considering for how long and how intensely Yeats was obsessed with his speculations, it is extraordinary how deft he became, especially in the works written after *A Vision* was begun, in keeping them to the genres to which they belong: the essay, treatise, gnomic poem, and the few 'texts for exposition'. In this matter he practised a discipline which was never learnt by his master Blake. The kinds of precision characteristic of the Yeatsian system—diagrams, classifications, formulae, technical terms, and citations from authorities—were utterly different from those which a drama requires in order to conform to its own mode of being: setting, costume, movement, speech, and the needs of actors. A glimpse into the systematized thought may show what it was that the barriers of the drama stood firm against, and will serve to introduce the themes common to the three plays.

There are four principal prose-writings in which Yeats wrought into system his ideas on the life of the dead. These are, in the order of their composition, the essay entitled 'Swedenborg, Mediums, and the Desolate Places', which was written about 1914 and printed in Lady Gregory's *Visions and Beliefs in the West of Ireland* (1920); the 'Anima Mundi' section of the treatise entitled *Per Amica Silentia Lunae* (1918); and a portion in each of the editions of *A Vision*: Book IV ('The Gates of Pluto') in the edition of 1925, and Book III ('The Soul in Judgment') in the edition of 1937. The essay in Lady Gregory's collection is a jumble, but it cites the authorities that Yeats was busy collating with his own spiritualistic experiences in castle and cottage. They include Plato, the neo-Platonists (Plotinus, Porphyry, Proclus, Synesius, Philoponus), the Cambridge Platonists (Henry More, Glanvil, Cudworth, Joseph Beaumont), Swedenborg, Allen Cardec and Jackson Davis (French and American Swedenborgians), numerous modern writers on psychical research (in a note Yeats mentions a dozen names), the Noh Ghost plays in the Pound / Fenollosa versions, Irish folk-lore, and the 'fat old woman', a medium in Soho, who would 'tell in Cockney language how the dead do not yet know they are dead'.[3] In *Per Amica* some of these names recur, but Yeats has purged his text of much of the confusion which they had wrought in the earlier essay. He now adopts a more personal and dogmatic approach to the subject, a style richer in metaphor and allusion. The obscurity here is of a different kind: an argument is not unfolded; it is glimpsed by snatches. Twenty-two brief numbered sections behave like detached meditations, *pensées* flying off at a tangent from one another. The allusiveness is not designed to persuade the intellect of the truth of what is being said but to lead us to an 'O altitudo' whereby judgement is suspended. Here, for example, is section xii in its entirety:

The dead living in their memories, are, I am persuaded, the source of all that we call instinct, and it is their love and their desire, all unknowing, that make us drive beyond our reason, or in defiance of our interest it may be; and it is the dream martens that, all unknowing, are master-masons to the living martens building about church windows their elaborate nests; and in their turn, the phantoms are stung to a keener delight from a concord between their luminous pure vehicle and our strong senses. It were to reproach the power or the beneficence of God, to believe those children of Alexander, who died wretchedly, could not throw an urnful to the heap, nor Caesarion murdered in childhood, whom Cleopatra bore to Caesar, nor the brief-lived younger Pericles Aspasia bore—being so nobly born.[4]

The criteria for such a passage are those applicable to the prose-poem, and in general *Per Amica* is as much about the prose-poet's emotion as he contemplates the profundity and grandeur of it all as about the subject itself. The 'untidy room' has not been swept; instead Yeats exults in its rich confusion.

It is not until 'The Gates of Pluto' and its second version in the second edition of *A Vision* that Yeats shakes himself free of the cloud of witnesses and his own crowding emotions. In writing *A Vision* he was experimenting with yet another genre, which is characterized by the use of technical vocabulary. This was not a complete innovation, because technical terms had appeared here and there in the two preceding documents, but in *A Vision* it is the essential manner of proceeding. Contrast, for example, this passage from 'The Gates of Pluto' with the passage I have just quoted from *Per Amica*:

The *Spirit* first floats horizontally within the man's dead body, but then rises until it stands at his head. The *Celestial Body* is also horizontal at first but lies in the opposite position, its feet where the *Spirit's* head is, and then rising, as does the *Spirit*, stands up at last at the feet of the man's body. The *Passionate Body* rises straight up from the genitals and stands in the centre. The *Husk* remains in the body until the time for it to be separated and lost in the *Anima Mundi*. The separation of the *Principles* from the body is caused by the *Daimon's* gathering into the *Passionate Body* memory of the past life—perhaps but a single image or thought—which is always taken from the unconscious memories of the living, from the *Record* of all those things which have been seen but have not been noticed or accepted by the intellect, and the *Record* is always truthful.[5]

This is entirely dogmatic and arbitrary, but internally coherent.

87

It makes use of terms which often have the opalescence of poetic imagery but do not shift their meaning when once they have been defined. In *A Vision* Yeats has found a form to match his thought. It is that of the metaphysical treatise, part Plotinian, part Swedenborgian. It was the right form. If you think like Swedenborg or Plotinus, then you might as well write like them too. The other documents in the case are a learned essay obfuscated by its anxiety about authorities, and a 'Religio Poetae' which cannot do justice to the System's conceptual elements because it is continually distracted by poetic excitement.

From this point of view, then, it is fair to describe the evolution of the System, in so far as it bears upon Yeats's beliefs about the condition of the dead, as a choice amongst kinds. All of them are, however, far distant from the dramatic kind, and the choice that proved most successful—the neo-Plotinian treatise—is the furthest away of all. Although they have a root in the one mind, the forms through which the thought of the System evolves and grows clearer is a branch which springs continually away from that other branch, the three ghost-plays and *their* formal evolution. There is no sense in which the plays are transcriptions of the documents that I have discussed. If comparison there is to be, it must take place at a point below that from which the disparate branches spring; and if transcription there was, it took the form of two different transcriptions of a common theme, which afterwards developed, in the prose-treatises and in the plays, two different ways of living.

As it is stated in the first of the prose documents, 'Swedenborg, Mediums, and the Desolate Places', this common theme has already become much more minutely detailed than it is in the earliest of the plays, *The Dreaming of the Bones*, although Yeats was able in his prose-note on that play to put it precisely enough as 'the world-wide belief that the dead dream back, for a certain time, through the more personal thoughts and deeds of life'.[6] So in 'Swedenborg, Mediums, and the Desolate Places', the dead live 'an earth-resembling life [which] is the creation of the image-making power of the mind, plucked naked from the body, and mainly of the images in the memory':[7]

All spirits for some time after death, and the 'earth-bound', as they are called, the larvae, as Beaumont, the seventeenth-century Platonist, preferred to call them, those who cannot become disentangled from old habits and desires, for many years, it may be for centuries, keep the shape of their earthly bodies and carry on their old activities, wooing or quarrelling, or totting figures on a table, in a round of dull duties or passionate events.[8]

Per Amica uses again some of the picturesque examples of this state which had been cited in *Visions and Beliefs*:[9]

Spiritism, whether of folk-lore or of the séance-room, the visions of Swedenborg, and the speculations of the Platonists and Japanese plays, will have it that we may see at certain roads and in certain houses old murders acted over again, and in certain fields dead huntsmen riding with horse and hound, or ancient armies fighting above bones or ashes.[10]

The dead, declares Yeats, must not be thought of as 'living an abstract life for it is the living who create abstraction which "consumes itself away"'.[11] Their condition, as they live through the passionate events, is ever more clearly seen as one of purgatorial expiation: 'the toil of the living is to free themselves from an endless sequence of objects, and that of the dead to free themselves from an endless sequence of thoughts':[12]

The dead, as the passionate necessity wears out, come into a measure of freedom . . . gradually they perceive, although they are still but living in their memories, harmonies, symbols, and patterns, as though all were being refashioned by an artist, and they are moved by emotions, sweet for no imagined good but in themselves, like those of children dancing in a ring; and I do not doubt that they make love in that union which Swedenborg has said is of the whole body and seems from far off an incandescence.[13]

The expiatory condition is one of several stages of purification in the first edition of *A Vision*, and is there described with a comparative absence of technicalities:

it is now that, according to ancient and modern tradition, the murderer may be seen committing his murder night after night or perhaps upon the anniversary of its first committal; . . . or it may be that the dream is happy and that the seer but meets the old huntsman hunting once more amid a multitude of his friends . . . the man must dream the event to its consequence as far as his intensity permit; not that consequence only which occurred while he lived, and was known to him, but those that were unknown, or have occurred after his death. The more complete the exploration, the more fortunate will be his future life, but he is concerned with events only, and with the emotions that accompanied events. Every event so dreamed is the expression of some knot, some concentration of feeling separating off a period of time, or portion of the being, from the being as a whole and the life as a whole, and the dream is as it were a smoothing out or an unwinding. Yet it is said that if his nature had great intensity, and the consequence of the event affected multitudes, he may dream with slowly lessening pain and joy for centuries.[14]

In the second edition of *A Vision* this passage has disappeared to make way for bleaker categories and more complex distinctions.

This indicates the character and some of the details of the theme which the three plays have in common. Elizabethan plays had their ghosts, but in the hard task of giving theatrical life to the dead, Yeats could not follow that example.

II

He went, indeed, to quite another tradition for *The Dreaming of the Bones* and sought a model in the type of Noh play which dramatizes the 'meeting with ghost, god, or goddess at some holy place or much-legended tomb', the supernatural stories which reminded him of 'our own Irish legends and beliefs'.[15]

A young revolutionary soldier, in flight from the enemy after the Easter Rising, comes to a desolate, hilly place on the borders of Galway and Clare. There he encounters the shades of Dermot and Dervorgilla, who 'brought the Norman in'.[16] They are imprisoned in their own remorse, punished by longing for each other but held from union by the memory of their crime. Gradually they reveal their identity to the soldier and tell him how their pain can be relieved:

> They were not wholly miserable and accursed
> If somebody of their race at last would say:
> 'I have forgiven them.' [17]

But the soldier cannot forgive them, and the play ends with their dance of unappeased longing.

In 1917 Yeats thought that this was 'the best play I have written for years', and he was still enthusiastic about it fourteen years later.[18] Yeats has successfully learnt the lesson of the Noh as it was taught by Fenollosa, with its emphasis on intensity and purity of a kind that might well appeal to the author of *Deirdre*.

The beauty and power of Noh lie in the concentration. All elements—costume, motion, verse, and music—unite to produce a single clarified impression. Each drama embodies some primary human relation or emotion; and the poetic sweetness or poignancy of this is carried to its highest degree by carefully excluding all such obtrusive elements as a mimetic realism or vulgar sensation might demand. . . . Now it is brotherly love, now love to a parent, now loyalty to a master, love of husband and wife, of mother for a dead child, or of jealousy or anger, of self-mastery in battle, of the battle of passion itself, of the clinging of a ghost to the scene of its sin, of the infinite compassion of a Buddha, of the sorrow of unrequited love. Some one of these intense emotions is chosen for a piece, and, in it, elevated to the plane of universality by the intensity and purity of treatment.[19]

This concentration and unity of mood is more noticeable in *The Dreaming of the Bones* than in any of the Yeatsian Noh plays discussed in the preceding chapter. It is achieved by imagery, by the description of setting and locale, and by construction.

In his essay on the Noh plays Yeats claimed to have detected in the examples with which he was familiar 'a playing upon a single metaphor, as deliberate as the echoing rhythm of line in Chinese and Japanese painting'.[20] In *The Dreaming of the Bones* it is the hour before dawn. Yeats uses an iterative image-cluster which evokes the sounds of the haunted night and holds them in contrast against the longed-for crowing of the cock that heralds the coming of the day. In the Musicians' speech and songs appear the birds that 'cry in their loneliness', the 'tomb-nested owl', the 'cat-headed bird' crying out in the shadow below the hills.

> The dreaming bones cry out
> Because the night winds blow

and the 'music of a lost kingdom', a wandering, airy music 'heard in the night air',

> Runs, runs and is suddenly still.
> The winds out of Clare-Galway
> Carry it: suddenly it is still.

These sounds contrast with the crowing of the cocks, bringing danger to the soldier and dismissal to the shades, as in the refrain of the Musicians' song:

> Red bird of March, begin to crow,
> Up with the neck and clap the wing,
> Red cock, and crow,

and spilling over into several allusions in the dialogue. Finally, this cluster of images appears as a coda in the last lines of the play.

Another controlling and unifying device is the detailed evocation of the setting amidst 'cold Clare rock and Galway rock and thorn'. The setting is more specific and the use of place-names more generous than in any of the other Yeatsian Noh plays, and closest to *The King's Threshold*. But, according to Yeats, he had improved on that play with the help of his Japanese models and the example of the emotion felt by the Japanese poets for 'tomb and wood', which he compared to the 'sense of awe that our Gaelic-speaking country people will sometimes show when you speak to them of Castle Hackett or of some Holy Well'.[21] And so the play is steeped in the sense of place, of rocks, ruined abbey, and the view over town, islands, and sea.

It is divided, like many of the Japanese Noh plays themselves, into two portions, separated by an interlude during which the shades guide the soldier to the hill-top where he is to watch for the boat that comes to take him away to safety. But the unification of the episodes depends upon the way the ghosts gradually reveal their identity and the nature of their suffering. As in *Nishikigi*, the ghosts tell their story but 'they do not say at first that it is their own story' (Fenollosa).[22] As in that play, the traveller does not seem to notice their ancient attire or their heroic masks. This is perhaps because at first the scene is dark—a darkness imaginatively rendered by the blowing out of the soldier's lantern. During the first episode he learns first that the place is haunted, and by a particular variety of spiritual being: those who must 'live through their old lives again'. More is slowly unfolded during the second episode. The shade of Dermot alludes to Donogh O'Brien, buried in the ruined graveyard; he

> rebelled against the King of Thomond
> And died in his youth.

But the crime for which *these* spirits suffer is much more hateful than rebellion, and because of it they are confined to an accursed solitude. Not until the whole story of Dermot and Dervorgilla has been recalled and the two phantoms begin to re-enact their agony in the final dance does the soldier realize, as the light of dawn breaks over Galway, who his guides have been:

> Why do you dance?
> Why do you gaze, and with so passionate eyes,
> One on the other; and then turn away,
> Covering your eyes, and weave it in a dance?
> Who are you? what are you?

To end the play with the dance of the unappeased shades was to imitate *Motomezuka,* one of the Noh plays to which Yeats refers most often. His own words are: 'Instead of the disordered passion of nature there is a dance, a series of positions and movements which may represent a battle, or a marriage, or the pain of a ghost in the Buddhist purgatory.' [23]

It was, then, by a fairly faithful transposition into an Irish key of some of the devices that he most valued in the Noh that Yeats dramatized the supernatural life in this play. The particular phase of the discarnate life that Dermot and Dervorgilla are caught in can be identified, if we wish to do so, from documents other than the play itself.* But a gloss of this kind is not really needed for *The Dreaming of the Bones.* Yeats supplied in the text itself all of

* According to the second edition of *A Vision* (the classifications are some-what altered from the first edition), there can be three states in the second stage of the life of the discarnate spirit: the *Dreaming Back,* the *Return,* and the *Phantasmagoria.* The last is distinguished from the first two partly by its being 'self-created' by the spirit, which undergoes during it emotional suffering due to remorse for sin committed in life (*A Vision,* 1937 edn., pp. 225–31). The punishments which it must live through are its 'own conscience made visible' (*A Vision,* 1925, p. 225). This phase must be exhausted before the spirit can proceed to the next stage. Dermot and Dervorgilla seem to belong to this phase, and it is linked with them in that Yeats should so often have cited as an example of the phase the sufferings of the spectre in *Motomezuka* which is 'set afire by a fantastic scruple, and though a Buddhist priest explains that the fire would go out of itself if the ghost but ceased to believe in it, it cannot cease to believe' (*Per Amica, Essays,* 1924, p. 521: compare the places cited from *A Vision* above, as well as *Visions and Beliefs,* II. 334 and *Four Plays for Dancers,* p. 129).

his thought that was theatrically viable and all that was needed to render the condition of the ghosts moving and intelligible:

> These have no thought but love; nor joy
> But that upon the instant when their penance
> Draws to its height and when two hearts are wrung
> Nearest to breaking, if hearts of shadows break,
> His eyes can mix with hers; nor any pang
> That is so bitter as that double glance,
> Being accursed . . .[24]
>   when he has bent his head
> Close to her head, or hand would slip in hand,
> The memory of their crime flows up between
> And drives them apart.[25]

Nor did Yeats spoil the completeness of his tragic form by representing the life of his spirits as only one amongst many stages of discarnate existence. That type of distinction belongs to the mode of the neo-Plotinian treatise rather than of the drama. The soldier's forgiveness, had it been granted, could only have mitigated their suffering not ended it. Even if some act of forgiveness had made possible the passionate union of the shades, their union would not at all have corresponded to the *Shiftings*, the third discarnate stage, to which the ghosts, if they had been conforming to *A Vision*, might have proceeded.

But peace and reconciliation amongst the dead, brought about by the intervention of the living, would have been a peripeteia in no way alien to the Noh tradition itself. One thinks of the priest's prayer in *Nishikigi* and the union of dead lovers that follows it, or of the exorcists in *Awoi No Uye* who drive the demon away and bring the dead woman peace. It would not have been foreign to Yeats's own art either, as 'Ribh at the Tomb of Baile and Aillinn' and its various analogues bear witness. That no event of this kind happens in *The Dreaming of the Bones* is due to its basic conception, and draws attention to the important element in its construction that has yet to be discussed.

In *The Dreaming of the Bones* there is a political element which at first sight seems incongruous. Yeats made somewhat worried mention of it in a letter to Lady Gregory and elsewhere.[26] The play is timed just after the Easter Rising, and there are many

references to war and destruction. When he sees the dispossessed
and ruined abbey the soldier exclaims:

> Is there no house
> Famous for sanctity or architectural beauty
> In Clare or Kerry, or in all wide Connacht
> The enemy has not unroofed?

The soldier himself is a somewhat surprising substitute for the
neutral intercessor to whom in the Noh plays ghosts often manifest themselves. But the point that Yeats is making is clear enough.
The hunted patriot and the destruction everywhere must be
recognized as the direct consequences of the sin committed seven
centuries ago:

> What generations of old men had known
> Like their own hands, and children wondered at,
> Has boiled a trooper's porridge. That town had lain,
> But for the pair that you would have me pardon,
> Amid its gables and its battlements
> Like any old admired Italian town.

The enemy whom the soldier fights is that same 'foreign army
from across the sea' which Dermot and Dervorgilla 'brought in'.
The Easter Rising, one of those occasions which fans the sequel
of continuous misery into a disastrous blaze, may be supposed to
aggravate the torment of conscience in which the lovers have 'lost
themselves'. They are like the girl in *Motomezuka*, whose 'Ghost
tells a Priest of a slight sin which seems a great sin because of its
unforeseen and unforeseeable consequences' [27] (in her case the
suicide of a rejected lover); or like the ghost in *A Vision* who must
'dream the event to its consequence'.[28]

But there is no suggestion in the play that intenser consequence
and sharper suffering are, as they are in *A Vision*, a purgatorial
therapy which will smooth out and unwind the pain. In this way
the play folds in upon itself. The antique story is tied to the
present moments of flight and disaster because they proceed from
it; the lovers inhabit a landscape of ruin which they made themselves; they address their hopeless appeal to the traveller whom,
as revolutionary and fugitive, they fathered. There is, as it were,
no room for a peripeteia. The soldier himself is caught inside this

tight circle; he is one of the consequences of their transgression and cannot forgive the authors of the evil which he fights and curses.

It is of him, however, that they ask forgiveness. This introduces at the end of the play a moral dilemma, an element entailing a choice and a possible development therefrom. These are things which the play's construction and the soldier's inherited role otherwise preclude.

It is not easy to decide whether this modifies the design of *The Dreaming of the Bones* in the wrong way. It seems to be in accord with Yeats's thought that the remorse of the dead may be lessened by some intervention on the part of those descendants of the dead man who have been affected by unforeseen consequences of his original crime. This is a theme which Yeats was to explore in *Purgatory*, although I do not know of anywhere else in his writings where it is explicitly treated. In *The Dreaming of the Bones* forgiveness is the intervention proposed. During the spirits' dance of agony the soldier does nearly forgive them:

> I had almost yielded and forgiven all—
> This is indeed a place of terrible temptation.

This moment certainly increases the tension at the end of the play, and this perhaps is its justification. But it does so at the cost of introducing inconsistency into the soldier's role. Throughout—although it is to him that the tale is told—he is never, except on this occasion, a mediator. He neither experiences nor transmits to the audience anything resembling pity or horror at the ghosts' fate. He is preoccupied with flight, danger, and hatred:

> It was men like Donogh that made Ireland weak—
> My curse on all that troop.

The dramatic method, too, has been to arouse pity and horror in the audience directly and not through his mediation, by what the ghosts say and the musicians shudder at, and not by what the soldier feels about what he hears.

Thus the soldier's moment of 'almost yielding' in some ways intensifies the theme by offering and then withdrawing a hope of relief, and so brings out still more cruelly the necessity imposed upon the shades of living through the old round unassuaged. But in other ways it makes for incongruity by allowing us to glimpse beyond this play a play with a different structure, one which admits both a purgatory and a peripeteia. This flaw, if it is one, detracts very little from a design that is moving because of its coherence, interlocking crime and consequence so that everything becomes intense and clear.

III

But *The Dreaming of the Bones*, which pleased Yeats perhaps because he had finally mastered the Noh models in begetting its autonomous life upon them, cannot have satisfied him entirely. Its mode of existence is closer to that of the lyrical poem than are the Noh plays which preceded it and followed it. In these, *At the Hawk's Well* and *The Only Jealousy of Emer*, there is found the untying of the knot by some movement of action which resolved a crisis and settled Cuchulain's or Emer's destiny. In *The Dreaming of the Bones* nothing is done or undone, and scarcely anything disturbs the intensity with which suffering winds in upon itself. The play is the nearest of the three to that 'pure presentation of the image in the theatre' which Frank Kermode sees as the rationale of all Yeats's adaptations of the Noh.[29] *The Words upon the Window-pane* is some sort of evidence that Yeats wanted to work in other modes as well, and it falls into place here because it also dramatizes the discarnate life.

Yeats had much experience of séances. The period between 1911 and 1916 seems to have been specially active. During those years the unpublished notebooks record details of many sessions and the work of many mediums.[30] In the introduction to *The Words upon the Window-pane* he declared that all the people in it 'were people I had met or might have met in just such a séance'.[31]

The scene is a Dublin lodging-house where six people are assembling for a séance with a visiting medium from London. Three of them, Corny Patterson, Mrs. Mallet, and the Reverend Abraham Johnson, are slyly amusing caricatures of typical addicts. Then there is the secretary of the group, Miss Mackenna, Dr. Trench, its president, and John Corbet, a visitor from Cambridge, who is writing a thesis on Swift. The house in which they find themselves had once belonged to friends of Swift's Stella; Trench shows Corbet the lines from Stella's birthday-poem to Swift which have been cut upon the window-pane, and they discuss the tragedy of Swift's personal life. The other characters, meanwhile, speak of what they hope for from the séance—news about heaven, advice from the late Mr. Mallet, the spiritual inspiration of Sankey and Moody—and allude to the way in which these expectations have been disappointed in preceding séances by the unwanted presence of two spirits who have gone through 'the same drama' on each occasion 'as if they were characters in some kind of horrible play'. Dr. Trench echoes Yeats's own thoughts when he speaks of earth-bound spirits who

think they are still living and go over and over some action of their past lives, just as we go over and over some painful thought, except that where they are thought is reality . . . if I were a Catholic I would say that such spirits were in Purgatory.[32]

The grotesque and the mysteriously painful are very dexterously combined in the protasis. Its themes are developed in the central episode of the play and help to make it intelligible. Here the medium, Mrs. Henderson, speaks in the voices of Lulu (her 'control'), of Swift, and of Vanessa. Between Vanessa and Swift the 'horrible play' is played through again: Swift's fear and loathing of procreation struggling with Vanessa's avowal of love and culminating in his terrible cry of 'who locked me in with my enemy?' This is followed by the calm of the spirit's long monologue addressed to Stella, in whom he seeks and thinks he finds moral assuagement and friendship for old age. The medium emerges exhausted from her trance; one by one the disappointed spiritualists file away, and the end of the play comes in sight.

To the effectiveness of the play on the stage there is testimony, although one wonders how many actresses would be equal to the part of Mrs. Henderson. Of the blending together in its structure of the story of the séance and the story of Swift and the tensions created by that method A. N. Jeffares has written perceptively.[33] I want to add some further thoughts about the way it is constructed and to consider the play in company with *The Dreaming of the Bones*.

'An excellent play about Swift'[34] has been the commentators' verdict, and it was as a play about Swift that Yeats referred to it in his letters. The choice of Swift as central figure arose from

Yeats's new interest in the eighteenth century—the 'one Irish century that escaped from darkness and confusion'.[35] But in the play these representative qualities of Swift (which are considered at length in its Introduction) get very little mention. Into its dramatic centre Yeats put instead the darkness and confusion of Swift's private life, and we are presented with an image of dis-carnate suffering which has the completeness and the same kind of infolded structure as *The Dreaming of the Bones*. Nor is the resemblance between the two plays much modified by the fact that the author of *A Vision* would have distinguished quite sharply between the shades in the earlier play 'caught in a winding labyrinth of conscience' and those in the later, who are re-living, as Dr. Trench explains, 'some passionate or tragic moment of life. . . . In vain do we write *requiescat in pace* upon the tomb, for they must suffer, and we in our turn must suffer until God gives peace.' The choice of a famous historical figure to play the role of suffering spirit is justified as much by the naturalistic Dublin setting as by an interest in Swift for its own sake. There is a sense in which anyone else whose life could yield the necessary perturbations would have done. But, having chosen Swift, Yeats was sufficiently obedient to the naturalistic tradition to provide all the realism of content that, within that tradition, makes for theatrical life.

There is also affinity with *The Dreaming of the Bones* in the final phase of the play. The last words of the shade of Swift are 'Yes, you will close my eyes, Stella. O you will live long after me, dear Stella, for you are still a young woman, but you will close my eyes.' After the others have gone, Corbet, the expert on Swift, who is unconvinced that anything he has heard has been the work of spirits, attributes to Mrs. Henderson a knowledge as great or greater than his own and tries to discuss Swift with her:

MRS. HENDERSON

Swift? I do not know anybody called Swift.

JOHN CORBET

Jonathan Swift, whose spirit seemed to be present to-night.

MRS. HENDERSON

What? That dirty old man?

JOHN CORBET

He was neither old nor dirty when Stella and Vanessa loved him.

MRS. HENDERSON

I saw him very clearly just as I woke up. His clothes were dirty, his face covered with boils. Some disease had made one of his eyes swell up, it stood out from his face like a hen's egg.

JOHN CORBET

He looked like that in his old age. Stella had been dead a long time. His brain had gone, his friends had deserted him.*

This conversation completes the Swiftian tragedy and makes a self-subsistent image out of it. The words upon the window-pane ('Late dying, may you cast a shred / Of that rich mantle o'er my head'), the prediction that Stella will close Swift's eyes, the flight to Stella for a refuge from his 'enemy' Vanessa and from the perilous consequences and responsibilities of physical love—these hopes are now seen to have been false and to have led only to madness and despair. By balancing the Stella episode against the conversation of John Corbet with Mrs. Henderson, Yeats completes his structure, and completes it with an irony comparable with that in *The Dreaming of the Bones*. The moment of appeasement represented by the communion with Stella resembles the relief that the lovers in the earlier play hope for from the pardon for which they ask the soldier. In *The Dreaming of the Bones* the soldier, as 'unforeseen consequence' of their sin, is a part of what torments the shades. So, too, in *The Words upon the Window-pane*, Stella herself is only a part of the lonely ghost's memories. Her voicelessness is significant; she is not present, as Vanessa is, and does not speak, as Vanessa does, through the medium, presumably because her spirit has long ago proceeded to some purer stage of

* We must infer, I think, that Yeats imagined that all the 'dreaming-back' recorded through the medium's mouth earlier in the play was the activity of the shade not of the younger Swift, of the same age as he was when the events took place in his life, but of the old, mad, deserted Swift. In old age he is imagined as dwelling on his memories, and these memories were the painful thoughts that were the substance of his madness. In death, therefore, his shade assumes this form and relives those painful thoughts. The ghost in the play is the equivalent of the mind of the mad, older Swift. Lulu refers to the shade, even during the Vanessa episode, as a 'bad *old* man', and his physical form, as glimpsed by Mrs. Henderson, is that of the aged Swift.

the discarnate life. She cannot pardon or release; Swift, like the bride in *Purgatory*, is 'alone in [his] remorse'.[36] The condition of the ghost's life is that he must live through the whole round of his painful thoughts that are his memories and may not find a place to stay and hide in any one of them. In a similar fashion, the continual consciousness of their sin is the condition of the life of the dead in *The Dreaming of the Bones*. But, as not in that play, there is in this one a hint from the author of *A Vision* (through the mouth of Dr. Trench)[37] that all this pain is expiatory and will pass away. It is a hint so slight that it does little to impair the cruel integrity of the tragic image.

There is a final twist of the knife, or pinnacle added to the construction, after Corbet leaves the stage. Yeats stretches the naturalistic mode by giving Mrs. Henderson what almost amounts to a soliloquy. The exhausted medium, trying to make herself a cup of tea, speaks suddenly in Swift's voice again and uses, amongst others, words recorded as having been spoken during his insanity: 'Perish the day on which I was born!' These are the last words of the play. As the only direct address to the audience in the play, the theatrical effect is all the greater. It deliberately shocks the audience into casting its mind back over the rationale of the whole affair.[38]

We know something of how Yeats would have explained Mrs. Henderson's last actions, because he tells us in his Introduction, warning us at the same time that he has not put this explanation into the play. Mediumship, he writes, is dramatization. The medium works like the actor by creating a 'secondary personality':

Perhaps May Craig [the actress who played Mrs. Henderson], when alone in her room after the play, went, without knowing what she was doing, through some detail of her performance. I once saw an Abbey actor going up the stairs to his dressing-room after playing the part of a lame man and saw that he was still limping.[39]

I do not fully understand the pages in which this idea is worked out, but Yeats is not, I think, doubting that in certain cases and under certain conditions the spirits of the dead many manifest themselves at mediumistic séances. The method by which the medium, whether false or genuine, works is the same. The difference between the false and the genuine is comparable, perhaps, to the difference between the bad actor who fakes and the good actor who conveys the reality in his part. By this reading, therefore, Mrs. Henderson's final actions need not cast any doubt upon the actuality of the shades or suggest that she is, as John Corbet supposes, 'an accomplished actress and scholar', except in so far as every medium is, in Yeats's view, an actress, a dramatizer, more or less accomplished.

But since the explanation that Yeats supplies in the Introduction is carefully excluded from the play itself, the audience is left to its own deductions. Because the dramatist has so provided, these will be mostly sceptical. The favourite one is likely to be, not that Mrs. Henderson is a mere fraud, but that she has been the unconscious receiver and dramatizer of the thoughts of John Corbet, the Swift scholar, whose somewhat obtrusive presence in the play seems designed to foster just such a conclusion. And even when he has left the stage she is still, in her exhausted state, subject to his influence, his last ruminations about Swift as he leaves the house. This type of event was accepted by Yeats as likely enough to occur during a séance.* Nor need Yeats's own explanation in the Introduction of Mrs. Henderson's last speech at all exclude the possibility that something of the kind has happened. There is always in mediumship a 'secondary personality' and several different ways in which it can be begotten. That traces of it cling to the dramatizing medium after the show is over can tell us nothing about the genuineness or otherwise of the show itself.

Yet the play is so designed that it is impossible to rest in this scepticism. It has been carefully indicated in the protasis that Corbet is now attending for the first time, that there have been three previous séances, and that the last two have both been spoilt by the 'horrible play' in which Swift and Vanessa have gone through the same drama and said the same words. We are set wondering again. Is the room in which Stella played cards and cut her verses on the window-pane truly revisited by her lover's shade? Do Mrs.

* He speaks in the Introduction of an occasion when 'the mind of an old doting general [one of the sitters] turned all to delirium', and in *Per Amica* writes of spirits who transmit through a medium finding it difficult to 'speak their own thoughts and keep their own memory . . . [they] readily mistake our memory for their own, and believe themselves whom and what we please. We bewilder and overmaster them' (*Essays*, 1924, p. 531).

Henderson's last words mean that she is still subject to the reve-
nant, and is likely to be as long as she remains in the haunted
house? The audience is deliberately left uncertain, in a frame of
mind which corresponds to that of Miss Mackenna and of Yeats
himself:

> I have seen a good many séances, and sometimes think it is all coinci-
> dence and thought-transference. . . . Then at other times I think as Dr.
> Trench does, and then I feel like Job—you know the quotation—the
> hair of my head stands up. A spirit passes before my face.

In dramatizing the modern séance-room Yeats was forced to
adopt the naturalistic mode. He seems to calculate the expectations
that his audience will bring to a play about this subject, and avoids
what might have been a temptation inherent in it: the writing of
a tract for or against spiritualism. In the manner of a problem-
play dramatist he keeps his audience's intellectual faculties working, but also in presenting the completed tragedy of Swift he
endeavours to move it as he had in *The Dreaming of the Bones*.
Yeats has made a finished image of suffering and set about it a
naturalistic problem-play on spiritualism. It is in this sense that it
is a 'play about Swift'.

IV

' "And another time I saw Purgatory. It seemed to be in a level
place, and no walls around it, but it all in one bright blaze, and
the souls standing in it. And they suffer near as much as in Hell,
only there are no devils with them there, and they have the hope
of Heaven." ' So spoke the old Galway villager, commemorated
in *The Celtic Twilight*, 'who can see nothing but wickedness. Some
think him very holy, and others think him a little crazed.' [40] For
his last play on this theme Yeats chose an image which goes back
to his younger years, to Castle Dargan, and the 'ruined castle lit
up'.[41] From a ghost-story that Yeats himself told, about a family
ruined by drink, a castle burnt down, and an 'ashen woman' re-
peatedly seen by her descendants living through her act of suicide,
Yeats borrowed other main themes for *Purgatory*,[42] weaving the
diffuseness of the old story into a tight dramatic narrative. The
shades in this play, haunting the ruined mansion, are nearer to

the audience than the mythological and historical figures of Dermot, Dervorgilla, and Swift, because they derive from the popular tale.

The scene is 'a ruined house and a bare tree in the background'.[43] A wandering pedlar and his bastard son stand in the moonlight before the ruin, while the old man reveals its history to the boy. In this house the pedlar had been born, the son of a great lady who had married a drunken groom. After his wife's death in child-birth, the groom had squandered the estate, but his son had been taught to read and had got a haphazard education. The boy listens enviously to the tale of riches and learning. When the old man was sixteen, the groom had burned down the house in a drunken frenzy and his son had stabbed him to death in the ruins and fled to escape trial. When this exposition is finished, the action begins.

It is the anniversary of the mother's wedding-night. Her remorseful shade must act the occasion through again and again, tortured by her knowledge of the ruinous consequences of her marriage. The old man hears the hoof-beats of the bridegroom's horse on the gravelled drive, and the figure of the bride appears at a lighted window of the ruin. The boy his son, meanwhile, can see and hear nothing, and mockingly accuses the old man of madness. A long speech from the old man divides the play into two portions, as he describes the wedding-night, cries out vainly to his mother's shade 'Do not let him touch you!', and meditates on the mystery of her re-enactment of the sexual act. But his meditation is interrupted by the boy, who had seized the chance of stealing the bag of money from the pedlar's pack and is making off with it. The catastrophe approaches in intensifying violence.

They struggle for the money, which is scattered on the ground, and the boy threatens to kill his father. While this is going on, the figure of the bridegroom appears at the window, leaning there like 'a tired beast'. The boy can see this apparition;* as, filled with horror, he hides his eyes, the old man stabs him to death. The window in which the apparition stands now darkens,

---

* The boy can see this second apparition perhaps because he, like his grandfather the groom, represents the evil, degenerate element in the family-story. He cannot see the apparition of his grandmother because his evil nature cannot 'dramatize' it.

and it seems as if the phantom, the 'nothing' that is the 'impression on my mother's mind', has been exorcized. Another stage-effect (which is seen to be equally ironic when the true catastrophe occurs, follows: the dry tree that emblematized when it was green the rich life of the prosperous family now appears bathed in white light on the darkened stage. As the old man looks at it standing there 'like a purified soul' he explains why he killed the boy. It was to put an end to the chain of consequence, the polluted blood that would have 'Begot, and passed pollution on'. As he bends to pick up the scattered money, the bridegroom's hoof-beats are heard again. The old man realizes in despair that the dream of the dead woman cannot come to an end:

> Twice a murderer and all for nothing,
> And she must animate that dead night
> Not once but many times!

The play ends with his prayer to God to release the tormented soul from its dream, for 'Mankind can do no more'.

In this play, the conscience of the shade compels her to re-enact her transgression at that moment when it initiated the chain of consequence that fills her with remorse: the begetting of a child. This is the knot the old man strives to cut. The souls in Purgatory, he says, that 'come back to habitations and familiar spots'

> know at last
> The consequence of those transgressions
> Whether upon others or upon themselves;
> Upon others, others may bring help,
> For when the consequence is at an end
> The dream must end; upon themselves,
> There is no help but in themselves
> And in the mercy of God.

The consequence of her crime upon 'others' that is most vividly presented in the play is the dynastic one, represented especially by the character of the boy. He is ignorant, amoral, thieving, a potential parricide, and—it is hinted—lecher. The boy, then, is to be killed, to be 'exorcized' like the grandfather, and the degenerate stock wiped out. Otherwise, he will repeat the pattern of his polluted father's career, which began at sixteen, the boy's age, with the murder of the groom, and went on to the begetting of

a bastard 'Upon a tinker's daughter in a ditch'. And so on to
generations unborn. When the boy is killed, the mother's spirit
is momentarily assuaged. This is emblematized by the tree's becoming 'like a purified soul':

> All cold, sweet, glistening light.
> Dear mother, the window is dark again,
> But you are in the light because
> I finished all that consequence.*

But, after the death of the boy, there yet remains the consequence of the crime 'upon themselves'. This is also a ground of
the remorse that the spirit suffers. The crime that the woman
committed upon herself was the fouling of her own nature by
lust, as the old man explains in the central speech of the play
when he imagines the bridal night:

> She has gone down to open the door.
> This night she is no better than her man
> And does not mind that he is half drunk,
> She is mad about him. They mount the stairs,
> She brings him into her own chamber . . .

This, and the meditation that follows, is an extremely crucial part
of the play, to which I shall return. For the moment, it must be
clear to the audience that into *this* re-enactment no action of the
old man, of the living 'others', can possibly enter in order to cut
its knot. The point is stressed by the old man's ineffectual cry 'Do
not let him touch you! . . . Deaf! Both deaf!' The woman cannot

---

* The tree is a family-'tree' and also stands for the condition of the shade's
soul. Fifty years ago it had 'Green leaves, ripe leaves, leaves thick as butter,
Fat greasy life'. Then it was blasted and became the bare tree of the play, which
resembles the image of the tree seen in the bitter glass held up by demons
before the woman who barters her beauty in 'The Two Trees'. Through its
branches fly the 'ravens of unresting thought':

> For there a fatal image grows
> That the stormy night receives,
> Roots half-hidden under snows,
> Broken boughs and blackened leaves.
> For all things turn to barrenness
> In the dim glass the demons hold.
>   (Variorum edition of the *Poems*, p. 135)

be freed from that aspect of her crime which is equivalent to her self-degradation. For this act, even after death, brings with it pleasure as well as remorse, as the old man suggests. The remorseful spirit must, in order to be free of it, repeat, explore, or dream through the crime which it committed during life; but in this case the renewal of the act, because of the nature of the act, renews the self-degrading pleasure that accompanied it. Thus the very consequence from which release is sought—self-degradation—is entailed upon the mother's spirit each time she lives through her transgression. It is as pretty an entanglement as Yeats ever devised. There is none like it in *A Vision*, perhaps because he had not yet seen, when he wrote that work, into what complexities his notion of the dead who are obliged to live through their transgressions might be developed if only the transgressions were complicated enough. The case is one, as the old man at length perceives, which only the 'mercy of God' can solve. Hence his final prayer. Yeats—can it be said?—has at last found a use for God. He is called in because the Yeatsian dead can no longer manage by themselves, so extraordinary has their private purgatory become. There is no God amongst the discarnate spirits of *A Vision*.

The subject of *Purgatory* is an extension of one that had been touched upon in *The Dreaming of the Bones*. Both plays are concerned with the remorse of the dead, and in the earlier one there is a hint that the living, the 'others' who suffer the consequences of the crimes of the dead, may help them. In *The Dreaming of the Bones* the soldier's forgiveness might have assuaged the torment of Dermot and Dervorgilla. The whole subject of *Purgatory* is such an assuagement, which is indeed accomplished, although under the conditions making for final frustration that have just been examined. That in this play the act of intervention is a murder, not pardon, is necessitated by the story chosen. It affords a measure of the difference between the finished, melancholy and somewhat self-conscious beauty of *The Dreaming of the Bones* and the squalor, sexuality and violence of *Purgatory*.

The development on this scale of a theme which *The Dreaming of the Bones* merely sketches meant that Yeats had to find a fresh dramatic form. The making of a self-subsistent image of phantasmic suffering such as he gives us in *The Dreaming of the Bones* and at the centre of *The Words upon the Window-pane* can no longer be his aim. His subject, which is now chiefly about an attempt at intervention by the living in the life of the dead, requires that he concern himself with the living, with the unfinished life, not with the intense rendering of an unearthly suffering. The story told in *Purgatory* is one that leaves on the ears of the audience a cry reaching outside the play to God, unlike the final words of both *The Dreaming of the Bones* and *The Words upon the Window-pane*, which fold the plays back upon themselves so that they contemplate their own stories. *Purgatory* is an image deliberately left incomplete, a human image, rather than one that shows the dead trapped in the vortex of their own suffering. Compared with the earlier plays, it is, as it were, slewed round; ghosts and men have exchanged positions. In *Purgatory* the man is what we see first, and beyond and through him the voiceless shades pose in a window like lantern-slides upon which he discourses. This is very different from *The Dreaming of the Bones*, where Dermot and Dervorgilla dominate a human being whose representative status matters more than his individuality, and from *The Words upon the Window-pane*, where Mrs. Henderson, asleep in her chair, mediates to us the full force of the passionate shade. In *Purgatory* we are deeply engaged with the old man.

One of his functions is to tell us what the apparitions mean and to what realm they belong. He thus performs the task allotted to Dr. Trench in *The Words upon the Window-pane* and to the conversation between the soldier and the lovers about the different kinds of hauntings in the first portion of *The Dreaming of the Bones*. His speech, therefore, part of which I have quoted on page 105, explains all that the spectator needs to know about the condition of the dead in the play. But it could not have been spoken by an entirely naturalistic character. If the old man really 'knew' all that, he would not have acted as he does, or at least would not have been surprised that his action was ultimately without effect in releasing his mother's shade from its dream. This is one of those carelessnesses about orthodox realism that also occur in *The Death of Cuchulain* and convey, however mysteriously, a sense of theatrical power. This does not mean that the old man and his whole situation are not sharply individualized with the aid of as much graphic detail as the miniature size of the play permits. His description of the groom's murder,[44] for example, carries conviction:

just so might the brutal country tragedy have happened. When
the old man speaks of it, possessed though his mind is with heredity and phantoms, he looks round to make sure that no one can
overhear, and similarly, when he kills the boy, he makes certain
that nobody, except the phantom groom, is watching.

There are things, then, which the old man both 'knows' and
does not *know*, and what he does not *know*, or does not fully
understand, is an important element in his tragedy. He has learning, which he obtained in spite of his polluted origin, and he
cherishes the things of learning and ancestral beauty. He speaks
of the 'great people' of the old estate, their love of the demesne
and the flowering trees that were cut down by the degenerate
inheritor, and of his own education:

> some
> Half-loved me for my half of her:
> A gamekeeper's wife taught me to read,
> A Catholic curate taught me Latin.
> There were old books and books made fine
> By eighteenth-century French binding, books
> Modern and ancient, books by the ton.

But at a crucial moment this sort of learning becomes a crazy
parody of itself. In the long central speech, during which the consummation of the fatal marriage is re-enacted, the old man tells
the audience enough for them to understand the nature of the
mother's self-degradation, the consequence that she commits upon
herself; but he does not understand it himself.

> she must live
> Through everything in exact detail,
> Driven to it by remorse, and yet
> Can she renew the sexual act
> And find no pleasure in it, and if not,
> If pleasure and remorse must both be there,
> Which is the greater?
> I lack schooling.
> Go fetch Tertullian; he and I
> Will ravel all that problem out
> Whilst those two lie upon the mattress
> Begetting me.

The call for Tertullian is a kind of witless joke on his part. F. A. C. Wilson's straight-faced comment that he 'refers to Tertullian's treatise on the mixed nature of the soul, *de Anima*' [45] seems to me to miss the point. The point is that the old man is unable to relate what is happening with what as a character inside the play's action he does not *know*, namely, that the dead

> know at last
> The consequence of those transgressions
> Whether upon others or upon themselves . . .
> upon themselves,
> There is no help but in themselves
> And in the mercy of God.

If he were able to collate his two kinds of knowledge, which being in a state of crazy half-knowledge, he is not, he would know his mother's condition to its depths; he would not suppose that the killing of the boy could do more than momentarily assuage her torment. This state of half-knowledge is his hereditary condition entailed upon him by his polluted blood. It is his tragic fate. It is that which engineers the catastrophe, just as Cuchulain's movement of courage in *At the Hawk's Well* frustrates itself because of his fate. The old man, the son of a groom, conceived in drunkenness, cannot be a sage, although there are moments when he pathetically tries to behave like one.

All the old man's qualities are quartered with his vices in this way. He acts to save his mother, but has brutalized his son, and given him, as he tells him:

> the education that befits
> A bastard that a pedlar got
> Upon a tinker's daughter in a ditch.

He is capable of vision, but breaks away from it to struggle with the boy for the bag of money. His past is like this, too: the gently-nurtured boy who killed his father and hid the body in the burning house. That he can say that he is 'a wretched foul old man' is his noble trait, because it expresses his awareness of degradation, which is not present in the boy his son yet further degenerated from the stock; but it is also the truth.

The central figure is thus hereditarily endowed with worth and vileness, and these are interlocked in his nature as Othello's nobility is interlocked with his crime or Coriolanus's manhood with his childishness. I think that we are meant to be aware of this when we contemplate his final acts. He kills the boy in order to break the links of consequence, but the act itself partakes of his double nature. It is done by all that is good in him, but it is done in the condition of half-knowledge necessitated by what he is, and it is also a horrible crime. This last is true if I am right in thinking that the dramatist did not mean us to regard it in a coldly theoretical way simply as something done by the living for the sake of the dead and therefore justifiable even if largely ineffectual. The image of the father killing his son duplicates too dreadfully the earlier image of the son killing the father; the knife with which it is done is the same knife, the vile knife which 'cuts my dinner', like the Blind Man's knife in *The Death of Cuchulain*; the hand which drives it is the same hand:

> My father and my son on the same jack-knife!

'He stabs again and again', says the stage-direction. The act is a crime because it explicitly shares features with the parricide which, when he was sixteen, was the old man's first manifestation in action of his tainted stock. The nursery-rhyme which he chants as he murders the boy adds a special ghastliness. The sacrifice turns out to be murder after all.

There is great irony in it, too. For this act, which is designed to finish 'all that consequence', and indeed does so, is also a fresh addition to the links of consequence. Instead of a lengthening chain, it makes of them a circular band of horror, a wheel of fire: the son kills the father, the father kills the son. And all this has failed to break the suffering spirit's bondage. Thus the old man, as this realization breaks upon him and he turns away from his acts to pray, does rightly in that he prays for the living as well as for the dead:

> O God,
> Release my mother's soul from its dream!
> Mankind can do no more. Appease
> The misery of the living and the remorse of the dead.

Purgatory is the most successful of Yeats's three attempts to dramatize one stage of the progress of the soul from grave to cradle, or from grave to beatitude. He chose the only one of the visionary phases which could be adapted for human theatrical life. The imagination that conceived the 'dreaming back' had that much in common with the dramatic imagination. The purgatorial state was made to fit forms so different from one another as the Noh, the naturalistic play in prose, and a Shakespearian tragedy in miniature.

There is room for another comment on the relation between playwright and philosopher. In *The Words upon the Window-pane* Yeats has suspended his own convictions for the play's sake, and we are invited to put our own interpretation on what we have seen. But the convictions remain there rigidly in the centre of the play in the image of Swift's ghost and its suffering and re-enactment. This makes the rest of the play seem merely the scaffolding for the central event, the mystery. The human observers are grouped in a circle round the appalling, unreachable voice; the construction of the play mirrors the arrangements for a séance, or a revelation. As in *The Resurrection*, Yeats has turned the tables upon the naturalistic drama by exploding it from inside; from its shattered ruins there arises the terrible image of an utterly different kind of life. But in *Purgatory* the convictions are dissolved into the life of the protagonist; our attention is fixed upon the old man's story and his divided nature. The dead of *A Vision* and of the other plays live, although their condition is vividly enough rendered, a schematic life, each in the appropriate circle of their purgatory; but in the last play the old man's attempt to break into the circle, driven by furious pity and by jealous hatred of his own evil as embodied in his son, is his own story and no ghost shares it.

Chapter Six

For Reason, Miracle

All things have value according to the clarity of their expression of themselves.

I

THE two plays about Christianity, *Calvary* (1921) and *The Resurrection* (begun in 1925 and later rewritten), are often coupled together, and have been used mainly, if not entirely, as clues to Yeats's philosophy of history, his theism, or atheism.[1]

On Christianity, so far as they are relevant to the plays, his thoughts can be described briefly, without doing them very much injustice. He saw the pagan world, in particular the world of Greece and Rome, as a *primary* civilization; at the time of Christ's coming it was drawing to its foreordained end in the cyclical movement of history and was becoming subject to the loss of control which heralded the birth of the next age. This next, or Christian, age was *antithetical* to its predecessor. It begins with the Annunciation of a God who seeks to live like a man while teaching that man must seek to live like God. Yeats's favourite gnomic phrase for this, which he uses at the end of *The Resurrection* and elsewhere, was a saying borrowed from Heraclitus: 'God and man die each other's life, live each other's death.' This riddling aphorism, which can be shown to have a connexion with the lines in 'Byzantium'

I hail the superhuman,
I call it death-in-life and life-in-death,

113

can be sorted out, and the chief *loci* indicated, in this way:

(1) God dies man's life, or life-in-death: the dead God is like a live man (the resurrection, the journey to Emmaeus, the beating heart of the resurrected Christ in *The Resurrection*).

(2) God lives man's death, or death-in-life: the eternal God becomes a man, and dies.

(3) Man dies God's life, or life-in-death: the dead man is like a living God; he cannot die, or cannot find the death appropriate to man (Lazarus in *Calvary*).

(4) Man lives God's death, or death-in-life: the living man endeavours to live like an immortal, spiritual creature, to 'ascend to Heaven', or to be, like the resurrected Christ, 'a phantom with a beating heart'. In this way man diminishes his humanity, and the self no longer claims

> as by a soldier's right
> A charter to commit the crime once more.[2]

Man renounces the self and tries to live according to a pattern drawn from the God who dies. The saint and the anchorite who retire to the desert and whose 'joy is to be nothing, to do nothing, to think nothing'[3] become the supreme models for humanity:

> Fix every wandering thought upon
> That quarter where all thought is done.[4]

They become vessels filled with the divine life, not their own life; their desert-world is 'changed into featureless clay and can be run through the fingers'.[5]

The Resurrection, in particular, if suitably correlated with other documents, can be made to yield much complicated information about such matters as the historical cycles, Yeats's views on Babylonian astronomy, or his knowledge of what a certain fourth-century sophist, whose words are recorded in Eunapius's life of Aedesius, said about 'a fabulous formless darkness tyrannizing over the fairest things on earth'.[6]

Calvary and *The Resurrection* are partial and dramatic actualizations of this complex of ideas, especially as it bears upon the role of Jesus the Man-God. But they are not 'texts for exposition', and there is some danger that their properties as plays may go unexamined.

A writer of drama must observe the form as carefully as if it were a sonnet, but he must always deny that there is any subject-matter which is in itself dramatic—any especial round of emotion fitted to the stage, or that a play has no need to await its audience or to create the interest it lives by.⁷

It would, of course, be pointless to deny that these are plays of ideas, and that the first impulse that the student of Yeats's work as a whole is likely to feel when he encounters them will be one of curiosity about Yeats's readings of religion and history. If this were all, they could, by such tests as the poet himself was normally willing to apply, be written off as dramatic failures. But the fact that they are plays of ideas (a respectable enough theatrical kind) has its own aspect of formal significance. Do they create the interest they live by?

II

Little attention has ever been paid to *Calvary*. Sturge Moore, when he was designing the cover for *Four Plays for Dancers*, liked it least of the four.⁸ It is certainly in a different category from the other plays in that collection. In it, Christ 'dreams His passion through' and is confronted with images of those whom he cannot save: Lazarus, Judas, the Three Roman Soldiers, who ask nothing of God, and Heron, Eagle, and Swan, which are content in their solitude. With its Musicians' songs and descriptions of the scene, its bare stage, masked actors, and final dance (of the Roman soldiers round the Cross), the play has the familiar Noh features. It also has the iterative image-cluster—this time of bird and animal—which Yeats believed to be a principal device of the Noh. In a play on so tiny a scale everything counts, and this imagery contributes much to its structure.

The first song for the folding and unfolding of the cloth about the heron staring at its own image in the moonlit water, with its refrain 'God has not died for the white heron', is not the key to the meaning of the play. It is the first of four variations on the theme of Christ's powerlessness to save those who can live without salvation. The play consists of these four variations; the theme itself is not heard except through them. It is important, if obscurity is to be avoided, that the playwright should show us how each variation relates to the common theme. The refrain of the song about the heron is clear enough; it is more doubtful if the full thematic significance of the rest of it can be grasped at a first hearing, although the notion of crazy self-absorption is plainly put:

> Although half famished he'll not dare
> Dip or do anything but stare
> Upon the glittering image of a heron,
> That now is lost and now is there.[9] *

The songs in *Calvary* have other functions to perform in addition to constituting the first variation on the common theme. It follows that they relate to that theme differently from the way in which the three self-contained episodes of Lazarus, Judas, and the Roman Soldiers relate to it. Their chill detachment expresses the 'subjectivity' of a world detached from Christ; it also holds the play within a frame and helps to give it the quality of 'distance' which Yeats admired in the Noh plays.[10] By establishing its bounds so clearly the songs order the life of the play, and maintain this control by means of the image of the heron, which recurs in

---

* No music for the songs in *Calvary* is printed in *Four Plays for Dancers*. Yeats had once believed in the possibility of establishing a right relationship between words and music in his plays:

If a song is brought into a play it does not matter to what school the musician belongs if every word, if every cadence, is audible and expressive as if it were spoken . . . One must ask . . . for music that shall mean nothing, or next to nothing, apart from the words (*Plays and Controversies*, pp. 129–30).

But he despaired of finding an adequately submissive musician, and had by now, as he put it in his 'Commentary' on *The King of the Great Clock Tower* (Dublin, Cuala Press, 1934, p. 18), 'given up the fight', and cynically resigned himself to the fact that no audience would ever be able to hear properly any words of his which were accompanied by music. His cynicism took the form of regarding his songs as 'secrets'—always in the sense that he did not expect the words to be heard in the theatre (but they could be consulted in the book), and sometimes also in the sense that the song was *about* a mystery or secret. This hidden meaning could also be solved by 'turning to a note' (see *Four Plays for Dancers*, p. 135; the Cuala Press edition of *The King of the Great Clock Tower*, p. 19). The degree of 'secrecy' in the meaning of the songs seems to vary from play to play, but they are not often as obscure as they are in *The Resurrection*, where the songs have a special history (see below p. 127). For the songs in *The King of the Great Clock Tower* and *A Full Moon in March*, see below, p. 162.

the body of the work. Such strict ordering is the more needed here because the play has no single central action, as *The Dreaming of the Bones* has, nor structural core, as *The Words upon the Window-pane* and *Purgatory* have. It simply presents us with a series of events; each of these are of the same length and importance, and there is no 'working to a climax'.[11] The danger that the series will break down into arbitrary and inconsequential incidents is avoided by what the songs do.

There is a contrast, not of theme, but of style and feeling, between the songs and the other elements in the play. These other elements are centred on the rendering of Lazarus, Judas, and the Soldiers. The songs are impersonal, remote, and symbolic; Lazarus and the others are individually, almost naturalistically, done. So, too, is the Musicians' description of the scene when it is compared with their opening song. A similar contrast is observable between Christ and the other characters.

It is important to understand that the play does not attempt to actualize Christ's suffering. The play is his 'dreaming-back':

> Good Friday's come,
> The day whereon Christ dreams His passion through.
> He climbs up hither but as a dreamer climbs.
> The cross that but exists because He dreams it
> Shortens His breath and wears away His strength.

This theme is not used in the way it is used in the plays discussed in the preceding chapter, but in order to make the suffering remote rather than actual. Christ's speeches are all very short (the longest is of four lines) and they often take the form of oracular utterances, majestic and theophanic: 'I have conquered death And all the dead shall be raised up again'; 'I do my Father's will'; 'My Father put all men into my hands'. Christ is at the centre of the scene not as a tortured victim but as the pantokrator, Byzantine and unrealistic, rigid like the figure in an icon. There is only one place where he betrays this role: in the Musician's description of the three Marys casting their tears upon the ground before his blood-dabbled feet.[12]

By contrast, Lazarus and Judas are both individualized. The part of each builds up towards a longer speech in which this individuality and realism come to a climax. Lazarus reproaches Christ for dragging him up to the light, demands Christ's death in exchange for the one he has been robbed of, and describes (with one of the animal-images that run through the play) how the theft was accomplished:

> Alive I never could escape your love,
> And when I sickened towards my death I thought
> I'll to the desert, or chuckle in a corner
> Mere ghost, a solitary thing. I died
> And saw no more until I saw you stand
> In the opening of the tomb; 'Come out!' you called;
> You dragged me to the light as boys drag out
> A rabbit when they have dug its hole away;
> And now with all the shouting at your heels
> You travel towards the death I am denied.

Lazarus, unlike Christ, is visualized; his face is death-hungry, and the crowd shrinks from him. He beats in vain against the marmoreal stillness of the central figure.

So also with Judas. Lazarus is an emotional figure, thirsting after the personal death beyond his reach. Judas is intellectual; his business is to conduct a theological dispute with Christ during which he says fifty words to every two or three of the other speaker. He betrayed Christ in order to be free of him, in order to be himself again and not an object of the all-powerful God. Christ's statement that God had determined from the beginning that somebody should betray him produces Judas's long assertion of identity, corresponding to Lazarus's speech:

> It was decreed that somebody betray you—
> I'd thought of that—but not that I should do it,
> I the man Judas, born on such a day,
> In such a village, such and such his parents;
> Nor that I'd go with my old coat upon me
> To the High Priest, and chuckle to myself
> As people chuckle when alone, and that I'd do it
> For thirty pieces and no more, no less,
> And neither with a nod, a look, nor a sent message,
> But with a kiss upon your cheek. I did it,
> I, Judas, and no other man, and now
> You cannot even save me.

Browning might have written in this fashion had he attempted a dramatic monologue for Judas. But all this intellectual energy is at a discount. Christ keeps his marble repose. During the final episode of the Roman Soldiers he speaks only two lines. The Soldiers are those who cast all upon the throw of the dice, asking nothing of Providence because they are content with Fortune. Their dance before the motionless figure on the cross repeats the contrast between stillness and movement.

These contrasts between the active and fixed, personal and impersonal, suffering which reaches out in gloating and accusation and suffering which is withdrawn and symbolic, are the formal devices fundamental to the play. They are also, of course, its larger meaning. The forms have been used to convey the ideas in this play of ideas. These are individuals who reject Christ because they cling to their selfhood, personal death, and freedom from the invading God who wants to turn them into what he is; they are 'subjective' men in the special Yeatsian sense.

The construction, both formal and conceptual, is completed by what we discover about Christ. Just as Lazarus, Judas, and the Soldiers form one movement, so Christ and the birds of the Musicians' songs form the counter-movement. The birds are the completest symbols of self-sufficient isolation:

> The geer-eagle has chosen his part
> In blue deep of the upper air
> Where one-eyed day can meet his stare;
> He is content with his savage heart.

> God has not appeared to the birds.

God has not appeared to them, but this God is like them. By this subtle collocation (the songs are finally seen to be *about* Christ as well as about the birds), Yeats makes his last points. The stillness and loneliness of Christ are enhanced, and the songs are tied into the main antithesis of the play. As Yeats would have put it when writing in another mode, it is the subjective God who calls upon men to be his objects, who pours his own spirit into them. During a phase of civilization such as the Greek and Roman was, men are permitted to be their own objects: 'Man . . . remains separate. He does not surrender his soul. He keeps his privacy' (The Goddess, in Yeats's favourite Homeric image, takes Achilles by his yellow hair, not by his soul). During the Christian era, God, unique and solitary as the Eagle, which is the King of Birds, seeks, like the heron in the stream, to find everywhere his own image and to change what he loves into himself, unlike the lovers in *A Vision* who 'would not change that which we love'. When God acts towards men he acts towards his own image in them. Thus, 'the Good Samaritan discovers himself in the likeness of another, covered with sores and abandoned by thieves . . . and in that other serves himself'.[13] God pities men to the degree that they are not like him and must, for example, die; so he raises Lazarus. His power is absolute, so he can make Judas into his instrument. In *Calvary* both Judas and Lazarus are conceived as relics of the elder civilization; they do not want to be completely God's objects but to remain themselves; they want to keep their subjectivity and selfhood, their privacy, and are not willing to 'sacrifice everything that the divine suffering might . . . descend into one's mind and soul' and to allow 'God . . . to take complete possession'.[14] The playwright's mind, as well as his eye, has seen Christ as the pantokrator in the Byzantine dome looking everywhere and asking for everything.

III

Calvary is successful in giving the 'feel' of the ideas upon which it is a play, although these are not given in the terminology of the metaphysical treatise. They are presented as movement round a medial stillness, as vortices of the intellectually active, death-hungry, or dancing selfhoods arranged about the god. The play does not quicken or deepen as it grows; it shows what it is by standing still and is short enough for the audience to hold it in its mind as a whole and range back and forth over it as they speculate on its meaning. This is an unusual form for a play of ideas, where normally we expect the ideas to be developed dialectically. In *The Resurrection* there is much more development of the dialectical variety. Some of the ideas are directly expressed in debates between the characters; the characters themselves are representative men, explaining what they represent instead of, as in *Calvary*, leaving it to be deduced from the way they describe what they have done. *The Resurrection* is more, however, than merely a discussion-play. Events are shown, not just talked about. And all the explanatory talk and commentary are in the end subordinated to the showing forth of their own meaning which is done by the events themselves. These events are arranged in a more ordinary dramatic pattern than the one to be found in *Calvary*. It is not a static pattern, ordered by interlocking contrasts, but a sequential one of exposition, conflict leading to mounting tension, and exploding into a catastrophe.

Yeats worked hard to achieve just this. In 1925, we are told, a first sketch of the play was read out 'to a few people, a Cabinet minister among them, who were frigid'.[15] This was the 'chaotic dialogue' of which he wrote in a letter to Mrs. Shakespear in December, 1930: 'But now I have dramatic tension throughout.'[16] The narrative design and many of the ideas are curiously adumbrated in a passage written nearly thirty years before (in 1904). Its imagery suggests the Christian referents at the back of the writer's mind:

A Civilisation is very like a man or a woman, for it comes in but a few years into its beauty, and its strength, and then, while many years go by, it gathers and makes order about it, the strength and beauty going out of it the while, until in the end it lies there with its limbs straightened out and a clean linen cloth folded upon it. That may well be, and yet we need not follow among the mourners, for it may be, before they are at the tomb, a messenger will run out of the hills and touch the pale lips with a red ember, and wake the limbs to the disorder and the tumult that is life. Though he does not come, even so we will keep from among the mourners and hold some cheerful conversation among ourselves; for has not Virgil, a knowledgeable man and a wizard, foretold that other Argonauts shall row between cliff and cliff, and other fair-haired Achæans sack another Troy?[17]

The notion of holding 'some cheerful conversation' while an era lies dead seems a little touch of Lewis Carroll in the night of Yeats's later imagination of disaster as famously expressed in 'The Second Coming'. But in *The Resurrection* the allusions to the messenger, the mourners, and the Virgilian prophecy are made actual.

The play begins in a bustle of apparently unrelated movements; it is only gradually that we learn the rationale that makes a single event of them. The eleven apostles, unseen by the audience, are gathered in the upper room after the crucifixion. The mob is 'busy hunting Christians', but three followers of Jesus, a Hebrew, a Greek, and a Syrian (absent from the stage when the play begins) are ready to defend the stairway with their lives. Meanwhile another mob, the followers of Dionysus, are out in the streets dancing and worshipping as they carry the image of their dead god.

There is further movement in the argument between Greek and Hebrew. Both are subjective men, like Lazarus and Judas in *Calvary*. To the Greek, Jesus was not a man but a spirit:

We Greeks understand these things. No god has ever been buried; no god has ever suffered. Christ only seemed to be born, only seemed to eat, seemed to sleep, seemed to walk, seemed to die.[18]

The gods do not covet earthly bodies, but are discovered only through contemplation; God does not 'die man's life'. The Hebrew is shocked because the Greek thinks of Jesus's life as only a simulacrum of human life, and of the crucifixion as a shadow-play. To the Hebrew, it was the suffering of a man, 'the best man who ever lived', who 'some day when he was very tired . . . thought that he himself was the Messiah'. In his way, the Hebrew is glad that this has now been proved to be the case by the defeat and death of the supposed Messiah; earlier, when he acknowledged the Messianic claim, he had anticipated with dread the terrible burden this was going to impose on him, robbing him of his subjectivity and making him simply an object of the immanent God:

One had to give up all worldly knowledge, all ambition, do nothing of one's own will. Only the divine could have any reality. God had to take complete possession. It must be a terrible thing when one is old, and the tomb round the corner, to think of all the ambitions one has put aside; to think, perhaps, a great deal about women. I want to marry and have children.

He no longer has to become an anchorite and retire to the featureless desert.

If this were all, we would have the ideas clearly expressed but not dramatically presented. But Yeats relates this ideological argument between Greek and Hebrew both to the events of the plot and to a meaningful thematic accompaniment. Out of these three elements he contrives a dramatic unity. Thus the Hebrew is made to state the Christian position from the point of view of a believer in it who has just received proof of its falsity; he has reverted to what he was before the failed Messiah came. The Greek, meanwhile, is waiting for the proof of *his* position:

THE HEBREW

Proof?

THE GREEK

I shall have proof before nightfall.

THE HEBREW

You talk wildly, but a masterless dog can bay the moon.

The Greek has sent the third man, the Syrian, to the tomb 'to prove that there is nothing there', and he expects the messenger to return with the certain news that 'Jesus never had a human body',

that he is a phantom and can pass through that wall; that he will so pass; that he will pass through this room; that he himself will speak to the apostles.

It is his confidence in this that prepares for the moment of intense excitement at the end of the play. Thus the Hebrew, with his 'proof' drawn from the crucifixion, and the Greek, with his 'proof' drawn from the resurrection, are not merely debating incompatible points of view; in judging by events, they relate their argument to a narrative sequence; the events in their turn share in the debate because they are assimilated into it as proofs. Sequence and debate are both put into time and await resolution by it.

The debate is joined to the accompaniment of a background of 'irrational force' and 'animal chaos'—the phrases are used in *A Vision*—which is represented by the worshippers of Dionysus in the street below. Their rattles, drums, and cries, and their song ('Astraea's holy child') sound at intervals throughout the play. The worshippers abandon themselves to their god and become completely his objects; 'three days after the full moon, a full moon in March, they sing the death of the god and pray for his resurrection'. Although the parallels do not escape the audience, the Greek

and the Hebrew are quite unaware of them. The self-abandon-
ment, the monstrous ceremonies, the boys from the theatre
dressed as girls, the barbaric din are merely disgusting, the work
of mad, ambiguous creatures, 'such a thing [as] had never happened in this city before'. In providing an accompaniment of this
kind Yeats was doing more than supplying factitious excitement
or indulging himself in an exercise in comparative religion. There
are, of course, good reasons in *A Vision* for the presence of such
sectaries at such a moment in time,* but they are not given in
the play. What the audience is given, in place of this kind of
detail, is the juxtaposition of two characters to whom religion is
a matter for individual response, definition, discussion, and proof,
with the worshippers of the dismembered god, to whom it is a
matter for collective howling, drumming, and orgiastic frenzy.
This is a contrast, achieved by formal antitheses (speech and song,
beaten drums and anxious talk), which is similar in kind to those
in *Calvary* between one mode of being and another. It generates
the sense that the world of *The Resurrection* is throbbing with
forces that make the stance, even the intellectuality (their power
to argue about the issues), of Greek and Hebrew things which
belong to a habit that is threatened and about to pass away.

But in *The Resurrection*, as not in *Calvary*, the spectator is made
to participate by having the argument demonstrated upon his
own pulse. The Greek awaiting his proof and the issue that hangs
in the air between the reasoners and the worshippers, the frenetic
sect and the ordered cities, cohere together as they move together
into a final event of compelling theatrical authority, the most con-
summate moment of its kind in all Yeats's plays. The Syrian messenger returns; Yeats must have been sorry that he could not call
him a Babylonian, but he got as near to this as he could. 'Like a
drunken man' he announces the tale told him by the Galilaean
women, of the appearance of Jesus to them, and of the empty
sepulchre. He is convinced that something has happened which is

* Yeats believed that the Second Annunciation (the first was that to Leda)
was preceded by obscure intimations in the form of the oriental cults of the
Roman empire which were influenced by Babylonian astrology and astronomy.
These were the 'peacock's cry', the final loss of control of the old primary
civilization as it was transformed into the antithetical Christian era (see *A
Vision* [1937], p. 268).

outside the kind of knowledge and order to which the other two men are clinging. His excitement, contributing a note of hysteria to the argument, makes it intenser in tone and more rapid in pace, for the Greek and Hebrew had been doing their duty as defenders of the apostles in a spirit of last-ditch, disciplined Stoicism:

THE SYRIAN

... What if at the moment when knowledge and order seem complete that something appears? [*He has begun to laugh.*]

THE HEBREW

Stop laughing.

THE SYRIAN

What if the irrational return? What if the circle begin again?

THE HEBREW

Stop! He laughed when he saw Calvary through the window, and now you laugh.

THE GREEK

He too has lost control of himself.

THE HEBREW

Stop, I tell you. [*Drums and rattles.*]

THE SYRIAN

But I am not laughing. It is the people out there who are laughing.

THE HEBREW

No, they are shaking rattles and beating drums.

The Greek's laughter was close to the philosopher's cackle at a well-conducted argument; the Syrian's to the hysteria of the wor-shippers' self-abandon, merging into the noise in the streets.

Both Greek and Hebrew refuse to accept the implications of his message. To the Hebrew, it is the wishful 'dreams of women'; to the Greek, it is his proof at last, that Jesus was a phantom, whose reappearance will show that God does not overwhelm man with miracle but permits him to keep his privacy. Meanwhile, the Dionysans, who have gone away to bury their god, are re-turning through the streets with their cry of 'God has arisen'.

Their dance is suspended suddenly as they turn eyes blind with
ecstasy towards the house; two religions melt into one as the converging lines of the drama touch and what was an analogue becomes the thing itself. The dramatic climax shows Yeats combining his long-held idea that men seek reality with the slow toil
of their weakness and are smitten from the boundless and unforeseen with a technique learnt from the Japanese Noh; for, as Earl
Miner has observed, 'the climax occurs at the point where the
supernatural being (Christ) reveals his true form and brings, as in
nō, spiritual enlightenment'.[19] Even after the figure of Christ has
made its silent entry, the empirical Greek is determined that what
his senses will tell him will be the truth that he expects:

There is nothing here but a phantom, it has no flesh and blood. Because I know the truth I am not afraid. Look, I will touch it. It may
be hard under my hand like a statue—I have heard of such things—
or my hand may pass through it—but there is no flesh and blood.
[*He goes slowly up to the figure and passes his hand over its side.*] The
heart of a phantom is beating! The heart of a phantom is beating!
[*He screams. The figure of Christ crosses the stage and passes into the inner
room.*]

It is one of the oddest critical misjudgements that a dramatist
who can contrive a moment so supremely thrilling as this—one
in which all the movements of the play blaze up together into
meaning and theatrical effect—should have been accused of writing plays which 'are little more than charades'.[20] 'I felt', Yeats
wrote, recording how he encountered the original of the incident
in Sir William Crookes's *Studies in Psychical Research*, '. . . the
terror of the supernatural described by Job.'[21] He successfully
administers to his audience the 'violent shock' which induces a
sense of spiritual reality.[22] The 'terror of the supernatural', which
Miss Mackenna merely talked about in *The Words upon the
Window-pane* passes before the face: 'Belief comes from shock and
is not desired.'[23]

As plays of ideas, *Calvary* and *The Resurrection* are different in
method, although they use a roughly similar set of ideas. *Calvary*
presents its audience with an image for it to contemplate and does
not attempt to draw its hearers into it more than is needed to get
them to pay attention. *The Resurrection* is more dynamic; by

increasingly converging lines of movement Yeats brings the spectator into position so that he can administer his 'violent shock'. Each play follows its chosen form 'as carefully as if it were a sonnet'. Yeats was willing to experiment, especially after he had discovered the Noh and completed *At the Hawk's Well* in 1916. The Noble Plays themselves were after all, he said, something that 'need absorb no one's life'. When he had done enough in that kind he would 'record all discoveries of method and turn to something else'.* [24]

* I have not discussed the two songs with which *The Resurrection* opens and closes. Famous as poems from their inclusion in *The Tower* (1928), they were an addition to the original scheme of the play (see *Wheels and Butterflies*, p. 111); the last of the four stanzas was a still later addition, post-dating *The Tower*. Although, except for this stanza, they are lyrical meditations on the theme of the play, intelligible in the light of it, they seem completely detachable from it, unlike the songs in *Calvary*.

Chapter Seven

The Beasts

---

hoping to find once more,
Being by Calvary's turbulence unsatisfied,
The uncontrollable mystery on the bestial floor.

I

'F OR years', Yeats wrote in the Introduction to *The Resurrection*, 'I have been preoccupied with a certain myth that was in itself a reply to a myth' and went on to say:

I do not mean a fiction, but one of those statements our nature is compelled to make and employ as a truth though there cannot be sufficient evidence. When I was a boy everybody talked about progress, and rebellion against my elders took the form of aversion to that myth. I took satisfaction in certain public disasters, felt a sort of ecstasy in the contemplation of ruin.[1]

The sense that the world was awaiting a revelation that would destroy old things and bring a different order to birth was one that persecuted him as much as it inspired him. It grew slowly more elaborate, aided and transformed by the discovery of images. Destruction acquired its complement: the generation, out of a violent reversal of the old order, of a new time.

The poets, rebels, and outcasts, who are the central figures in the early stories in *The Secret Rose* and *The Tables of the Law* (1897), are impelled to reject the life around them and travel the 'roads of the world', searching, like the old man in 'The Heart of

128

Spring' for something they cannot define, 'the secret of life', the 'Great Secret'.[2] They choose 'that beauty which seems unearthly',[3] and discover that there is something in their natures which cannot be content with ordinary loves—one of the themes of 'The Wisdom of the King', where the monarch who has been gifted with the feathers of the magical hawk instead of hair strides from his palace into the unknown world and is never seen again. Red Hanrahan is a wanderer and outcast of this kind; persecuted and inspired, he is a victim as well as a teacher and poet. His visions are of the Sidhe, Cathleen ni Houlihan, and a Celtic Valhalla whose music is 'the continual clashing of swords'.[4]

Lady Gregory had helped to purge the Red Hanrahan stories of some of their excessive ornament and to make his story part of a familiar Irish landscape, and it is the tales about Owen Aherne and Michael Robartes that bring us closest to Yeats himself at this time. They are filled with confusion, argument, and colour—faked patrology, alchemical rites, sacred books with jewelled covers that enshrine Byzantine paintings. The character of Aherne expresses most completely the 'consuming thirst for destruction' which also entails the destruction of the self:

More orthodox in most of his beliefs than Michael Robartes, he had surpassed him in a fanciful hatred of all life, and this hatred had found expression in the curious paradox—half borrowed from some fanatical monk, half invented by himself—that the beautiful arts were sent into the world to overthrow nations, and finally life herself, by sowing everywhere unlimited desires, like torches thrown into a burning city.[5]

The world and the future that Robartes and Aherne seek are never very clearly seen. The stories dramatize the seeking rather than the finding: 'I know nothing certain as yet but this', Aherne cries, 'I am to become completely alive, that is, completely passionate, for beauty is only another name for perfect passion':

I shall create a world where the whole lives of men shall be articulated and simplified as if seventy years were but one moment, or as they were the leaping of a fish or the opening of a flower.[6]

And the search is attended by nightmare terrors, visions of evil as well as of supernatural good, like the great worm which seems to clutch Aherne in its folds, as it had clutched Red Hanrahan in another story.[7] The narrator fights against being swept away 'into an indefinite world which fills me with terror':

a man is a great man just in so far as he can make his mind reflect everything with indifferent precision like a mirror. . . . I command you to leave me at once, for your ideas and phantasies are but the illusions that creep like maggots into civilizations when they begin to decline, and into minds when they begin to decay.[8]

But Robartes and Aherne continued in attendance, waiting their opportunity, which came in 1917 when Yeats discovered what he was for a time to call their 'papers'. He went back over the old stories about them in the inductions to *A Vision*. By then it had all become precise:

'Have I proved that civilisations come to an end when they have given all their light like burned-out wicks, that ours is near its end?' 'Or transformation', Aherne corrected. [The narrator answers affirmatively.] 'If you had answered differently' said Robartes, 'I would have sent you away, for we are here to consider the terror that is to come.'[9]

The prophecies of destruction were now combined with the notion of the historical cycles, and there formed about them a rich cluster of attendant images: the annunciations, the 'rough beast' which is also demiurgic, the harlot of the new dispensation who supplants the virgin of the old. Catastrophe is everywhere interlocked with renewal, and accepted with terror and joy.[10]

This complex of ideas satisfied Yeats's desire to 'arrange in one clear view'. It contributed much to the force and splendour of a few poems such as 'The Second Coming', 'Leda and the Swan', and 'The Gyres', and in *The Resurrection* a part of it achieved theatrical expression. But the other plays in which Yeats sought to employ it are much less successful. Although he toiled at them arduously, neither *Where There Is Nothing*, nor *The Unicorn from the Stars* nor *The Player Queen* are as interesting as some of the plays into which Yeats put less of the persecuting abstracts. One inherent disadvantage of the theme, from the point of view of both playwright and storyteller, was its prophetic character. Where everything moves towards a measureless consummation that is to take place in the future, the characters tend to be reduced to evangelists and sectaries; and it is difficult for the divine event for which everyone is waiting to be wrought into the business of the stage. Even in *The Player Queen*, where Yeats had much success in turning his *preparatio* into an intrigue, the feeling that a good deal is necessarily withheld from the audience is frustrating when the last curtain falls. *The Resurrection* does not suffer from this because it is a history-play and it was possible to put into it the revelation towards which it builds.

In *Where There Is Nothing* (1903) Yeats to some extent overcame this difficulty by stressing the fortunes of the hero, who is another version of the outcasts in *The Secret Rose*. Paul Ruttledge is a celibate country gentleman who has begun to see his relatives and fellow-magistrates as just an ungenial collection of barnyard fowl. He has dreams of destruction in which he identifies himself with 'Laughter, the mightiest of the enemies of God'. It is a beast which he wishes to overtake, a 'very terrible wild beast, with iron teeth and brazen claws that root up spires and towers'.[11] After he has repudiated his old life and its established society and changed clothes with Charlie Ward the tinker we see him in the second Act a member of the tinkers' gang, learning from them and trying to teach them. Repudiating another worn-out emblem of civilization, he marries the tinker girl Sabina Silver by 'lepping over the tinkers' budget', and in the next Act demoralizes the whole village with free drink. This makes him very popular with the tinkers, but less so with the magistrates. When they attempt to put a stop to it all, Paul and the tinkers seize them and subject them to a mock trial:

You have come into a different kingdom now; the old kingdom of the people of the roads, the houseless people. We call ourselves tinkers, and you are going to put us on our trial if you can. You call yourselves Christians and we will put you on your trial first.[12]

All the Christian magistrates are convicted of 'breaking the doctrine they boast of'. At the beginning of the fourth Act the tinkers take Paul, who is ill, to be looked after in a monastery. Five years pass, and he has become an heretical monk and has acquired a few disciples. Emerging from a trance, he preaches a sermon to them —a portion of the play that gave Yeats much trouble—in which the history of mankind is sketched as a gradual decline from God-given joyous impulse to a society immured by institutions and victimized by 'all the animal spirits that have loved things better than life'. But 'the Christian must live so that all things shall pass away':

We must destroy the World; we must destroy everything that has Law and Number, for where there is nothing, there is God.[13]

Banished from the monastery, his teaching beyond the grasp of his own disciples (who wish to re-create institutions in order to live in greater comfort), Paul at length dies at the hands of a superstitious mob.

Una Ellis-Fermor found much to admire in both the characterization and the sentiments of *Where There Is Nothing*.[14] In a play whose design is that of the life-story everything seems to depend upon what the playwright achieves with his protagonist. Neither Yeats nor his collaborators (Douglas Hyde and Lady Gregory) were able to make Paul Ruttledge potent or interesting enough. There are moments when he is talking to Father Jerome in the first Act and to Charlie Ward and the other tinkers in the second Act when it seems as though he may be coming to life. These are some of the quieter passages in the play, and Paul's animation is agreeably correlated with the growing signs of affectionate puzzlement or respectful tolerance that the other persons feel for him. Paul, too, is successfully kept in the centre of the action; as rebel, as teacher, and as victim he seems to have the possibility of complex life. But all is vitiated by his inexpressiveness. Unprovided with either friend or foe, he is a Richard without Buckingham, or without the soliloquies. He is surrounded by lifeless people. The curse of this play, as of several others, is Yeats's taste for hosts of minor characters; the more they crowd the scene, the more they drain the life from it. Paul can address them only in a public voice, with sentiments out of Blake, Nietzsche, and Tolstoy. But this eloquence is unpersuasive because it proceeds from a character who gives us so little of his own inner travail. To Yeats himself Paul soon appeared to be 'arid and dominating'. The play's faults of construction, such as the clumsy attempt to solder the break between the tinker's camp and the monastery, do not need emphasis.

Where There Is Nothing was hurriedly put together by the three collaborators 'spurred by an external necessity' (which was the fear that George Moore would steal the plot).[15] It was admired by many people, including Shaw. Yeats himself repudiated it, partly because of its faults of construction and its unsympathetic hero, partly because of what he came to consider the 'crude speculative commonplaces' of the 'trial'-scene in Act III, and he would not allow Bullen to reprint it in the Stratford edition,[16] where it was replaced by Lady Gregory's new version of the theme, *The Unicorn from the Stars* (1908). The collaborators have reduced the tangled life-story of Paul Ruttledge to a single action: Martin Hearne's vision of the trampling unicorn, the fabulous beast whose destruction of the old order fills Martin with joyful terror, his entanglement with the outlaws who interpret his teaching in acts of drunken anarchy that terrify all the respectable folk, and his final vision, before he is shot in a scuffle with the constables, that the battle of ruin and rebirth is to be fought in the human mind, in mental fight:

MARTIN

It was but a frenzy, that going out to burn and to destroy. What have I do with the foreign army? What I have to pierce is the wild heart of time. My business is not reformation but revelation.

JOHNNY

If you are going to turn back now from leading us, you are no better than any other traitor that ever gave up the work he took in hand. Let you come and face now the two hundred men you brought out daring the power of the law last night, and give them your reason for failing them.

MARTIN

I was mistaken when I set out to destroy Church and Law. The battle we have to fight is fought out in our own mind. There is a fiery moment, perhaps once in a lifetime, and in that moment we see the only thing that matters. It is in that moment the great battles are lost and won, for in that moment we are a part of the host of heaven.[17]

In *The Unicorn from the Stars* the symbolism is much more coherent and meaningful. Martin's destruction of the golden state-coach which he has been building is the poet's destruction of his own artefact, the deed which chooses that 'heavenly mansion', 'perfection of the life' and not of the work;[18] yet it proceeds with substantial realism from the coachbuilder's artisan that he is in the play. The reduction of the visionary's rank from country gentleman to tradesman resulted in further unities of setting and society. It was in the development of Martin's two uncles and of Father John that Lady Gregory showed most skill. Thomas Hearne, the respectable coachbuilder, is much more actual than the ninepins which Paul Ruttledge knocks over, and in Father John and the second uncle, Andrew Hearne, the possibilities of Thomas Ruttledge and Father Jerome in *Where There Is Nothing* are effectively developed. They are men who, through learning or temperament or both, have themselves experienced something of Martin's visionary turbulence; they exemplify those 'strange souls born everywhere to-day', of whom Yeats wrote in *The Trembling of the Veil*, 'with hearts that Christianity, as shaped by history, cannot satisfy'.[19] They help the audience to believe in and sympathize with Martin. There is no doubt that in so decisively preferring *The Unicorn from the Stars* to its earlier version Yeats showed sound judgement as a theatrical craftsman.

II

Yeats's note on *The Player Queen* explains a good deal about its origin and theme:

I began in, I think, 1907, a verse tragedy, but at that time the thought I have set forth in *Per Amica Silentia Lunae* was coming into my head, and I found examples of it everywhere. I wasted the best working months of several years in an attempt to write a poetical play where every character became an example of the finding or not finding of what I have called the Antithetical Self; and because passion and not thought makes tragedy, what I made had neither simplicity nor life. ... At last it came into my head all of a sudden that I could get rid of the play if I turned it into a farce; and never did I do anything so easily, for I think that I wrote the present play in about a month.[20]

Yeats's doctrine of the Mask, the notion that each man can find his hidden opposite, his anti- (or antithetical) self, is his best-known 'myth'. The mask of the anti-self, to be sought out with courage, is worn by those 'who are no longer deceived, whose passion is reality';[21] * it bring happiness:

* The last phrase appears, from its context, to mean 'who have a passion for (specifically) religious truth'.

all happiness depends on the energy to assume the mask of some other life, on a re-birth as something not one's self, something created in a moment and perpetually renewed.

The finding of the Mask is one of Martin Hearne's 'fiery moments'; the wearing of it at last defines what Owen Aherne meant by saying 'I must become completely alive'. Another passage in *Per Amica* bears directly on *The Player Queen*:

When I had this thought I could see nothing else in life. I could not write the play I had planned, for all became allegorical, and though I tore up hundreds of pages in my endeavour to escape from allegory, my imagination became sterile for nearly five years and I only escaped at last when I had mocked in a comedy my own thought.[22]

In *The Player Queen* the finding of a Mask is linked to the miraculous end of an era and the coming of a new dispensation—all that is symbolized in *Where There Is Nothing* by the beast with iron claws and in *The Unicorn from the Stars* by the trampling, milk-white unicorn. The combined themes are transformed into Yeats's nearest approach to a neo-classical comedy of sexual intrigue. The poet, teacher, victim, and evangelist divide into a humour-character and a grotesque, while other grotesques abound. The setting is removed from Ireland to a nameless country whose only visible political institutions are a queen, a mob, and a comic prime minister. By these means Yeats's thought is made to dance in a sufficiently gay and extraordinary fashion.

To mock one's own thought is not necessarily to achieve an escape from allegory; it need not mean more than the substitution of a comic allegory for a serious one. By altering the temper and tone of his chosen images (putting, for example, a silly goose like the Queen in *The Player Queen* into the place of a tragedy-queen) Yeats may have hoped to transform the thought into comedy and so escape from its sombre and exalted appeal, which threatened to become a persecuting obsession. In the essays on Blake and on 'The Symbolism of Poetry' Yeats had long before suggested that thought and image can and should be wrought into symbol; and perhaps, if that is done, then all that is needed to mock one's thought is to transform the symbol. Yeats may have considered that a transformation of that kind was at work when he re-wrote the play as a comedy. We must grant that Yeats did not wish merely to present the old, sombre notions dressed up in gladder rags. But it is doubtful whether thought and image had been wholly wrought into symbol. The transformation, since it is only a comicalizing of the image, leaves the basic tone and temper of the thought unaffected, and perhaps the relation between image, character, and story on the one hand and the persecuting abstract on the other remains essentially akin to that which obtains in allegory. Comic character and behaviour and all that is meant by the development of an intrigue, at least, although they may be intended to convey by what they are and do the meanings that are being mocked, still contain patches of uneasiness and of great obscurity.

Some of the qualities of *The Player Queen* give evidence of the survival of old perplexities. First, there is some inconsistency in the method of characterization and the behaviour of individual characters; sometimes they play intelligible roles in a comic matter which does convey its own meaning, sometimes their gestures or concernments fail to convey meaning to any but the most initiated spectator (who has to go outside the play for a gloss).[23] Secondly, some of the implications of the story have a melancholy resonance which is out of accord with the impudent events and the farcical fortunes. It begs the question to declare that the clothes are gay but that *au fond* the spirit is grave, but there is more than a hint of bitter conclusions which suggest that Yeats had not really succeeded in mocking his own thought. There are strange inconstancies of tone, which may derive from uncertainty—the author's uncertainty unconsciously betrayed to the spectator—about the genre. The 'comedy' is a 'farce' as well, and a farce, Yeats reminded Lady Gregory, is 'comedy with character left out'. But character, in the sense of the discrimination and definition of individuality, is no more absent from *The Player Queen* than it was absent from *Deirdre*. In this respect, *The Player Queen* fits Yeats's definition of farce no better than *Deirdre* fitted his definition of tragedy. Perhaps we should be content to call it a tragi-comedy: a label which is unsatisfactory only because Yeats would have regarded it as a contradiction in terms.

There are, as Becker has pointed out, two stories in the play. They are carefully interwoven, one being centred on Septimus the drunken poet and the other on his wife Decima the player queen. They are members of a company of players which has arrived at the castle of the Queen and is to perform, by order of her Prime Minister, a play called *The Tragical History of Noah's Deluge*. The first Act belongs mainly to Septimus. He is a comic *poète maudit* and parodies the central characters in the *Secret Rose* stories; his drunkenness is a literalized and comical version of the spiritual intoxication of Paul Ruttledge and Martin Hearne, drunk with the grapes of wrath. Like them, he has his vision: of the chaste, noble, and religious unicorn, the 'hidden, flying image' of all that he is not, his Mask. His 'humour' is to make tipsy speeches about it in enamelled rhetoric. Before he stumbles on to the stage looking for his wife Decima, whose disappearance threatens the performance of the morrow's play, two old men have been commenting on the disturbance made by rioters in the night-time streets. Septimus's quarrel with the two 'bad, popular poets' whom he encounters (as they are returning apparently from a brothel) underlines his role as a proud outcast. He goes to sleep in the gutter, but is disturbed by a crowd of citizens who are rioting against the Queen. They say that she has never been seen outside her castle during the seven years of her reign; she must be a bad, evil-living witch; there is a story told by a goat-herd who looked through her window and saw her coupling with a great white unicorn, which on another occasion he shot at and wounded. Septimus gets up to defend the chastity of the unicorn, but is soon knocked down by one of the peasants, who have decided to break into the castle and strangle the Queen. Then the crowds disappear when the Old Beggar is reported to be coming in their direction. The Old Beggar is a grotesque parody of the evangelist who announces the new dispensation. His back begins to itch, he looks for straw to lie upon, and brays like a donkey every time the crown changes. His back is itching now, he explains to Septimus, and poet and evangelist go off the stage together.

This Act is clearly an ingeniously contrived preparation for what is to come. The parodic roles of poet and prophet are obvious, although the characters are of different types—one is purely a symbolic grotesque, the other is a comic humour-character. Similar matchings occur in some of Jonson's plays and seem awkward there too. The audience is presumably expected to wait patiently or eagerly for the mystery of the unicorn to be disclosed: which is right about it, Septimus or the crowd, and are they talking about the same thing? But the crowd itself dashes the comedy down into ugliness and bestiality. Their superstitious brutality and gloating chatter about the strangling of witches show that Yeats has not been able to rid his imagination of the tempestuous squalor that accompanies the falling-apart of an old era as the new one approaches. Here the tone of comedy is lost.

The second Act opens with an angry Prime Minister demanding that the missing Decima be found:

I know her sort; would pull the world to pieces to spite her husband or her lover. I know her—a bladder full of dried peas for a brain, a brazen, bragging baggage.[24]

This splutter is interrupted by the entrance of the Queen. She is a nun-like creature, ascetic and badly dressed, devoted to Holy Saint Octema, and has reluctantly agreed to show herself to her people, although quite persuaded that this will result in her martyrdom at their hands:

I have now attained to the age of my patroness, Holy Saint Octema, when she was martyred at Antioch. You will remember that her unicorn was so pleased at the spectacle of her austerity that he caracoled in his excitement. Thereupon she dropped out of the saddle and was trampled to death under the feet of the mob. Indeed, but for the unicorn, the mob would have killed her long before.

The unicorn is still an emblem of destruction, although the Queen does not recognize this. What is to her symbolic union with an image of chastity and austerity is bestial witchcraft to the brutish crowd and supplies the main reason why they wish to kill her as the Saint was killed. This seems to be an attempt, though not perhaps a very successful one, to turn the unicorn into a comic or ironic antinomy.

The Prime Minister despairs of ever making the Queen appear sufficiently queenly; she is utterly unfitted for her role in life and seeks only to run away to a convent. But he has a plan, as yet undisclosed, that will make her acceptable to the people. When they go off the stage, Nona, the other leading actress of the company, appears with a lobster and a bottle of wine and lures the hungry Decima from her hiding-place under the throne.

What follows is a long, rapidly developed scene of comic

intrigue, with Decima as the heroine of more than a comedy of humours. She refuses to play the part allotted to her in *The Tragical History of Noah's Deluge* (an old tale of the destruction, or preservation, of the world), in which she has been cast for the role of that old harridan Noah's wife, whom 'a foul husband beats with a stick because she won't clamber among the other brutes into his cattleboat'. In refusing to wear the mask of this brutish role she seeks one antithetical to it: 'the only part in the world I can play is a great Queen's part'. Nona replies scornfully:

You play a Queen's part? You that were born in a ditch between two towns and wrapped in a sheet that was stolen from a hedge.

Thus in Decima there are interwoven from her first appearance her two roles as a 'ditch-delivered drab' and as an artist or heroine seeking her anti-self. Her song, which she attributes to the 'mad singing-daughter of a harlot', combines these two subjects, as well as the theme of the sexual conjunction of woman and bird as it appears in 'Leda and the Swan', the symbolic poem concerned with the annunciation to Leda that 'founded Greece' and was followed next in the series by the annunciation made to the virgin that founded Christendom:[25]

> She pulled the thread and bit the thread
> And made a golden gown,
> She wept because she had dreamt that I
> Was born to wear a crown.
>
> 'When she was got,' my mother sang,
> 'I heard a seamew cry,
> I saw a flake of yellow foam
> That dropped upon my thigh.'

The significance of the Harlot as the 'virgin' of the post-Christian annunciation has been explained by Giorgio Melchiori and by F. A. C. Wilson, chiefly by collating it with Yeats's story 'The Adoration of the Magi', a first version of which appeared in 1897. This story is about a Parisian prostitute, who is visited by the Three Wise Men, those Magi who, in the poem of that title, are 'by Calvary's turbulence unsatisfied'.[26] In the 1925 version of this story the girl gives birth to a 'cold, hard, and virginal unicorn', the emblem of the new era.[27]

It may fairly be claimed that in *The Player Queen* itself Yeats leaves this aspect of Decima impenetrably obscure. William Becker, who praised the play as a 'clear candidate for popular acceptance' (because its meaning emerges through its dramatic context), missed the aspect of Decima as Harlot, because he did not make the necessary connexion with 'Leda and the Swan' and 'The Adoration of the Magi'. It is therefore all the harder to see how any audience could penetrate so far, except the group to whom Yeats dedicated *Reveries over Childhood and Youth*: 'those few people mainly personal friends who have read all that I have written'.[28]

Yeats indeed shaped his second Act round another subject. He concentrated on the process whereby Decima is stripped of everything in the old life so that she may live the new one. By this method the material becomes human comedy, for the process is rendered as a traditional intrigue, although the theme itself is constantly recurring in Yeats, and is seriously treated in *The Hour-Glass*, *Where There Is Nothing*, and elsewhere:

To seek God too soon is not less sinful than to seek God too late; we must love man, woman or child, we must exhaust ambition, intellect, desire, dedicating all things as they pass, or we come to God with empty hands.[29]

Decima loses her man Septimus and her part in *The Tragical History* to Nona. In passages where the two women needle each other jealously about their hold over Septimus, Nona reveals that Septimus is her lover and that she was in bed with him when Septimus composed the verses to Decima which Decima carries next to her heart. Decima therefore feels, or pretends to feel, free to choose a new man. When the players come in, dressed for their animal parts in the Noah play—Bull and Turkey are the two animals mentioned, the first combining (being a pantomimic bull) two men—she considers their possibilities, and then all the players dance while she sings about Pasiphae and Leda:

> Spring and straddle, stride and strut,
> Shall I choose a bird or brute?
> Name the feather or the fur
> For my single comforter?

According to Wilson, this is a dance of 'sexual invitation to God-

head',[30] and this is what we might expect of the Harlot/Leda of
the new annunciation. But it seems capable of being interpreted
in another way: as just as much an emblem of her old life as it is
of the new one that is being prepared for her. For what else is her
choice amongst the player-beasts but another attempt to 'clamber
among the other brutes into [Noah's] cattle-boat'? The farmyard
animals are analogous to the barnyard creatures in *Where There
Is Nothing* whom Paul Ruttledge actualizes in nightmare and
in topiary-work,[31] and eventually repudiates. Certainly, from the
position of this episode in *The Player Queen* it is a fair inference
that during it Decima is still clinging to the old life, because,
although she has ostensibly given Septimus up, she none the less
tries desperately to keep him in the next part of the scene. The
point is left obscure because the dance is broken off when Septimus
comes in.

He is still half-drunk, has much in mind the impatient mob
gathering outside the castle, and is radiant with a new idea about
the unicorn:

I announce the end of the Christian Era, the coming of a New Dispensation, that of the New Adam, that of the Unicorn; but alas, he is
chaste, he hesitates, he hesitates. . . . I will rail upon the Unicorn for his
chastity. I will bid him trample mankind to death and beget a new race.

Here Seanchan's Nietzschean race of the future and Martin
Hearne's unicorn of destruction have bcome assimilated to the
godhead as beast, and to the theme of the anti-self. As Melchiori
explains the latter point:

The Unicorn is chastity itself. Copulation and begetting are its opposite, its Mask. Now, the consummation by the Unicorn of an act of
lust would mean reaching its own opposite, its Mask; and this is outside
the range of natural possibilities, it is miracle . . . Only miracle can
produce the end of an era and the advent of a New Dispensation.[32]

But so far as the action of this play is concerned, the change of
crowns itself is effected not by miracle but by the development
of the story of Decima as a personage in a comic intrigue.

She does her best to retain Septimus ('If you would be faithful
to me, Septimus, I would not let a man of them touch me'), but
Septimus eventually follows Nona out through the door that
Decima has locked, but of which Nona has recaptured the key.

Septimus is characterized as a man who knows the truth, but lacks courage and energy for the measureless consummation. He piles the images of his art upon his back, and chooses a woman who is not, as Decima is, 'terrible' to him,[33] and takes flight from the wrath to come, carrying in his hand the high-crowned hat of Noah the preserver. At the same time he has had his vision. He still dreams that he will aid the unicorn to accomplish its anti-self and become the image to which man may unite himself (the theme of Byzantium, and the Byzantium poems).

When we have put all in safety we will go to the high tablelands of Africa and find where the Unicorn is stabled and sing a marriage song. I will stand before the terrible blue eye.

But 'putting all [the properties of *The Tragical History*] in safety' is hardly compatible with surrender to the apocalypse, and the unicorn is conveniently remote. He will never visit the unicorn but will continue to dream about it, a *poète maudit* to the end, who, by renouncing Decima, unintentionally leaves her free to accomplish her destiny. Irony engulfs him. He is at bottom a tragic figure; he both withdraws from the heart of the story (the life of Decima) and is extruded by it. All his comic drunkard's rhetoric does not conceal this, but allows us to perceive the difference between gay clothes and the frustrated hero, a Cuchulain of the poetic life.

Decima is now completely deserted, and when the Old Beggar enters, still looking for his straw, she is thinking about plunging the wardrobe-mistress's scissors into her breast. He urges her not to, and gives her a glimpse of the life after death which takes away the last hope and curiously controverts the substance of *The Dreaming of the Bones* and *Purgatory*:

DECIMA

I have been betrayed by a man, I have been made a mockery of. Do those who are dead, old man, make love and do they find good lovers?

OLD BEGGAR

I will whisper you another secret. People talk, but I have never known anything to come from there but an old jackass. Maybe there is nothing else. Who knows but he has the whole place to himself?

This perhaps is 'mocking one's own thought', but we can see that the result is not necessarily gay. Reduced to this gloomy and empty vision, Decima is about to stab herself: 'a hero loves the world till it breaks him'.[34]

Then the Queen comes in. They quickly agree to change clothes and roles; Decima finds her Mask in a flash. This is a point on the play where the λύσις, the sudden untying of the tangled skein traditional in neo-classical comedy, perfectly matches the thought, for the Mask is found 'in a moment', one of Martin Hearne's 'fiery moments': 'the antithetical man works by flashes of lightning'.[35] Decima assumes the Queen's role expecting to die in her stead at the hands of the mob:

O, your Majesty, I shall die whatever you do, and if only I could wear that gold brocade and those gold slippers for one moment, it would not be so hard to die.

For she has become 'completely alive'.

It is difficult to be sure what mood dominates at the end of the play and whether or not all the preceding themes achieve completion and resolution there, although events can be clearly set down. The Prime Minister comes back, after he has disclosed to the mob the plan to save the situation that he had mentioned earlier to the Queen: it is that he should marry her. This has kept the people quiet—in Act I a citizen had cried, 'When [the Queen] is dead we will make the Prime Minister King.' He is amazed to find Decima in the Queen's place, but she can play the role as though she had been born to it (as indeed she has). Her majestic beauty instantaneously overawes crowd and Minister, who begins to desire her. The bray of a donkey is heard and the Beggar-evangelist is dragged in. He is packed off to prison as an impostor, for it is now policy to maintain that the real Queen has not disappeared and that the crown has not changed hands; Septimus (who ineffectually attempts to disclose the truth) and the other players who know who the new Queen really is are expelled from the kingdom. In the revised edition (1934) Decima addresses them in a farewell speech; during it, both symbolically and for the purposes of disguise, she wears the mask of the sister of Noah who in *The Tragical History* had refused to enter his 'cattle-boat' and had been drowned in the flood of destruction.

The ending is comic in so far as Decima finds her Mask, and happiness; the donkey's bray and the mask of Noah's sister make it plain that the crown has truly changed, and that a new dispensation has arrived. But the annunciation is kept secret and ironically muddled; the Prime Minister takes various measures to conceal what has really happened, as does Decima herself, and the crowds that acclaim her are utterly deceived, for they suppose that the new Queen is only their old one writ finer than they had expected and are unaware that their revolt against their chaste and virginal ruler because of her imputed witchcraft and harlotry has landed them with a witch and harlot indeed.

Decima's status as harlot of the new annunciation seems, as before, a matter which can hardly be explained without external aid. F. A. C. Wilson is prepared to make the necessary inference: 'We are left to infer that the form in which divinity is to descend to Decima is that of the unicorn, the disguise under which it manifests in this palace.'[36] This may be right, but one of the objections to it is that throughout the play the unicorn in its aspect of immanent beast-deity is the property of Septimus's imagination and has, as it were, gone off with him when he withdrew from the story. Decima, after all, does not marry a unicorn, or even talk about one; she marries the Prime Minister, who has been ruling the kingdom for seven years already. It is true that his reign appears to be over, since it is apparent that Decima will stand no nonsense from him; but what is this farcical figure doing in the new era? He proposes, suggests Wilson, to 'usurp the function of Godhead',[37] and this sounds much more like the real ending. But you cannot easily have it both ways: Decima cannot be both the bride of God and the bride of his usurper; and if Yeats is hinting that the Prime Minister is to be God's unwitting surrogate, like Congal and his men in *The Herne's Egg*, the theme is so darkly rendered in *The Player Queen* as to require exegesis from a sequel written fourteen years later. It may be, finally, that it is by means of this episode that the sense in which the play is the farce that Yeats called it is made most plain. Decima, expecting death, finds instead her anti-self and her happiness; but a condition of this seems to be that she must unite herself with a buffoon. Below the farce, as is the case with Septimus's drunken rhetoric, there lurks the hint of tragedy.

On various grounds, then, *The Player Queen* seems an imperfect achievement, if we attempt to judge it as the comedy Yeats thought he had written. The point is worth making boldly, in view of the tendency amongst recent commentators to single it out for special approval. The great interest of the play is, of course, Decima; she is the new Deirdre and was, if allegory had not frustrated all, to be her successor in the repertoire of Mrs. Patrick Campbell; like Deirdre she had the courage and 'energy of soul' to assume the role that would alter her story after the bitter experience of playing parts devised for others' stories; and like Deirdre she achieves her imaginative triumph in the face of death. For Deirdre's stately passions are not merely 'mocked' and 'got rid of' by Decima's wit and sensuality. The resemblance, as well as the difference, between the pair are the index of a vast, potential enlargement of the woman's place in Yeats's drama—the shadowing forth of a figure various enough to comprise both Deirdre and Crazy Jane. Such a figure, Yeats's unwritten Cleopatra, did not after all appear, and the more's the pity if Decima was, as we may suspect, the original impulse of *The Player Queen* when it was started shortly after the success of *Deirdre* and proceeded to run foul, as we have seen, of the 'persecution of the abstract'.

It is probably this persecution that makes it, despite the liveliness and assurance of its writing and characterization and the highly successful scene of neo-classical comedy between Nona and Decima, inferior to works on a much more modest scale such as *Purgatory*. 'Aesthetically speaking', Professor Edgar Wind has said, 'there can be no doubt that the presence of unresolved residues of meaning is an obstacle to the enjoyment of art.' [38] It is still possible for a commentator, to offer an account of the play by freely interpreting its character and plot and disregarding its theme and history.[39] But most spectators are likely to keep restlessly enquiring 'Now what exactly does the playwright mean by *that*?' Too often the answers cannot be provided from the play itself. Apart from the larger problems, some of which I have discussed, there is a continuous spray of surface detail which it is not impertinent to call substantially allegorical still. This at least seems to make *The Player Queen* a poor choice for an audience that expects meanings to be conveyed through the dramatic context.

III

In November, 1935, Yeats wrote to Dorothy Wellesley about his new play, 'as wild a play as *Player Queen*, as amusing but more tragedy and philosophic depth'. Originally planned as a three-act tragedy, it eventually became *The Herne's Egg*, in six Scenes, 'the strangest wildest thing I have ever written'.[40]

The animal presences and the sexual themes are responsible for the first impressions of strangeness. There is much that seems like the games of children—the stylized battles, Corney scolding his life-size toy-donkey, the village-children catechizing Attracta, Congal's six child-like men—and this is oddly conjoined with the sexual theme, rape and the sacred marriage. *The Herne's Egg* is crowded and stagy, too, not a play for the drawing-room, but more on the scale of the old Abbey plays and *The Player Queen*, with its different locations, its fourteen speaking parts, and an abundance of properties and stage-effects. The absence of a chorus brings us face to face with a protagonist in a way that had scarcely been attempted since *The King's Threshold*, except in *The Player Queen*.itself. These piquant contrasts and lavish arrangements to some extent conceal a concern, similar to that in the Cuchulain plays, with the working out of an individualized hero's destiny and with a fable which is almost as regular as one of Ovid's: a man commits sacrilege against a god by stealing his sacred objects and violating his priestess, and is suitably punished with metamorphosis. Yeats gives this ancient tale of mortal hubris and divine implacability 'philosophic depth' by making his hero's stubbornness an intransigent assertion of his human self and un-christened heart. Congal claims.

> as by a soldier's right
> A charter to commit the crime once more.

What makes Congal's story complex and ironically determines the nature of his struggle is that he does not understand the god against whom he makes war. It is made plain in the play that this failure of understanding is inseparable from his role as man, sol-dier, and chieftain. The bird-god, the Great Herne, is known only to his initiate the priestess Attracta. Congal is precluded by all that he is, by every occasion on which he employs the weapons of his manhood, from being an initiate. He is therefore different from Cuchulain or Emer, who know what they contend with, even when it is supernatural. The god in *The Herne's Egg* can terrify but not convert Congal. The hero fighting the god under these conditions is also a kind of fool; when he releases his grip on the life he lives, he is turned into a donkey. It is in accord with this that Congal should be set in the context of much brash and oafish life, and that events and properties should seem to mock at him. The contrast between this element and Attracta's exalted and sacerdotal role enforces the theme as well as the vitality of the play.

In the first Scene Congal, King of Connaught, and Aedh, King of Tara, conclude a peace after their fiftieth drawn battle. Theirs has been a prelapsarian world, like Red Hanrahan's Heaven, whose music was the 'continual clashing of swords'. In the next Scene Congal and his men visit the abode of the Great Herne, where lives the promised bride of the god. They pillage the eggs from the hernery as a delicacy for the supper at Tara which is to celebrate the peace. This act is at first largely unmotivated, the impulse without which the play cannot move, but it soon assumes a different character. Congal behaves as an unbeliever in the face of the god's and his priestess's claim. Must old campaigners forego a delicacy because

> a woman thinks that she
> Is promised or married to a bird?[41]

Attracta's marriage to the god is a perverted fancy arising from frustration:

> Women thrown into despair
> By the winter of their virginity
> Take its abominable snow,
> As boys take common snow, and make
> An image of god or bird or beast
> To feed their sensuality.

The cure for this condition is the experience of human sexuality. Happiness, replies Attracta, is to be found only in communion with the god: 'There is no happiness but the Great Herne'; but

Congal denies her right to say so, because she does not know what human pleasure is:

> pick,
> Or be picked by seven men,
> And we shall talk it out again.

Similarly, when the curse is pronounced upon him, that he must be changed into a fool and die at a fool's hand, it means nothing to him:

> That I shall live and die a fool,
> And die upon some battlefield
> At a fool's hand, is but natural,
> And needs no curse to bring it.

The saving clause 'upon some battlefield' shows the degree of his misunderstanding; he easily twists the sinister literalism of *fool* in the curse into a harmless, worldly generality. In all this, Congal blunts the supernatural by interpreting the signs of its immanence rationally and psychologically. Nothing in his conduct so far suggests that making war on the god would make sense to him.

When Congal and his men go, the audience is brought closer to the reality he has disregarded by Attracta's discourse on her mysterious marriage, addressed to the girls. They describe her trance. The priestess becomes the instrument of the god, vacated of all human will; she goes away carrying the hen's egg, which she has taken from one of the girls' baskets, and which is to destroy the harmony of Congal's life and initiate the curse. The god is present when his tune 'The Great Herne's Feather' is played, and in Scene iii, before the gates of Tara, the Great Herne flies over Congal's troop while they try to stone and slash him, taking him more for an angry bird than for an enraged divinity. And then (Scene iv) Congal bursts from the feast at Tara in a drunken rage, accusing Aedh of having insulted him by substituting a hen's egg for the hernes' eggs which every other man has had. Since they have given up their arms, the two kings fight with legs broken from the tables, and Congal kills Aedh, bringing to an end the condition of heroic equilibrium which they enjoyed before the curse began:

> I would not have had him die that way
> Or die at all, he should have been immortal.
> Our fifty battles had made us friends.

And there are fifty more to come.
New weapons, a new leader will be found
And everything begin again.

MIKE

Much bloodier.

CONGAL

They had, we had
Forgotten what we fought about,
So fought like gentlemen, but now
Knowing the truth must fight like beasts.

Congal acknowledges his Fall. The truth that they know is certainly not any mystical truth acquired through the consumption of the sacred eggs (which anyway no one will have had time to consume), but the 'truth' about war as hatred ending in death, not a gentlemanly contest between equally matched technicians; it is something which is not 'legal' and is 'bloody'. Congal guesses at why it has all happened:

Maybe the Great Herne's curse has done it.
Why not? Answer me that; why not?

This is Congal's first acknowledgement of the god's comminatory power over him, and it is followed by the entry of Attracta, still entranced and carrying the missing herne's egg that should have been on Congal's plate. Her presence and her continued possession by the god are the sign that what now happens is his will. The troopers realize the part she has played and wish to take their revenge, but in a manner consonant with their claim to be gentlemen. As James says,

All that have done what she did must die,
But, in a manner of speaking, pleasantly,
Because legally, certainly not
By beating with a table-leg.

When Mike reminds Congal that Attracta is dedicated to the god, James's argument is reinterpreted in an important speech by Congal. It sums up what he has learnt from the experience so far, acknowledging the god's handiwork and introducing the theme of the war against god for the first time:

> I had forgotten
> That all she does he makes her do,
> But he is god and out of reach;
> Nor stone can bruise, nor a sword pierce him,
> And yet through his betrothed, his bride,
> I have the power to make him suffer;
> His curse has given me the right,
> I am to play the fool and die
> At a fool's hands.

The difference between dying like a fool 'upon some battlefield' and *playing the fool* shows how far Congal's acknowledgements have carried him.

He constitutes himself a court, and decides that the seven men shall violate the priestess 'in the name of the law'. It is to be a 'pleasant' and 'legal' undertaking, an attempt to recapture the prelapsarian equilibrium, a refusal to accept the bloody and illegal irrationality which has crumbled away the old heaven. When his followers hesitate, he reproves them:

> Whoever disobeys the Court
> Is an unmannerly, disloyal lout,
> And no good citizen.

For 'A Court of Law is a blessed thing' and 'everything out of balance accursed':

> When the Court decides on a decree
> Men carry it out with dignity.

The restoration of psychological balance is also reasserted and earlier definitions of it maintained when Congal claims that the violation will do 'a great good' for Attracta:

> Melting out the virgin snow,
> And that snow image, the Great Herne;
> . . . when it melts
> She may, being free from all obsession,
> Live as every woman should.

At the end of the scene, Attracta's song, as she stands motionless in her trance, affirms as a contravention of all this the mystery and unreason of the divine marriage.

In this scene Congal's 'law' itself may be read as the consequence of his fall into disorder and hence as incompetent to restore the old equilibrium. Attracta's condition during it, furthermore, suggests that all he does is done at the god's behest, that he is already playing the fool, ironically unaware that law and reason and revenge against the god are simply the motives that the Great Herne uses to effect his own end, which is the consummation of the marriage.

But, as the play develops, the stress falls more on Congal's stubborn refusal, or inability, to judge his own acts as other than they seem to him, and on his continuing conviction, despite his terror, that he can of his own choice fight the god who (to another than Congal—the audience, for example) appears to determine everything the hero does, even his fighting. Thus Congal resembles one of those Renaissance perspective toys where the shape seen depends upon the angle of vision. He is one way a fool; but another way, because the understanding that the audience has of the rigidly god-determined world in which he lives is withheld from *him*, a hero asserting his freedom and selfhood against the thunder and the curse.

This works out in the two remaining Scenes. When Scene v begins Congal thinks that he has proved a point: Attracta has been done great good:

> No more a herne's bride, a crazed loony,
> Waiting to be trodden by a bird,
> But all woman, sensible woman.

Corroboration is to hand in the claim of the six other men; they have indeed lain with the priestess. Attracta affirms that 'My husband came to me in the night', and in response to her prayer the round heaven declares in thunder that the darling of the god is 'pure'. The terrified men, all except Congal, proceed to retract:

MATHIAS

I was a fool to believe myself
When everybody knows that I am a liar.

151

Attracta threatens them with punishment for what they have said (not for what they have done): after death they will all be changed into gross animal-shapes; the thunder is heard again, confirming the sentence. This drives even Congal to his knees, but not to retraction:

> I held you in my arms last night,
> We seven held you in our arms.

Unlike Mathias, Congal must believe himself. This is an aspect of his heroic selfhood. And what he says is true, for the mystery of the sacred bride-bed is that the men have acted as the surrogates of the god. Therefore Attracta is also right in her claim that she has suffered no violation. This mystery Congal cannot perceive. He fights an enemy whose absolute power he comes to acknowledge but whose mystery is hidden from him. But the fight is a real one to him and makes the sort of heroic sense which he understands—the untamed self striving against supernatural odds. As long as he remains a hero, he can see his relationship with god as a fight with him, though in the god's perspective it can be no such thing, but only a rigid sequence of offence and punishment. Congal heroically rationalizes this sequence as a series of bouts with the god, which he thinks he can win or lose. This is his way of saying in his own language how he lives; he is not to know that it somewhat imperfectly expresses his place in the macrocosmic rationale.

Throughout the play the offence has been the theft of the hernes' eggs. This has to work itself out through the fulfilment of the original curse ('And to end his fool breath / At a fool's hand meet his death') before the punishment for 'saying' that he has lain with the priestess is brought to bear. In the last Scene Congal is alone on the mountainside with Tom the Fool, a grotesque creature out of the kitchen, armed with a spit and the lid of a cauldron. This Fool, although he is sent by the god (he whistles 'The Great Herne's Feather'), is picturesquely incompetent, and Congal does not really expect to die at his hands. But now he sees the situation as the last of his three bouts with the god:

> He won the first, I won the second,
> Six men and I possessed his wife.
> . . . she said that nobody had touched her,

> And after that the thunder said the same,
> Yet I had won that bout, and now
> I know that I shall win the third.

The first bout was the fall into disorder and the death of Aedh, and the second the violation of Attracta. Thus Congal asserts to the end what is true to the self and the senses, unable to see the mystery of the rape that is a sacred marriage. He re-asserts also his claim to have made the god 'suffer', although he no longer talks rationally and psychologically, because now the god's terribleness is fully known to him—what began as disregard ends as defiance —and he has a nightmare vision of the Great Herne's implacability when he thinks of the endless, sinister carnival of Fools that will be sent up against him:

> And I, moon-crazed, moon-blind,
> Fighting and wounded, wounded and fighting.
> I never thought of such an end.

The war against the god is very different from the heroic battle-field.

This curse is not to be evaded unless the hero himself can disrupt its cruel logic. This is the way in which Congal is to win and lose his last bout:

> though I shall die
> I shall not die at a Fool's hand . . .
> If I should give myself a wound,
> Let life run away, I'd win the bout.

Then the thought strikes him:

> Fool! Am I myself a Fool?
> For if I am a Fool, he wins the bout.

His answer is, like 'I am Duchess of Malfi still', a final assertion of identity in the face of those who wish to destroy him by stealing his Name:

> I am King Congal of Connaught and of Tara,
> That wise, victorious, voluble, unlucky,
> Blasphemous, famous, infamous man.
> Fool, take this spit when red with blood,
> Show it to the people and get all the pennies;
> What does it matter what they think?
> The Great Herne knows that I have won.

This claim is of the same kind as the one made after the thunder spoke in Scene v and several times during this Scene:

> I held you in my arms last night,
> We seven held you in our arms.

It picks out of the whole truth that part of it which is the hero's truth. Congal is King Congal of Connaught and of Tara, and not a Fool. But just as the rape was a sacrament, so the hero is a fool, and has worked out his destiny according to the first stave of the curse:

> He that a herne's egg dare steal
> Shall be changed into a fool.

In the god's perspective everything from the death of Aedh to his own self-destruction has been Congal's fool's play. As Attracta says,

> You were under the curse, in all
> You did, in all you seemed to do.

But this is not the audience's perspective. They can discern what Conrad called 'the accent of heroic truth' [42] as well as the fool's play. Congal's last words are of the victorious bouts he knows and not of the logic of defeat which he is precluded from grasping:

> But I have beaten you, Great Herne,
> In spite of your kitchen spit—seven men—
> *(He dies.)*

The account I have given of the play so far has done no justice to the characterization of Attracta. She convinces us of the reality of her mystical life by her human dignity and warmth and the way in which these contrast, when she is in her trance, with the harsh and terrified abandon of her welcome to the god. Nor has another element in the play had much attention—that which is best represented by Corney, Attracta's servant, and his donkey, formerly a highwayman. The theme is developed at the end of the last Scene, after Congal's death. Because Corney's donkey has broken from where it was tethered further down the mountain and is coupling with another donkey, the hero's soul is destined to be reborn in that shape. The last words of the play are Corney's:

> All that trouble and nothing to show for it,
> Nothing but just another donkey.

154

This is more than a cynical footnote or afterthought, because the presence of Corney and his donkey throughout the play prepares for it. Congal's metamorphosis accords with the other indignities that cock a malicious eye at the Yeatsian Prufrock—the fight with the table-legs, the drawing of lots for Attracta, the god who is a heron and a thunder-bogy, death on a kitchen-spit. As a theme, too, metempsychosis is worked into the narrative at an earlier stage (in Corney's chatter about his donkey's past); Congal fears what the Great Herne 'May do with me when I am dead', and Attracta predicts this final punishment for his hubris (which he must share with the other campaigners who have insulted her) in Scene v. The episode may be objected to, not because it is incongruous or inconsequential, but for other reasons.

First, it turns the play in the direction of moral allegory, as any epiloguizing which insists too confidently on the protagonist's *final* place in the macrocosm will tend to do (consider the difference between *Doctor Faustus* and *Othello*). It upsets the delicate equilibrium between the god's perspective and the hero's perspective which has been the audience's angle of vision. The play begins to look like a parable about the superiority of the mystical to the heroic life: those who choose to be heroes rather than adepts will be re-born in lower forms; the mystic is released from the wheel of incarnations. With such matters Yeats was preoccupied at the time when he wrote *The Herne's Egg*. But, although in a game as in a drama one side or the other may legitimately be said to win, it seems much riskier to say that victory has proved the victor right. That is a theory which appertains to trials by combat, ideological wars, and the moral play.

Secondly, the part played by Attracta in the episode is obscure and contradictory. Congal, afraid of being put 'Into the shape of a brute beast', begs her to protect him against the Great Herne. Attracta believes that the god, whose knowledge she shares since her mystic marriage with him, has not yet determined Congal's fate, and therefore says to Corney:

> Come lie with me upon the ground,
> Come quickly into my arms, come quickly, come
> Before his body has had time to cool.

But Corney, frightened of the Herne, hesitates; his donkey breaks free, and it is too late:

CORNEY

King Congal must be born a donkey!

ATTRACTA

Because we were not quick enough.

In the light of her previous role as the god's agent, Attracta's action is inconsistent, and indeed inexplicable. For why should she attempt to frustrate his purposes? Yeats seems to have been betrayed into muddling his own design through the influence of his sources.* And the reason given for failure—'Because we were not quick enough'—suggests, with a cynicism which is jarringly ungenerous to both god and hero as they have been depicted in the play, that the Great Wheel, like other kinds of machinery, can be halted by the most trivial forms of accident.

If images are structural, what is being criticized here is structure itself. This is a measure of the seriousness with which *The Herne's Egg* needs to be taken, compared with the other plays discussed in this chapter. When *The Player Queen* was found in patches intolerably obscure this seemed to be because some parts of the plot, characterization, and symbolism had not achieved the right relation with the theme which other parts jibed with; they were bits that had fallen off or not been used, and so could not be considered part of the structure at all. They were bad because, like builder's débris, they spoiled the look of the place. In *Where There Is Nothing* there is very little that is solid at all—a mist of ideas imperfectly enclosed in a ragged envelope. But in *The Herne's Egg* all runs sweetly up to the pinnacle, which is firmly set

---

* As F. A. C. Wilson explains it (*W. B. Yeats and Tradition*, p. 108), Attracta has become since her divine union a Swedenborgian angelic spirit and in this condition tries to protect Congal. But why should an angel attempt to frustrate the god? Wilson also shows on pp. 102–4 that her presence at Congal's death also owes something to Ferguson's Lafinda in his *Congal*. Another reason for the episode may be that it allows Yeats to make a further technical discrimination between the divine marriage and human sexual union (see her speech 'I lay with the Great Herne' on p. 72). This theme, however fascinating (it is important in the Ribh poems in 'Supernatural Songs'), seems here an intrusion from the philosophical mythology.

and made of congruent material, but is wrong none the less—a wrong design for a structure which conforms to another mode of design; a moral-play epilogue to a drama of the Shakespearian kind. But its possession of this last quality, so far as it can be limited to a compassionate sense of human dignity amidst the travesties of it and the terrors, distinguishes *The Herne's Egg* from the other two plays, as it distinguishes *Purgatory*.

Chapter Eight

The Image in the Head

For wisdom is the property of the dead.

I

YEATS wrote the prose-dialogue of *The King of the Great Clock Tower* 'that I might be forced to make lyrics for its imaginary people'.[1] Ezra Pound declared that the play was 'putrid', but Yeats was unrepentant:

> From all that makes a wise old man
> That can be praised of all;
> O what am I that I should not seem
> For the song's sake a fool.[2]

He rewrote the play in verse, and then produced a second version of the same story, *A Full Moon in March*. *The King of the Great Clock Tower* was performed at the Abbey in July, 1934: '. . . send the enclosed cutting to Ezra that I may confound him. He may have been right to condemn it as poetry but he condemned it as drama. It has turned out the most popular of my dance-plays.'[3]

A common man, 'Stroller and Fool', appears before the King and Queen:

A year ago somebody told me that you had married the most beautiful woman in the world, and from that moment I have had her image in my head, and month by month, it has grown more and more beautiful. I have made poems about her and sung them everywhere, but I have never seen her.[4]

158

He swears, or prophesies, that the Queen will dance for him, that he will sing for her, and that, as a reward, she will give him a kiss. The King, furious at the insult, orders him to be beheaded. The head is brought, and the King insists that the Queen shall dance:

Dance! Dance! If you are nothing to him but an image, a body in his head, he is nothing to you but a head without a body.

The Queen dances, the head sings, and the Queen 'presses her lips to the lips of the head'. The King kneels to her, lowering his sword. In *A Full Moon in March* there are only two characters, apart from the Musicians—Queen and Swineherd. The Queen orders the Swineherd to be beheaded because he has heaped 'complexities of insult' upon her. But she drops her veil and dances, holding the severed head, which sings. In all the versions, the Musicians' songs enforce the themes of the sexual joys of eternity, the 'miraculeuse nuit nuptiale' of Villiers de l'Isle-Adam's *Axël*, and of Baile and Aillinn,[5] and meditate upon the communion between the emblematic Queen and the foulness of the common man:

> What can she lack whose emblem is the moon?
> But desecration and the lover's night.

These plays have proved amenable to explanation on several different levels. For T. R. Henn, the Queen primarily represents Woman, obsessed with the sexual act, and eternally seeking ravishment; the story tells of the ultimate victory of Man over perverse and vicious Woman and her 'virgin cruelty', and of 'the poet triumphant after death through his magical and enduring art'.[6] For Frank Kermode, the Stroller / Swineherd is the *poète maudit*, and the Queen's beauty, or the Queen herself, is the Image, out of time and deathless; the dance with the severed head is a complex symbol of 'the Dancer in the special role of the Image that costs the artist personal happiness, indeed life itself'.[7] F. A. C. Wilson, while making room for Henn's interpretation, concentrates chiefly on a theological and Platonic one: the Stroller symbolizes 'spirit in its fallen condition, but spirit which is . . . nevertheless in love with the idea of Heaven', symbolized by the Queen; Eternity, too, is, in Blake's phrase, 'in love with the productions of time', and therefore the dance with the severed head 'is in one sense symbolic of the union of spirit with the principle from which it emanates'.[8]

I have mentioned these interpretations here—without, however, attempting to do them any sort of justice—because they are not incompatible with each other; something resembling the old system of tropological and anagogical readings has a highly practical value here. All interpretations of these plays are likely to share a common characteristic. The mode of existence and of action belonging to the characters is to be seen as representing something which is not overtly expressed in it. The persons behave in a manner analogous to that of participants in a rite, and the Musicians' songs can be compared to the psalms, hymns, or other prescribed chants, which accompany and, in this case, explain the general significance of what is being done. When we ask about the celebrant of a rite 'Why is he doing that?', the answer we expect is not one in terms of the priest's or the victim's personal motives or life-history but in terms of what the ritual lays down. Enquiries about the ultimate meaning of the actions are always in the end enquiries about the meanings attached to the ritual or the fable as a whole. (It is not necessary here to go into the complicated question about ritual's precedence over fable, or vice-versa.) If the priest plucks out the victim's heart, or drains the cup before the altar, explanations in terms of his cruelty or thirst are plainly out of court. The characters in these three plays are entirely submissive to the roles which the fable prescribes for them. These roles are designed not on the pattern of ordinary human action, or even in accord with such networks of recognizably human motivation and interplaying impulses as are labelled heroic legend or Noh play, but as projections of the multiple meanings of the story, Woman's Cruelty and Man's Desire, Accursed Poet and Romantic Image, Eternity and its Emanations.

In their more brashly emblematical forms the characters in this kind of drama can become like those gods and godlings which are illustrated in the Renaissance handbooks of mythology, the work of a Cartari or Natale Conti: the man with serpents instead of fingers, the woman with three animal heads, the naked man headed like a bird of prey.[9] The severed head which sings, although—or because—it has many antecedents in tradition, has an affinity with these fabulous creatures. They are mere monsters if the imagination permits them to become disjoined from the meanings which their queer properties emblematize.

It is this feature which differentiates *The King of the Great Clock Tower* and *A Full Moon in March* quite sharply from most of the plays discussed in the previous chapters. Their relation to their tale is not the same as the relation of Cuchulain or Congal, Deirdre or Seanchan, Decima or Emer, to their stories.

Indeed, a possible fault of these dance-plays is that what remains of ordinary human motivation is sometimes found in rather grotesque combination with its absence, just as mechanically realistic drawings of human anatomy or classical drapery furnish forth, in Cartari's woodcuts, creatures with vulpine heads or reptilian tails. The King in *The King of the Great Clock Tower* behaves like a jealous husband. The echo of this homely theme means nothing in the fable, but only confuses it. Yeats found the character altogether unnecessary and eliminated it in *A Full Moon in March*. I have seen no interpretation of the plays which makes it clear why the Queen should be considered, or should consider herself, insulted by the Stroller / Swineherd's somewhat tepid commendations of her beauty when at last he beholds it. What he sees when he still wears the muddy vesture of mortality and looks through corporeal eyes is not, of course, so fine as the 'image in his head' with which he will unite after death in 'the condition of fire', the conflagration of bodiless intercourse when he is 'transfigured to pure substance'.[10] He says so, and speaks boldly of that sacred dance and mysterious kiss. All this is in fitting accord with his several symbolic roles. But the Queen's reaction is less attuned to hers. In *The King of the Great Clock Tower* it is the King who is outraged by the Stroller's insolence. This is better than *A Full Moon in March*, where the Queen herself says:

> All here have heard the man and all have judged.
> I led him, that I might not seem unjust,
> From point to point, established in all eyes
> That he came hither not to sing but to heap
> Complexities of insult on my head.[11]

This is all very human and queenly, and provides the occasion for the Swineherd's punishment. But this Queen needs no excuses for her cruelty or witnesses to her justice. It is the dramatist who has

needed the insult-motif as an excuse to keep his story unfolding;
he 'must have severed heads',[12] and he must somehow contrive
that the Queen shall behead the Swineherd in order to organize
his central symbol. A touch of human motivation is introduced
into the rite. This contrasts with total submission to it on the
Swineherd's part. When he is told that he must die he is impassive;
his death is not personal; he is neither glad nor sorry, nor fearful,
nor brave; he is the Victim, and his death occasions prophecy.
Long before it is off, his trunkless head has already become an
emblem to himself.

These inconsistencies are forgotten by those who respond to the
power of the Musicians' songs. They are amongst the most compelling of all Yeats's later poems. He has now, with perhaps a
touch of pettishness, ceased to worry about whether or not the
music will distort the words and prevent the audience hearing
them:

I say to the musician 'Lose my words in patterns of sound as the name
of God is lost in Arabian arabesques. They are a secret between the
singers, myself, yourself. The plain fable, the plain prose of the dialogue, Ninette de Valois' dance are there for the audience. They can
find my words in the book if they are curious, but we will not thrust
our secret upon them. . . .'* [13]

There is one song in the plays which ought not to have the
same character as the others, because it is a part, or fulfilment, of
the action in a way that they are not. This is the song of the severed
head itself. It was not until the final version that Yeats hit upon the
effective way of doing this. There are two other versions of the
head's song (in the two versions of *The King of the Great Clock
Tower*), but they fail to be dramatic because they are like the other

* I interpret this passage differently from Wilson (p. 54), for whom it
implies that the understanding of the songs is purposively reserved for initiates
into the philosophical mythology. I think that the 'secret' which is to be kept
from the audience is what the words *are*, not what they are about; the curious
can discover the former if they wish and there is nothing to suggest that they
may not then be read as poems; as such, they are less obscure than other late
poems such as 'The Statues' and 'The Gyres'. Their function in the plays is
psalmodic, accompanying the ritual, so in theory it does not matter if they are
not heard in the theatre. But Yeats's apparent willingness to accept this expe-
dient is connected with his prolonged inability to get words and music in
what he considered right relation: see above, p. 116.

songs in the play, and are, indeed, interchangeable with them. But in *A Full Moon in March*, the song ('I sing a song of Jack and Jill') has the right air of inexpressive mystery—inexpressive because inexpressible like the notes sung to 'Heav'n's new-born Heir' by Milton's Cherubim. It is the depersonalized voice of phantasmic folk-song and nursery-rhyme, utterly different from the richer and more human note of amazement and longing heard in the Musicians' songs. As far as the central symbol, the dance with the severed head, is concerned, it is precisely this remoteness and inexpressibility that count. The moment has nothing at all in common with the rather frantic attempts of Oscar Wilde (which gave Yeats the hint) or of Arthur Symons to actualize the Salome incident—'Je la mordrai avec mes dents comme on mord un fruit mur', and so on.[14] All human character and circumstance sink away. Otherwise silly, shocking, or monstrous, it is clinically pure, if also rather dull, when it is related with exactitude to the mystery to come, like the Renaissance *icones symbolicae* of Chronos's self-emasculation or Saturn's eating his children. It is also, of course, extremely pagan, as the long struggle of Christianity against the Hellenizing of the incidents of the incarnation into abstract or neo-Platonic mysteries sufficiently shows. Yeats was well aware of this. In choosing an image which is, if wrongly read, morbid and offensive he was issuing a challenge, a heresiarch's demand for allegiance.

II

I have summed up the difference between these plays and most of the others as a difference in the way the characters are related to the stories. This distinction seems to be of the first importance in a general view of Yeats's drama. In *The King of the Great Clock Tower* and *A Full Moon in March* the personages are primarily projections of the fable's meanings. Their deeds and their attributes are simply clues to the meanings they are acting out. They are simulacra of human forms; they even simulate the human process by which desire leads to activity. But they have no individuality and no names, except ritual ones, any more than have Jack in the Green, the yearly Tammuz, St. George, or the Betty. Everything they do can, and should, be done again exactly as before.

There are signs in plenty of this mummer's play genre in Yeats's other dramas. *The Cat and the Moon* is perhaps the most obvious. More remotely related to the type are *The Dreaming of the Bones* and *Calvary*, especially the latter. In *The Dreaming of the Bones* the three characters combine to show forth an ancient wrong and its nexus of cause and ever-iterated consequence. But there the fixity of the roles, which is brought out by the characters' sufferings and struggles to escape, and by the soldier's momentary impulse towards departing from his own unforgiving hatred, is itself part of the play; forced to act out a meaning, the persons try to break free of the perpetual repetition of the dreadful anniversary. In *Calvary*, the play of Christ's 'dreaming-back', each character has its self-determined role; they are all paradigms of the Subjective Man's intolerance of an equally paradigmatic saviour. In other places, in the final moments of *The Herne's Egg* and in some parts of *The Player Queen*, we have noticed a similar relationship between character and the absolutely demonstrative. *The Hour-Glass*, too, a 'morality',[15] is related to this kind.

With Yeats's other plays it is no such matter. The persons confront a world which may be utterly strange to them and to us, Spenser's world of 'Infernall Hags, Centaurs, feendes, Hippo-dames', a Mareotic sea of Baconian εἴδωλα or neo-Platonic *icones*. It solicits weirdly, and often comprehensively denies human will or desire; but the characters are not its instruments, or, if they become so, it is not without a struggle in which individual motivation of a recognizably human kind is paramount. Deirdre, Cuchulain, Emer, Congal are individualized at least in so far as they have to choose their roles and to make, if they can, their own stories. Usually they are defeated by the world of Fand, Bricriu, Aoife and the Herne, but the protagonists themselves are not supernatural, not gods but heroes. Although 'At stroke of midnight God shall win', until that hour they endure their 'bodily or mental furniture'.[16] That is why it seems possible to discuss Yeats's drama in ways which often disregard his frequently expressed wish to 'empty' his work of the naïvely human. It is not until 'Mankind can do no more' that the personages become still, unmoving figures like Emer and Cuchulain (in *At the Hawk's Well*) and submit to 'God' or destiny or to their transformation into ghosts, animals, or images. 'I have beaten you, Great Herne' may be a deluded cry, but it is not a disillusioned one, nor, indeed, is 'Cuchulain, son of Sualtim, comes!' The supreme example of this seems to be *Purgatory*, the protagonist's struggle in 'the network of the stars', heredity and the inexorable conditions of the supernatural world. Unless we are to regard the old man's last words as merely the rhetoric appropriate to a curtain-line—which it may well be proper to do—the struggle has in this instance even transformed the God who 'wins' into a God who can be prayed to. The contrast with the Swineherd and the Severed Head is huge.

Purgatory and *A Full Moon in March*, both written in the same decade, are extreme examples of the contrary trends. They compose the antithesis on which it is entirely fitting to let any study of Yeats rest as best it may. The Severed Head knows all, and man is stricken deaf and dumb and blind:

No living man can drink from the whole wine

The old man in *Purgatory*, like the old Adam, struggles blindly, and sight, when it is finally purged, puts an end to his day's war, but

A living man is blind and drinks his drop.

Notes

THESE Notes are normally confined to references to quotations or allusions in the text, where some longer Notes (indicated by *) will be found. The following abbreviations are used for the more frequently cited works, all of which are by Yeats except the last five:

C.K.	*The Countess Kathleen and Various Legends and Lyrics* (London, 1892).
C.P.	*Collected Poems* (London, 1934 edn.).
C. Plays	*Collected Plays* (London, 1934)
C.W.	*Collected Works* (Stratford-on-Avon, 1908), eight volumes.
D.P.	*Dramatis Personae 1896–1902—Estrangement—The Death of Synge—The Bounty of Sweden* (London, 1936).
F.P.D.	*Four Plays for Dancers* (London, 1921).
Letters	*The Letters of W. B. Yeats,* ed. Allan Wade (London, 1954).
L.P.P.	*Last Poems and Plays* (London, 1940).
P. & C.	*Plays and Controversies* (London, 1923).
P.P.V.	*Plays in Prose and Verse Written for an Irish Theatre and Generally with the Help of a Friend* (London, 1922).
W. & B.	*Wheels and Butterflies* (London, 1934).
Ellis-Fermor	Una Ellis-Fermor, *The Irish Dramatic Movement* (London, 1954 edn.).
Henn	T. R. Henn, *The Lonely Tower—Studies in the Poetry of W. B. Yeats* (London, 1950).
Parkinson	Thomas Parkinson, *W. B. Yeats Self-Critic—A Study of his Early Verse* (Berkeley & Los Angeles, 1951).
Wade	Allan Wade, *A Bibliography of the Writings of W. B. Yeats* (London, 1951; 2nd edn., 1957).
Wilson	F. A. C. Wilson, *W. B. Yeats and Tradition* (London, 1958).

CHAPTER ONE

[1] *Samhain*, October 1901, p. 12.

[2] *D.P.*, p. 33.

[3] Lady Gregory, *Our Irish Theatre* (New York, 1914), pp. 20–1.

[4] *Literary Ideals in Ireland* (London and Dublin), 1899, p. 87.

[5] Quoted by Wade, p. 260.

[6] W. G. Fay and C. Carswell, *The Fays of the Abbey Theatre* (London, 1935), pp. 112–13.

[7] *D.P.*, p. 35.

[8] *P. & C.*, pp. 186–7.

[9] *D.P.*, pp. 34–5.

[10] *C.K.*, pp. 7–8.

[11] *P. & C.*, p. vi.

[12] *L.P.P.*, p. 80.

[13] Henn, p. 24.

[14] J. M. Hone, *W. B. Yeats 1865–1939* (London, 1942), pp. 87–8.

[15] *Letters*, p. 125.

[16] Maud Gonne, *A Servant of the Queen* (Dublin, 1950 edn.), p. 169. This was in 1891, according to Maud Gonne.

[17] *Letters*, p. 108. The 'folklore book' is *Fairy and Folk Tales of the Irish Peasantry* (1888)

[18] *P. & C.*, p. 287; compare *Fairy and Folk Tales*, p. 233.

[19] H. S. Krans, *W. B. Yeats and the Irish Literary Revival* (New York, 1904), p. 142, Cf. E. A. Boyd, *Ireland's Literary Renaissance* (London, 1923 edn.), pp. 146–7: 'the supreme moment of Kathleen's sacrifice passes almost unnoticed'.

[20] They were suggested to Yeats by a French drawing: see *Pages from a Diary Written in 1930* (Dublin, 1944), p. 19.

[21] *Poems* (1912 edn.), p. vi.

[22] A. Symons, *Plays, Acting, and Music* (London, 1909 edn.), p. 167.

[23] This alternative version was first printed in *Poems* (1912 edn.), pp. 315–19.

[24] Robinson, 'The Man and the Dramatist' in *Scattering Branches*, ed. S. Gwynn (London, 1940), p. 87.

[25] 'The Lover Tells of the Rose in his Heart', *C.P.*, p. 62.

[26] *P. & C.*, p. 218.

[27] *C.K.*, p. 79.

CHAPTER TWO

[1] *Letters*, p. 674.

[2] *Poems* (1912 edn.), p. vi.

[3] *Letters*, p. 409.

[4] See D. M. Hoare, *The Works of Morris and of Yeats in Relation to Early Saga Literature* (Cambridge, 1937), p. 120.

[5] Preface to Vol. III of *Plays for an Irish Theatre*. This acknowledgement was not repeated in any later edition.

⁶ See J. H. Pollock, *William Butler Yeats* (London and Dublin, 1935), p. 46.
⁷ *Literary Ideals in Ireland* (London and Dublin, 1899), p. 19.
⁸ *Poems 1899–1905* (1906), p. 279.
⁹ Ellis-Fermor, p. 94.
¹⁰ 'Among School Children', *C.P.*, p. 243.
¹¹ *P.P.V.*, p. 243.
¹² *P.P.V.*, p. 110; *C. Plays*, p. 141.
¹³ *Poems 1899–1905* (1906), pp. xi–xii.
¹⁴ This and the following quotations up to the end of the chapter are from the earliest version as printed in the 'Abbey Theatre Series', Volume V (Dublin, 1905).
¹⁵ Shakespeare, *Richard II*, II. i. 8.

CHAPTER THREE

¹ Hoare, *The Works of Morris and of Yeats in Relation to Early Saga Literature* (Cambridge, 1937), pp. 130, 131.
² Henn, p. 83.
³ L. MacNeice, *The Poetery of W. B. Yeats* (London, 1941), p. 191.
⁴ Ellis-Fermor, p. 115.
⁵ See R. Peacock, *The Poet in the Theatre* (London, 1946), p. 107.
⁶ Robinson, 'The Man and the Dramatist' in *Scattering Branches*, ed. S. Gwynn (London, 1940), p. 96.
⁷ *Letters*, p. 475.
⁸ *Essays* (1924), p. 328.
⁹ *P. & C.*, p. 124.
¹⁰ Parkinson, pp. 85–90
¹¹ *P. & C.*, p. 151.
¹² *P. & C.*, pp. 99–100.
¹³ *P. & C.*, p. 103.
¹⁴ *P. & C.*, p. 105.
¹⁵ *P. & C.*, p. 93.
¹⁶ *P. & C.*, p. 91.
¹⁷ *D.P.*, p. 89.
¹⁸ *P. & C.*, p. 158.
¹⁹ *D.P.*, p. 137.
²⁰ *P. & C.*, p. 120.
²¹ *P. & C.*, p. 126.
²² *P. & C.*, p. 20.
²³ *P. & C.*, p. 134.
²⁴ *P. & C.*, p. 117.
²⁵ *P. & C.*, p. 161.
²⁶ *P. & C.*, p. 158.
²⁷ *Essays* (1924), p. 338.
²⁸ *The Green Helmet* (*C. Plays*, p. 243).
²⁹ Ellis-Fermor, p. 86.

[30] *Essays* (1924), p. 297.

[31] Preface to *Plays for an Irish Theatre* (Stratford-on-Avon, 1911), pp. ix–x. This Preface, first printed in 1910 (see Wade, p. 99), is another version of the essay in *The Cutting of an Agate* (first published, New York, 1912) on 'The Tragic Theatre'.

[32] *Essays* (1924), p. 295.

[33] Preface to *Plays for an Irish Theatre* (1911), p. ix.

[34] *New Irish Comedies*, pp. 158–9, quoted Ellis-Fermor, p. 66.

[35] *D.P.*, p. 89.

[36] *D.P.*, p. 89.

CHAPTER FOUR

[1] *P. & C.*, p. 148.

[2] *L.P.P.*, p. 111.

[3] *Cuchulain of Muirthemne* (London, 1903 edn.), pp. 313–19.

[4] Parkinson, p. 80.

[5] See *Letters*, pp. 444, 595, 914.

[6] See, for example, V. K. Narayana Menon, *The Development of W. B. Yeats* (Edinburgh and London, 1942), p. 83.

[7] *In the Seven Woods* (Dublin, Cuala Press, 1903), p. 36.

[8] Parkinson, p. 54.

[9] *Poems 1899–1905*, p. 112.

[10] *Ibid.*, pp. 96–7.

[11] *Ibid.*, p. 102.

[12] *P. & C.*, p. 46.

[13] B. Bjersby, *The Interpretation of the Cuchulain Legend in the Works of W. B. Yeats* (Upsala, 1950), p. 33.

[14] *The Golden Helmet* in *C. W.*, IV. 67, 78.

[15] *Letters*, p. 674.

[16] *C. W.*, IV. 78.

[17] *F.P.D.*, pp. 17–18. All my quotations from *At the Hawk's Well* are from this edition.

[18] Henn, p. 263.

[19] *F.P.D.*, p. 42; *L.P.P.*, p. 119.

[20] Bjersby, *op. cit.*, p. 40; Pearce in *E.L.H.*, XVIII (1951).

[21] *L.P.P.*, p. 112.

[22] Praz, *The Romantic Agony* (London, 1933), p. 31.

[23] *F.P.D.*, p. 22.

[24] *F.P.D.*, p. 46.

[25] *W. & B.*, p. 75.

[26] *C. Plays*, p. 289.

[27] *F.P.D.*, p. 105.

[28] W. Y. Tindall, *The Literary Symbol* (Bloomington, 1955), pp. 181–2.

[29] Bjersby, op. cit., pp. 154–60.

[30] *W. & B.*, p. 69.

[31] Lady Gregory, *Cuchulain of Muirthemne*, ed., cit., p. 344.

[32] *Letters*, pp. 917–18.
[33] See *F.P.D.*, p. 86.
[34] Wilson, p. 163.
[35] *L.P.P.*, pp. 113–14. All my quotations from *The Death of Cuchulain* are from this edition.
[36] Wilson, p. 170.
[37] *Cuchulain of Muirthemne*, ed. cit., p. 332.

CHAPTER FIVE

[1] *Letters*, p. 627.
[2] Above, pp. 76–77.
[3] *Visions and Beliefs* (New York and London), II, 318.
[4] *Essays* (1924), pp. 526–7.
[5] *A Vision* (1925), p. 222.
[6] *F.P.D.*, p. 129.
[7] *Visions and Beliefs*, II. 300.
[8] *Ibid.*, II. 318.
[9] *Ibid.*, II. 302.
[10] *Essays* (1924), p. 520.
[11] *A Vision* (1925), p. 221; compare the Severed Head's song, *A Full Moon in March* (London, 1935), pp. 38–9.
[12] *Essays* (1924), p. 520.
[13] *Ibid.*, p. 523.
[14] *A Vision* (1925), p. 227.
[15] *Essays* (1924), p. 287.
[16] The whole idea of the play, though with important variations, is sketched out in the story 'Hanrahan's Vision': see *C.W.*, V. 248–9.
[17] *F.P.D.*, p. 65. All my quotations from the play are from this text.
[18] *Letters*, p. 626, 653, 788.
[19] 'Fenollosa on the Noh' in *The Translations of Ezra Pound* (London, 1953), pp. 279–80.
[20] *Essays* (1924), p. 289; see also Miner, *op. cit.*, pp. 256–7.
[21] *Ibid.*, p. 287.
[22] *The Translations of Ezra Pound*, pp. 283–4.
[23] *Essays* (1924), p. 285.
[24] *F.P.D.*, p. 62.
[25] *F.P.D.*, p. 63.
[26] *Letters*, p. 626, 653.
[27] *A Vision* (1925), p. 225.
[28] *Ibid.* (1925), p. 227.
[29] Frank Kermode, *Romantic Image* (London, 1957), p. 78.
[30] See Virginia Moore, *The Unicorn* (New York, 1954), pp. 225–39.
[31] *W. & B.*, p. 31.
[32] *W. & B.*, pp. 47–8. All my quotations from *The Words upon the Window-pane* are from this text.

[33] A. N. Jeffares, *W. B. Yeats: Man and Poet* (London, 1949), pp. 263-4.

[34] R. Ellmann, *Yeats: the Man and the Masks* (London, 1949), p. 270.

[35] *W. & B.*, p. 7.

[36] *L.P.P.*, p. 106.

[37] In the passage quoted above, p. 98.

[38] I must here withdraw what I wrote about this topic in my *Towards a Mythology* (Liverpool and London, 1946), pp. 83-4.

[39] *W. & B.*, p. 32. For Yeats on 'dramatization' see also L. A. G. Strong, *Green Memory* (1961), pp. 249-51.

[40] *C. W.*, V. 59-61.

[41] *Autobiographies* (1926), p. 66; *W. & B.*, p. 37.

[42] See Hone, *W. B. Yeats, 1865-1939* (London, 1942), pp. 283-4.

[43] *L.P.P.*, p. 97. All my quotations from *Purgatory* are from this text.

[44] *L.P.P.*, p. 102.

[45] *Wilson*, p. 152.

CHAPTER SIX

[1] See especially Henn, pp. 194-5, 268-9; Ellmann, *The Identity of Yeats* (London, 1954), pp. 260-3; Wilson, pp. 58-68.

[2] 'A Dialogue of Self and Soul', *C.P.*, p. 266.

[3] *A Vision*, 1925, pp. 113-14.

[4] 'A Dialogue of Self and Soul', *C.P.*, p. 265.

[5] *A Vision*, 1925, p. 186. I have discussed the working of this idea in 'Demon and Beast' in *Irish Writing*, no. 31 (1955), pp. 42-50.

[6] See my 'Yeats and the Prophecy of Eunapius', *Notes and Queries*, New Series, I (1954), 358-9.

[7] Preface to *The Poetical Works* (New York, 1907), II. v.

[8] *W. B. Yeats and T. Sturge Moore*, ed. U. Bridge (London, 1953), p. 40.

[9] *F.P.D.*, p. 72. All my quotations from *Calvary* are from this text.

[10] *Essays* (1924), p. 278.

[11] Preface to *The Poetical Works* (New York, 1907), II. v.

[12] *F.P.D.*, p. 76.

[13] *A Vision* (1925), p. 187.

[14] *W. & B.*, p. 118; see below, p. 122.

[15] Hone, *W. B. Yeats, 1865-1939* (London, 1942), p. 417.

[16] *Letters*, p. 780.

[17] *P. & C.*, p. 99.

[18] *W. & B.*, p. 116. All my quotations from *The Resurrection* are from this text.

[19] Miner, *op. cit.*, p. 260.

[20] L. MacNeice, *Poetry of W. B. Yeats* (London, 1941), p. 196.

[21] *W. & B.*, p. 109.

[22] *W. & B.*, p. 110.

[23] *A Vision* (1937 edn.), p. 53.

[24] *Essays* (1924), p. 274.

CHAPTER SEVEN

[1] *W. & B.*, p. 101.

[2] *C.W.*, VII. 46.

[3] *Essays* (1924), p. 301.

[4] *C.W.*, V. 258.

[5] *C.W.*, VII. 145.

[6] *C.W.*, VII. 155.

[7] *C.W.*, VII. 260, V. 223.

[8] *C.W.*, VII. 117.

[9] *A Vision* (1937 edn.), p. 50.

[10] The best treatment of this side of Yeats's art is G. Melchiori, *The Whole Mystery of Art* (1960), pp. 35–98.

[11] *Where There Is Nothing: Being Volume One of Plays for an Irish Theatre* (London, 1903), pp. 46, 45. All my quotations are from this, the only, version.

[12] *Ibid.*, p. 65.

[13] *Ibid.*, p. 98.

[14] Ellis-Fermor, pp. 104–7.

[15] Yeats told the story of its origin and composition on several occasions: see *C.W.*, III. 220–1; *P.P.V.*, pp. 425–7; *D.P.*, pp. 70–3.

[16] *Letters*, p. 503.

[17] *C.W.*, III. 198–9.

[18] 'The Choice', *C.P.*, p. 278.

[19] *Autobiographies* (1926), p. 388.

[20] *P.P.V.*, pp. 428–9.

[21] *Essays* (1924), p. 493.

[22] *Essays* (1924), p. 496.

[23] The pioneer analysis of the play is that by W. Becker, 'The Mask Mocked: or, Farce and the Dialectic of the Self' (*Sewanee Review*, LXI [1953], 82–108). Becker seems to me to make the play sound better and clearer than it is. It will be obvious that I do not agree with his view that most of the plays by Yeats preceding it 'must be relegated to the dead past'.

[24] *C. Plays*, p. 404. All my quotations from *The Player Queen* are from this revised final edn.

[25] See p. 124 above, and *A Vision* (1937 edn.), p. 268.

[26] *C.P.*, p. 141.

[27] *Early Poems and Stories* (London, 1925), p. 522.

[28] *Autobiographies* (1926), p. 2.

[29] *Essays 1931–6* (Dublin, Cuala Press, 1937), p. 129.

[30] Wilson, p. 182.

[31] *Where There Is Nothing*, ed. cit., Act I.

[32] *The Whole Mystery of Art*, p. 67.

[33] *C. Plays*, p. 421.

[34] *Essays* (1924), p. 500.

[35] From an unpublished notebook, quoted by Jeffares, *W. B. Yeats Man and Poet*, p. 335.

[36] Wilson, p. 182.

37 Wilson, p. 183.

38 *Pagan Mysteries in the Renaissance* (London, 1958), p. 22.

39 N. Newton, 'Yeats as Dramatist: *The Player Queen*', *Essays in Criticism* VIII (1958).

40 *Letters*, pp. 843, 845.

41 *The Herne's Egg* (London, 1938), p. 10. All my quotations from the play are from this text.

42 For Conrad's comments on this phrase of Marcus Aurelius, see 'A Familiar Preface' to *A Personal Record* (London, 1946 edn.), p. xii.

CHAPTER EIGHT

1 *The King of the Great Clock Tower, Commentaries and Poems* (Dublin, Cuala Press, 1934), p. [iii].

2 *Ibid.*, p. [v].

3 *Letters*, p. 827.

4 *The King of the Great Clock Tower*, ed. cit., p. 3.

5 de l'Isle-Adam *Œuvres complètes* (Paris, 1923), IV. 263; see my 'Yeats's Supernatural Songs', *R.E.S.*, N.S., VII (1956).

6 Henn, p. 270.

7 *Romantic Image* (London, 1957), pp. 80–1, 73.

8 Wilson, pp. 71, 78.

9 See V. Cartari, *Le Imagini . . .* (Padua, n.d. [?1603]), pp. 105, 107, 400.

10 'Ribh at the Tomb . . .', *A Full Moon in March* (London, 1935), p. 61.

11 *Ibid.*, p. 12.

12 See *L.P.P.*, p. 112.

13 *The King of the Great Clock Tower*, ed. cit., p. 19.

14 Wilde, *Salomé* (London, 1927 edn.), p. 88; compare Symons, 'The Dance of the Daughters of Herodias', 'Salome' (*Collected Works* [London, 1924], II. 36, III. 239).

15 The play is thus subtitled in earlier editions (e.g. *C.W.*, IV. 3).

16 See 'Ribh Considers Christian Love Insufficient' and 'The Four Ages of Man', *A Full Moon in March*, ed. cit., pp. 66, 69.

Appendix: A Brief Chronology

For further information see G. B. Saul, *Prolegomena to the Study of Yeats's Plays*, Philadelphia, 1958.

* indicates plays in which Lady Gregory is known to have collaborated.

C.P. = published by the Cuala Press, Dublin.

Title of Play	Written	First Performed	First Printed
At the Hawk's Well	1915–	Lady Cunard's drawing-room, 1916	*Harper's Bazaar*, March, 1917.
Calvary	?1920		*Four Plays for Dancers* (London), 1921.
The Cat and the Moon	?1917	Abbey, 1926 (?); or 1931	*Criterion, Dial*, July, 1924.
* *Cathleen Ni Houlihan*	1901	St. Teresa's Hall, Dublin, 1902	*Samhain*, 1902.
The Countess Cathleen	1889–	Antient Concert Rooms, Dublin, 1899	*Countess Kathleen and Various Legends and Lyrics*, 1892.
The Death of Cuchulain	1938	Abbey, 1949	*Last Poems and Two Plays* (C.P.), 1939.
*Deirdre	1905–	Abbey, 1906	*Deirdre* (London and Dublin), 1907.
The Dreaming of the Bones	1917	Abbey, 1931	*Two Plays for Dancers* (C.P.), *Little Review*, January, 1919.

Appendix: A Brief Chronology

Title of Play	Written	First Performed	First Printed
Fighting the Waves	1927	Abbey, 1929	*Wheels and Butterflies* (London), 1934.
A Full Moon in March	1934		*Poetry* (Chicago), 1935.
The Golden Helmet	1907	Abbey, 1908	*The Golden Helmet* (New York), 1908; *Collected Works* (Stratford), 1908.
The Green Helmet	1909	Abbey, 1910	*The Green Helmet and Other Poems* (C.P.), 1910.
The Herne's Egg	1935–		*The Herne's Egg* (London), 1938.
*The Hour-glass [prose version]	1902–	Molesworth Hall, Dublin, 1903	*North American Review*, September, 1903.
The Hour-glass [poetic version]	1903–	Abbey, 1912	*The Mask* (Florence), April, 1913.
The King of the Great Clock Tower [prose version]	1933	Abbey, 1934	*The King of the Great Clock Tower Commentaries and Poems* (C.P.), 1934, *Life and Letters*, November, 1934.
The King of the Great Clock Tower [poetic version]	1934		*A Full Moon in March* (London), 1935.
*King Oedipus	1905–	Abbey, 1926	*Sophocles' King Oedipus* (London), 1928.
**The King's Threshold*	1903	Molesworth Hall, Dublin, 1903	*The King's Threshold* (New York), 1904, *The King's Threshold and On Baile's Strand* (London and Dublin), 1904.

175

Title of Play	Written	First Performed	First Printed
The Land of Heart's Desire	1894	Avenue Theatre, London, 1894	*The Land of Heart's Desire* (London), also Chicago, 1894.
Oedipus at Colonus	1926–	Abbey, 1927	*Collected Plays* (London), 1934.
On Baile's Strand	1901–	Abbey, 1904	*In the Seven Woods* (Dun Emer Press, Dundrum), 1903.
The Only Jealousy of Emer	1916	publicly staged in Amsterdam in 1922 by Albert van Dalsum	*Poetry* (Chicago), January, 1919.
The Player Queen	1908–	King's Hall, London (Stage Society), 1919	*The Dial*, November, 1922
The Pot of Broth	1902	Antient Concert Rooms, Dublin, 1902	*Plays in Prose and Verse* (London), 1922.
Purgatory	1938	Abbey, 1938	*Last Poems and Two Plays* (C.P.), 1939.
The Resurrection	1925–	Abbey, 1934	*Adelphi* (London), June, 1927.
The Shadowy Waters	ca. 1885–	Molesworth Hall, Dublin, 1904	*North American Review*, May, 1900.
The Shadowy Waters [acting version]	1906	Abbey, 1906	*The Shadowy Waters* (London), 1907.
The Unicorn from the Stars	1907	Abbey, 1907	*The Unicorn from the Stars and Other Plays* (New York), 1908.

Title of Play	Written	First Performed	First Pinted
* *Where There Is Nothing*	1902	Royal Court Theatre, London (Stage Society), 1904	*United Irishman*, 1902.
The Words upon the Window-pane	1930	Abbey, 1930	*The Words upon the Window Pane* (C.P.), 1934.

Index

LITERARY
PUBLICITY
The Final Chapter

Joseph Marich Jr.

DELMAR

TM

THOMSON LEARNING

Australia Canada Mexico Singapore Spain United Kingdom United States

DELMAR

™

THOMSON LEARNING

Literary Publicity: The Final Chapter
by Joseph Marich Jr.

Business Unit Director:
Susan L. Simpfenderfer

Executive Production Manager:
Wendy A. Troeger

Executive Marketing Manager:
Donna J. Lewis

Executive Editor:
Marlene McHugh Pratt

Production Manager:
Carolyn Miller

Channel Manager:
Wendy E. Mapstone

Acquisitions Editor:
Zina M. Lawrence

Production Coordinator:
Matthew J. Williams

Cover Design:
Dutton and Sherman Design

Editorial Assistant:
Elizabeth Gallagher

For permission to use material from this text or
product, contact us by
Tel   (800) 730-2214
Fax   (800) 730-2215
www.thomsonrights.com

Library of Congress
Cataloging-in-Publication Data

Marich, Joseph.
   Literary Publicity: The Final Chapter / by Joseph
Marich, Jr.
      p. cm.
   ISBN 0-7668-3113-2
   1. Authorship — Marketing. 2. Books —
Marketing. I. Title.

PN3355 .M29 2001
070.5'2 — dc21   2001023114

Dedication

This book is dedicated to all authors, new or used, young or old, good or bad. If this book actually gets published, I look forward to joining your ranks. This was very hard to do and you all served as my inspiration.

CONTENTS

PREFACE

I thought I would take a minute to explain the purpose of this book and my objectives in writing it.

The purpose of this book is to help authors create and execute their own publicity plans for their books. Period.

I wanted to create a book that would help the author decide whether she has the time and money to do this on her own, or if she should let someone else do it for her. I wanted to teach an author how to design an appropriate publicity plan; educate her on the various media outlets; show her how to create her own special press kit, figure out a budget that makes sense, and write an effective press release; guide her on making pitch calls; and cheer her on as she goes through this process. I think it is important for authors to know that they can do many of the things a professional publicist can do— and that it's well worth their time and effort. I thought it would be helpful for authors to know all this *before* they decide to dive in and do it themselves.

This is *not* a book about marketing, advertising, or book sales. That's not what I do. I wouldn't presume to know what those professionals know or attempt to teach someone those skills.

After reading this book, some of you may think I haven't spent enough time talking about what the first-time author can do to publicize his book. All the information contained in this book should be of equal interest to first-time authors and to more established authors. I am aware that many of you who read this book may think there is a huge difference between getting publicity for a more established author and a first-time author. I'll let you in on a little secret: It's not that big a gap. A good story is a good story. If it's worthy of media coverage, the media will probably cover it. Established authors may have a slight edge in getting in the media door, but with a solid plan, some basic skills, and a major dose of courage, first-time authors can get book reviews and feature stories just as easily as more established authors. After all, there are only a handful of mega-powerful, A-list authors and a lot of blank pages that have to be filled in newspapers and magazines and a lot of air time to be filled on television and radio. The percentages are in your favor.

It is true that A-list authors are of more interest to the media, but that doesn't mean that a first-time author can't work a little harder and get the media coverage he needs or wants. An A-list author may get on *Oprah*, but getting a huge article written about your book in your local paper can be just as effective—and it's a darn good place to start. Remember that the big-shot authors all started with articles in *their* local papers. You're no different from them; they've just had more time to move up the media food chain. Your patience and tenacity will pay off in the long run.

The publicity tactics are really no different for any book or any level of writer. There are things first-time authors will do that well-established authors won't do, but they are few and far between. The major difference concerns local media. Established authors do not have the time or the need to speak with a lot of local media; they go right to national media. However, the *principles* for written press materials (like press releases and so on), contacting the media, and follow-up work are exactly the same whether you're speaking at your local university or appearing on a national network program. *Exactly the same.* A first-time author can do *the same things* an established author can do, just on a smaller scale. The realistic expectations of a first-time author will be significantly different, but the tasks to be accomplished are the same.

Expectations are relative. A publishing house handling an A-list author may expect five major articles to run for that author's new book. If they only get two, they're upset. If a first-time author got those two major articles, she'd be thrilled. Who is more right doesn't really matter.

My objectives for this book are simple. I wanted to create a concise, easy-to-follow, basic, practical guide to literary publicity. I also wanted it to be fun to read. In four years of undergrad and two years of grad school, I have never read a textbook that didn't bore me to death. Informative shouldn't mean dull. Have you ever really reread one of your old textbooks? You may keep them "just in case," but have you ever really used them after final exams? (I mean other than as a spare leg for a wobbly end table.)

This book is meant to be an adjunct resource rather than a primary one. It is not meant to supersede standard textbooks. That's best left to the "publish-or-perish" crowd. I'm writing this as a professional who actually does this every day, not as an education professional. I hope any faculty members who read this will forgive my imperfections in grammar and writing style.

Some of you may not appreciate the humor I've tried to inject into this book. To you, I send my sincere apologies. I hope you can overlook this short-coming and use the information to your benefit and ignore my attempts at humor.

My greatest wish is that this book will never be sold as a used book. This is for philosophical as well as financial reasons. I want this book to stay with you and be dog-eared and coffee stained—and *used*. I want it on top of your desk and in your book bag for many years to come.

Or at least until I write a revised edition.

ACKNOWLEDGMENTS

I have the smartest, funniest, and wackiest group of friends and associates you could possibly imagine and all of them helped in the writing of this book. They helped by reading the manuscript and giving me very helpful notes, or by buying me many, many drinks. Both helped a lot!

I sincerely and gratefully acknowledge the following:

Robert Prete, for talking me off the ledge every single day. Fortunately, you readers have no idea how crazy I really am. Robert keeps me from having to take a lot of medication. Thank you.

Laurie Reis, my friend and my own personal computer help desk. She's very funny, extremely smart, and she laughs at my jokes. You couldn't have a better friend.

Linda Carlson, the best damned publicist on the planet. It's a good thing she doesn't do literary publicity. Her guidance was a blessing.

Mark and Judy. Thanks for your support and all your wonderful ideas. These two really know how to make great Cosmopolitans!

To my family, who get excited for me even when they don't know what the hell I'm talking about and compassionate when I'm not so excited. I also thank them for letting me drop off the radar screen while writing this book. Dan, your notes were great!

A special thank-you to my sister, Nancy, who always goes above and beyond to help me out, no matter how big or small the problem. Thank you also to Michael. Emily, you're my favorite!

Finally, thanks to all of the wonderful people at Delmar. Your kindness and understanding toward this first-time author has not gone unnoticed. I hope all your other authors know what they're doing, unlike you-know-who. I hope I did okay.

The author and Delmar wish to express their sincere appreciation for the following reviewers:

John Flynn, Ph.D.
Towson University
Towson, MD

Julia Gammon
University of Akron Press
Akron, OH

Gerry LaFemina
Kirtland Community College
Roscommon, MI

ABOUT THE AUTHOR

Photo courtesy of Lisa Ann Pedriana

Joseph Marich Jr. is founder and president of Marich Communications, Inc. With an emphasis in literary, entertainment, and consumer publicity, Marich has worked in public relations for more than 10 years, planning and executing national and international campaigns for more than 30 book launches; special events, fundraisers, and openings in the theater, art, fashion, television, and film industries. He has worked with major publishing houses such as Knopf, Warner Books, Simon & Schuster, Henry Holt, Ballantine, HarperCollins, and Delacorte Press.

Representing author-director-producer, Michael Crichton *(Disclosure, Jurassic Park)*, Marich coordinates media tours (domestically and internationally), personal appearances, interviews, and press kit production for Dr. Crichton, working closely with his publishers in New York, as well as his international publishers throughout Europe. He continues his public relations duties for his top-rated television series, "ER," with Warner Television and for Crichton's latest business endeavor, Timeline Computer Entertainment, which develop CD-ROM and Internet games.

Marich has also been involved in public affairs and crisis management for all the Warner Music Group labels and has provided counsel to Virgin Records, United Talent Agency, and Oracle Corporation, bringing special skills to the clients by preparing them in media training, special-projects presentations, and developing and producing electronic media kits for satellite feeds.

Before starting his own company, Marich worked as a special events producer for The Donahue Group in Beverly Hills, as director of the Literary Division at Rachel McCallister & Associates Public Relations, and for Edelman Public Relations Worldwide in their entertainment division. At McCallister, Marich worked with such distinguished clients as Rock the Vote, DC/Marvel Comics, New Line Television, and Alliance Communications. Virgin Records, Oracle Corporation, and United Talent Agency were among his clients at Edelman Public Relations.

This is Marich's first (and probably last) foray into professional writing.

INTRODUCTION

So you want to be a best-selling, big-shot author? You want fame, fortune, and everything that goes with it, do you? Only foreign sports cars go from zero to sixty in three seconds. There are many steps to take between writing a book and appearing on *Oprah*. Most first-time authors think that just because they wrote a good book, they will sell millions of copies and live happily ever after. Unfortunately, this is just not true.

Many factors come into play in making a book successful. The story has to be interesting and well-written, sure, but these days, with the thousands of books flooding the marketplace, the media and the consumer have to know that your book even exists and where they can buy it. Even in the television industry—the most cutthroat industry I can think of—there are a finite number of channels and a finite number of hours in the programming day. In publishing, the number of books that can be created is potentially infinite. The competition is fierce.

The number of variables an author must consider when writing a book is enormous. Which story should I tell? Who will be interested in this story? Am I capable of writing this story? Do I have the time to write this story and meet my deadlines? How do I get an agent? Which agent will best represent me? How can I tell if I'm getting a fair deal? Which publishing house is the best one for my book? Will they really be behind me once I turn in my final draft? What will they do to promote my book? How do I get stories in the newspaper or appear on a talk show to promote my book? Who will distribute my book? Will the distributors really back my book, or will they bury it in the back of the store? And on and on.

It can make an author's head explode just thinking about it.

I can't help you write a good book, get an agent, tell you which publishing house to go with, explain contract law to you, or help you with distribution and sales. There are other people who are more qualified than I to help you solve those problems and answer those questions. I poke my head in the door at the very beginning of the writing process and then disappear until your book is ready to be sold to the consumer. You're on your own in between.

Every time I am asked to speak at writer's conferences, the first sentences out of my mouth are always, "You need to think about *publicity* before you even begin working on your outline. If you don't, you might waste a year of your life writing a book that no one will know exists." No matter who is ultimately going to do the publicity for your book, your publicist needs certain things to help you make your book a success. We cannot make diamonds from coal.

As a publicist, here's what I need: A well-written book; written by an interesting, well-spoken author who doesn't second-guess me every step of the way; about an interesting subject that appeals to a great number of people; national distribution in brick-and-mortar stores; four to six months to work; and a lot of cash. That's the reality.

It is difficult for me to understand why many authors do not realize that publishing is a billion-dollar industry. It is a *business;* it is about the bottom line. I believe that if Austen, Byron, Dickens, Joyce, Fitzgerald, Hemingway, or Faulkner wanted to publish today, they'd have one heck of a time trying to get a book deal. You only have to look at the most recent best-seller lists to see what is being published these days and what consumers are actually buying to see the basis of this opinion. This is a business, your book is a product, and publicists have to scratch and claw their way to the consumer via the disinterested media.

If your book does not have a strong media angle, the chances for publicity are dramatically reduced—nearly to zero. You need to have realistic goals, a good story, and a dynamic publicity plan if you want to succeed.

Publicity is what I know and publicity is what I discuss in this book.

This book is a basic guide for planning and executing a grassroots publicity plan, specifically for authors who are just getting started and want to begin work on their own publicity. It can also be helpful for those of you who *can* afford to hire a publicist, but don't know what they should be doing for you. This book does not include every single thing I have ever learned about publicity and the media. It does include practical information so you can start doing something *right now.* I have included general principles of publicity, a little background information on the different types of media, a checklist or two, and some writing guidelines. If you grasp the underlying concepts and follow these steps, you should be able to create a press kit, write a press release, figure out who to contact and know what to say when you make follow-up calls to the media (i.e., television programs, radio programs, newspapers, magazines, and Internet Web sites).

I have tried to keep it simple, concise, and logical. I hope I have succeeded.

I'll give you a short version of who I am and why I wrote this book. You can learn a bit more about me by reading my one-page biography in the third part of this book. (That item also serves as an example for writing your own biography.) I've worked at two well-known public relations agencies, where I was responsible for executing the publicity campaigns for several major corporate accounts and some not-so-corporate accounts. I discovered that although I was good at it, I'm not really wired for "corporate" things, be they client or employer. I explained to one of my employers that the vest on a three-piece suit cuts off the circulation to my creativity. I was informed that my jeans cut off their ability to sign a paycheck. I wore a suit. For a while. (I still wear them, of course, but only when absolutely necessary.)

It was at one of the bigger agencies that I was given the daunting task of handling public relations for best-selling author Michael Crichton. That was right before a little book and film, called *Jurassic Park*, hit. I was scared to death, and a bit intimidated to be working with someone of Michael Crichton's caliber, but was relieved to find Dr. Crichton to be one of the most intelligent and humorous people with whom I have ever had the pleasure to work. He was the antithesis of my corporate clients.

Once I got the hang of doing this literary publicity thing, I began to take on more and more authors. I found that I genuinely like them. I like how they think, how they speak, and how passionate they are about their projects. I am also very good at helping them get media coverage. Some people are good at reattaching severed limbs. I'm good at getting media coverage. Everyone is special in their own little way.

After working for other people for a few years, I decided to open my own company. As of this writing, I have launched some 25 or 30 books, most by first-time authors. I have also acted in the capacity of "literary consultant" for more than 50 authors and their projects—story structure, agents, publishing houses, and so on. It's been a very busy few years.

I decided to write this book for two reasons. First, it is very expensive to hire a professional publicist—maybe too expensive for most first-time authors. It costs a lot to do a lot. The good news is that most professional publicists get results. The *less* good news: If you decide to hire a professional publicist later on, you should expect to pay a monthly retainer fee of $2,500 to $5,000, plus expenses... and prices are only going up! Most agencies also require a four- to six-month minimum. If the publicist is charging any less than $2,500, check his references thoroughly. As the saying goes, if it's too good to be true...

Generally speaking, consultation fees should range from $100 to $250 per hour. Some PR consultants will charge you for reading time and some will charge a one-hour minimum.

It is expensive for many reasons.

In case you're interested, my PR firm is on the higher end of both the monthly retainer and the consultation fee payment schedules. This is primarily because I work with a maximum of six clients at a time, and that means less opportunities to make a living. It's a practical matter. Burnout runs rampant in my industry. There is no way one publicist can juggle 14 clients without burning out. Burnout also increases staff turnover and increases training costs. Many agency publicists with whom I worked have left the agency business and taken jobs in politics, where they said it was *less stressful!* Me, I ended up smoking too much, drinking too much coffee, and forgetting how to laugh. Now that I own my own company, I still smoke, though not as much; still drink coffee, but now it's decaf; and laugh a lot more. My first piece of advice: Keep your sense of humor throughout this whole writing/publicity process. Remember that we're not saving the whales.

I also wrote this because I get calls from hundreds of people a month asking for advice about what they might do until they are able to afford a professional publicist. I thought it might be helpful to have a book that authors could keep at their desks, just as they would a dictionary, to refer to whenever the need arose.

Again, I ask that you please keep in mind that this is not everything there is to know about literary publicity. This is just to get you started. If you want to learn more about this industry, you might want to take a class at your local college (seriously!) or volunteer at a PR agency in your home town.

What this book is *not* is a book on marketing a book. I discuss some of the differences between marketing, advertising, and publicity in a few pages. If I knew more about marketing, I would write about it, but I don't, so I can't. There are many good books on the shelves that can help an author effectively market a book. I do not get involved with printing, distribution, special sales, subsidiary rights, or selling books out of the back of a car. What I do is get the word out to the media and consumer that a new book is ripe for the reading.

Also, for every rule there are a thousand exceptions. The exceptions, however, are based on the subtleties associated with human behavior, the changing landscape of print and electronic media, the fickleness of the American public, and the news events of the day. Learning about the exceptions takes time and experience.

I believe that if you follow the steps outlined in this book, you should be able to create a successful publicity campaign.

PART

1

※

BASIC
CONCEPTS OF
LITERARY
PUBLICITY

※

CHAPTER 1

ADVERTISING, MARKETING, AND PUBLICITY

T he first step in this process is to get a basic understanding about what publicity is—and, more importantly, what it is not. After all, you can't do something if you don't know what it is, right? There are three basic methods of getting the word out to consumers about your book. They are advertising, marketing, and publicity. These are *not* the same, and this book is about only one of them. Now is a good time to discuss, very briefly, the differences between advertising, marketing, and publicity. I'm going to grossly oversimplify, so don't send me letters!

ADVERTISING

You pay for advertising. You pay *a lot* for advertising. Some national magazines charge more than $40,000 for a full-page four-color ad. A four-color advertisement, or "ad," is the type of all-color advertisement that you typically see in any magazine. Many smaller newspapers, magazines, and newsletters charge significantly less, especially for a black-and-white ad, but you are spending money nonetheless. There are two good reasons for buying advertising in the less expensive publications. (1) It's relatively inexpensive; some newsletters and smaller publications only charge $50 for a full-page advertisement. (2) Most newsletters and smaller publications have a specific target demographic; they may have a smaller circulation than a major magazine, but you know its readers will be interested in your subject. Not a bad deal for less than $100.

Demographic information refers to a set of characteristics that describe who is reading a newspaper or magazine, listening to a radio program, or watching a television program. It includes basic information like age, sex, race, location, and salary range. A teen magazine may have a demographic of Hispanic girls between 13 and 17 years of age, primarily from urban areas. A television program on a major network television station may have a national demographic of white middle-class women between the ages of 45-55 and white middle-class men between the ages of 55-65 who earn between $45,000 and 55,000 per year. This information is critical for advertisers. If you were a denture cream company, you probably would not want to waste your money on advertising in a teen publication; if you were a skateboard company, you probably wouldn't want to run your commercial on that television program: very few 55-year-old women buy skateboards and very few 14-year-old girls wear dentures (we hope!).

The advantage of advertising is that you have *absolute* control over the message. You decide what, how, when, and where you want to say whatever it is you want to say, and they have to print it *exactly* as you request it. That is a huge advantage.

The disadvantage is that you have to pay for that control.

The most brilliant and effective print advertising campaign I've ever seen was created for the Broadway musical "Phantom of the Opera." One Sunday, while I was still living in Chicago, I was having a cup of coffee and reading the *Chicago Tribune,* when I came across this little tiny one-inch square black box with a picture of a funny-looking mask (now, of course, you'd have to have been in a coma for the last 10 years not to recognize "the mask"). I spent a couple of minutes trying to figure out what that mask meant. There was no accompanying text with the ad, just the mask. Having no luck, I moved on to something else.

Over the course of a couple of months, I kept seeing that darn mask. It started to drive me crazy. I kept asking all my friends if they knew what that mask was. Most of them had never given it another thought until I asked about it, and none of them knew any more than I did.

After a couple of months, the advertisers began adding text. I think it said something like, "Coming Soon," above the mask. Not much of a clue, but something. Over time, they dribbled more text and information into the ads. I was fascinated by all of this. It really caught my attention. I followed that ad for *months* until they finally announced that "Phantom" was coming to New York, and would have a touring company coming to Chicago in six months.

That ad campaign was a stroke of genius, for several reasons. It was clever. It created intrigue and mystery. It used the advertising budget wisely. Little one-column square ads are relatively inexpensive. As the time drew nearer for ticket sales, the larger the ad became.

Brilliant. I've remembered that ad for many years. I ended up seeing that show six times. Coincidence? I think not.

MARKETING

Marketing is the plan of action taken to get the physical books into people's hands. Marketing, just like its name says, is concerned with getting the book "to market." This includes distributing the book through the usual channels, like major chain bookstores and independent booksellers; and/or specialty markets like college libraries, medical associations, Internet sales, direct mail, infomercials, book club special sales, and the like. Marketing answers the question, "How and where are people going to buy this book?"

The explosion of alternative distribution channels for books over the last 5 or 10 years is astounding. It used to be that if you wanted a book, you went to a real bookstore and bought one. Period. Now you can order a book that's been out of print for 10 years with the click of a mouse, or download one in a few minutes. You can join a book-of-the-month club or even *listen* to a book while you're stuck in traffic. (The irony is that as reading levels continue to decline, book sales continue to rise. I don't know if authors are writing to match their reader's reading skills, or if the same people are just buying more books. I hope neither is true. Maybe the cup really is half-full, what do I know?) All of this means that publishers have to spend more time and money on marketing to all these different places.

Marketing has become more critical as the number of distribution avenues increases. Getting into or reaching new stores and new consumers (market penetration) has become a number-one priority for publishers. For example, they may try to get a bridal store to carry a book about preparing for a wedding. The bridal stores are typically concerned with wedding dresses, but now they may carry a line of books as well. That is an example of penetrating a new market for a publisher. Market penetration on the Internet is the latest distribution avenue to challenge the publishing industry. The publishers have to constantly adapt to the changing marketplace. If they can, they'll stay in business. If they can't, they'll be dead in the water.

I'm not sure I like this, because I think the effects are ultimately bad for authors. When publishers have to spend more money on marketing their existing lists, they have less to spend on developing new authors. I think I'd rather see fewer books, but better written books.

The first time I went into the offices of a major publishing house in Manhattan, I had to wait in the main lobby for a meeting to begin. I started looking at the thousands of books displayed on their bookshelves. I was shocked to see so many unfamiliar titles. I thought I was really up-to-speed on the publishing industry, but boy, was I wrong. After the meeting I asked someone who worked there about all those unfamiliar books and was told that the editor-in-chief "strongly believes that some books just have to be published, whether they'll sell a lot or not." This editor wants to leave future generations as many well-written books as possible. What a *mensch!* I'm not telling you who this was or exactly where this took place because I'd rather not be responsible for flooding this publishing house with a million manuscripts.

I tell you this story because if that publisher didn't have to spend so much money on marketing its A-list authors, it could spend some on marketing the "literary" books and we'd all be a bit smarter. Myself included. (I am a pulp fiction addict. Please keep that our little secret.) The flip side is that it's the income from those same A-list authors that pays for the advances for the more literary books. It really is a literary Catch-22.

The single greatest advance in marketing over the last decade is the infomercial, used extensively by Ron Popiel. I go as far back with Ron as his "Pocket Fisherman." Remember that? It made you just want to tie some flies, climb into those waders, and hit the open lake. My best friend, Bobby, got one for his birthday that year. I was so jealous. Even though we were living in a land-locked suburb of Chicago at the time, I still wanted one. Ron made fishing cool! (I saw Bobby at our 20th high school reunion and he's been hit with a severe case of male pattern baldness, whereas I still have a full head of hair...everything balances out in the end.)

Marketing using the infomercial has done for fishing, big thighs, and thinning hair what the Internet has done for books. It has created a completely new marketplace in which to purchase products.

PUBLICITY

Publicity is the means of generating interest and excitement about a product or service; in our case, an author and his book. The goal is to get as many people as possible to know as much as possible about your book so they will go buy it. Publicity attempts to cause a surge in book sales by increasing awareness and excitement about a new book. *How* you do this is discussed later.

The most common form of publicity with which you might be familiar is the celebrity public appearance, particularly when a new movie is about to be released. It's when you see the lead actor appearing on all the morning talk shows, *Oprah, Entertainment Tonight, David Letterman,* and the front section of your local newspaper. All of this is planned months in advance by the studios, and the appearances are often part of the actors' contract. They are contractually obligated to make public appearances to publicize the film.

This all begins with the "press junket." A press junket brings all the media to one place (usually a hotel) so they can efficiently interview all the important players from the film without traveling all over the country to get individual interviews. It is exhausting for the media and even more so for the talent. As a publicist, I'd rather donate a kidney than attend a junket, but that's part of my gig.

The celebrities may speak with more than 500 journalists over a two or three-day period! For the talent, the most irritating part of the whole thing is having to answer the exact same question 500 times. It sounds glamourous, but I am really glad I'm not the one being interviewed. I'm not that patient. There have been times when I've just wanted to scream, "Can't you think of one original question??!!" Fortunately, most journalists are very professional and friendly; some are not, that's out of your hands. You will find out for yourself when you start hitting the media circuit.

The reason for all these interviews is to generate interest in the latest movie so you will go and see it. A press junket is extremely effective, especially as most people are predisposed to see films starring their favorite actors. Most people who see Julia Roberts on *Entertainment Tonight* will think, "Oh, she's got a new movie out. I'll have to check it out." That is precisely what the studios expect. That's why they dump so much money into these junkets, just so you will be reminded to go buy a ticket. That is "free" publicity.

That is how it works for a film. For books, it is a little different.

ADVERTISING, MARKETING, AND PUBLICITY

- Advertising can be very expensive, but you have absolute control of the message.

- Marketing answers the question "How and where are people going to buy this book?"

- Publicity is the means of generating interest and excitement about a product or service—or a book.

CHAPTER 2

PUBLIC RELATIONS — AN OVERVIEW

Remember Karen Black's character in *Airport 1975*? In the movie, flight attendant-turned-pilot Karen couldn't land the plane because she didn't understand the basic *concepts* about flying a 747. Chuck Heston had to risk toupee loss and be dropped into a hole in the cockpit of a jumbo jet streaking across the sky at 500 miles per hour and save the day. Why him? *Because he knew how to fly the plane.* The same applies here. I'm not going to let you loose, sending out press releases willy-nilly, endangering the lives of journalists across the country, without some basic concepts about publicity. So sit back, bring your seat to the upright position, and lock those tray tables in place, 'cause we're gonna learn some publicity concepts here.

PUBLIC RELATIONS

Publicity and public relations are not the same thing. Surprised? Publicity is a specific tactic, or subsection, of the larger field of public relations. **Public relations** is the management, creation, and positioning of the client's reputation, visibility, and image. This includes things like developing a community relations or community outreach program, like DaimlerChrysler's "Stop Red Light Running" program that they took into communities and schools to teach drivers the dangers of running red lights. Most corporations have some type of community relations program to enhance their standing within the community and within their area of business.

Public relations also includes helping a company choose a third-party spokesperson, usually an expert in a related field, to tell everyone how great the company is. A company might get Ralph Nader, the famous consumer advocate, to give interviews telling people that this company's toys are the safest on the market. It sounds more official and less self-serving coming from an outside expert.

Crisis management is another specialty within the public relations field. A restaurant chain may hire a public relations firm to counter the bad publicity it got when an *E. coli* outbreak made several customers gravely ill. The PR firm creates a crisis plan that outlines exactly what the company is going to do now to rectify the problem and what it will do to prevent such an occurrence in the future. The restaurant chain needs to calm the fears of other patrons who eat at their restaurants, set up an internal chain of command, media-train company spokespersons (teach them what to say and how to behave in an interview situation), and so on.

PUBLICITY

Generally speaking, publicity is tied into media coverage, either directly or indirectly. It includes one-on-one media interviews (direct), and doing "write-arounds," which is taking the press kit materials (press release, background information, biographical information, etc.) and generating a story without speaking directly to the author (indirect). It also includes arranging media tours. This is when a client travels from place to place giving interviews to anyone who asks for one. Media "stunts" also fall under the heading of publicity—like the woman who lived in a tree for two years to attract attention to the destruction of the environment. We will discuss other forms of publicity throughout this book, focusing specifically on literary publicity.

New authors, or established authors with a new book, present many public relations challenges. Media (I use "media" as plural) tend to be interested in people or books about which they already know or subject matter that is topical. Most popular authors did not become household names overnight; rather, they went through a long and arduous process of starting small and growing in popularity over time. There are exceptions, but they are few and far between.

You can choose to do publicity that goes directly to the consumer, bypassing the media. This can be done through writer's workshops, other public speaking venues, Web site chat rooms, book clubs, or school clubs. You can talk to someone at your alumni association asking that they include a story about your new book in their monthly newsletter. Ask your doctors and dentist to keep copies of your book on the coffee tables in their waiting rooms. (Goodness knows they all could use some new reading material.) You can even send a copy in with your phone bill payment. All of these ideas are extremely valuable to start generating "buzz" about a new book. Well, maybe not the phone-bill thing, but you get the idea.

You spent a long time writing, writing, writing. Now you have to spend a long time talking, talking, talking. Talk to anyone breathing if they look like they may pony up the $24.99 for your book. Start every sentence at a cocktail party with, *"Well, since my new book just came out..."* It's irritating but effective. When those annoying telephone solicitors call, don't let them hang up until *you* tell *them* about your amazing new book. (Payback time!) Talk to anyone who will listen.

TANGIBLE AND INTANGIBLE RESULTS

Before we discuss who should execute a publicity plan for your book, we need to have a little discussion about the results of a publicity campaign. Every publicity campaign has tangible results and intangible results, either of which may not be immediately evident. Some only become evident months or years after the fact.

Tangible results are the ones you can link directly to an action taken as prescribed by your publicity plan. For example, you appear on a morning TV show on Monday. By Tuesday, your book has shot up to the top of Amazon.com's best-seller list. Chances are that the "bump" in sales can be directly attributed to your appearance on the television program. That is about as tangible as it gets.

Intangible results are a little more slippery to define. You may send your book out to 500 media people and not get one article written about you or your book. Have you failed? A little yes and a little no. You didn't get the story written about you now—but when you send your next book to them, they will probably remember your last one, maybe this time they'll do the story. Introducing yourself to the media for future projects is an important intangible result that is just as important—for a different reason—than getting a story written about your current book. This is sometimes impossible to explain to authors because they want to see results!

Another common intangible result, "the talking head," can occur if you are an author who is an expert on a particular subject. Here is a true story about one of my clients that should help illustrate my point. Bob is a 23-year-old, Nordic-looking, ex-frat guy who wrote a hilarious tongue-in-cheek book about cheating in college. It was really very funny and clever. We sent out more than 600 press kits and books to all types of media (television programs, newspapers, magazines, etc.) and only got a few "bookings" (interviews). He was disappointed that we didn't get more tangible results—so was I, but that's just how it goes sometimes. I tried to explain to him that you never know when an editor or producer is going to need someone to talk about cheating. "Chin up, big guy." And that was that. We both moved on.

Sixteen months later, one of my account executives poked his head into my office and said, "Someone from *Oprah* is on line two." OK. I couldn't think of which client they might be calling about, but you should never leave someone from *Oprah* waiting on hold for long. I picked up the phone and caught up with this producer whom I'd met a few years back. Out of the blue, she asked me if I could get in contact with Bob. *BOB?* Jeez, we hadn't worked with Bob for 16 months. I didn't even know if he was still living in the same apartment, but I said I'd find out.

Two days later, Bob was in the front row of the audience at the *Oprah* show in Chicago, talking about cheating. His time had finally come. He was sooooooo happy! Neither of us expected this in a million years! He called me from Chicago when the taping was finished and we were both screaming like two lottery winners, we were so excited.

There are other, less extreme cases when the media has contacted us about a former client months after our contract ended. The point is: You never know when the intangible results from your publicity campaign will turn into tangible results.

It is vital that you understand: *this is no guarantee that any article or inter-*

view will run. There are too many variables when dealing with the media. An article can be "killed" if a major news story hits the same day your article is scheduled to run. There is a strong chance that the opportunity will pass—permanently—if something "hotter" hits the news. Don't get discouraged. Keep plugging away. Fast is not always best.

What you can expect, at the end of the day, from your publicity campaign is a few tangible results and a few more intangible results. National media tend to cover nonfiction more than fiction; famous experts/authors rather than new authors; newsworthy stories rather than fluff. If you don't fit into one of those categories, you're going to have a more difficult time of it. This is something you should take into account before you start writing your book. If your goal is to write a successful book, why write a book that won't get media coverage? If no one can find out about your book, they can't go buy it.

If you are a new author, you should expect to get some media coverage from your local newspaper, a couple of speaking engagements for local organizations, a local radio interview or two, and maybe a guest shot on your local morning show—at least in the beginning. That may change as you send out more books and get more interviews. If you get a response from 1 percent of the media you sent your press materials and books to, that is considered successful by almost any standards.

Now you know what literary publicity is and what tangible and intangible results you can expect. The next thing you have to decide is who will execute a publicity plan for your book.

CHAPTER 3

CHOOSING A PUBLICIST

You have several options to choose from regarding who should do your publicity. Just as you have to choose the right tool for the right job, you have to choose the most effective option that is most likely to get the most media coverage for your book. You have three primary choices. All three have their strengths and their weaknesses:

1. Using an in-house publicist, the publicist that works directly for the publisher.

2. Hiring an outside public relations agency, that is not directly attached to one specific publisher.

3. Doing it yourself.

IN-HOUSE PUBLICITY

Most publishing houses, like most businesses, have limited time, personnel, and resources. Often the in-house publicity departments of the publishing houses take an approach that is quite routine and limited. They tend to do the same things, in the same manner, for every author they handle. I can't tell you how many times I have asked an in-house publicist for copies of the collateral material (press release, press clippings, biographical information sheet, etc.) for a book we were both working on, only to receive a one-page press release—they fold it in half, stick it inside the cover, and send the book out for review.

In today's competitive media marketplace, you have to do a little bit more. A full press kit is required, but it is costly, which is one of the reasons why they don't do this. The other reason they tend to do the bare minimum is that one in-house publicist may handle 10 to 20 authors *per month*. That's a lot of writing, mailing, faxing, and talking to ask of one person.

A benefit of using in-house publicists is that they can try to leverage one of their better-known authors for a new one—overtly or covertly. For example, they might call up a TV show and say, "Hey, Mr. Producer Person, good news. I think I can get Ms. Famous Author to do your show. *(pause)* And *listen,* we'd really like it if you could have our Mr. Less-Known Author on next week when you're doing that segment on *blah, blah, blah.*" Subtle, but everyone involved gets the subtext: If you want Ms. Famous Author, you're going to have to find a slot for Mr. Less-Known. It doesn't work most of the time. Producers hate having their arms twisted like this. I don't blame them and I don't recommend it. The book should be of sufficient interest to the program's audience on its own to warrant a guest appearance or interview.

The other benefit of using in-house publicists is that they have established relationships with editors and producers that will guarantee a return phone call, at the very least. Whether the in-house publicists bring these relationships with them when they are hired, or inherit them from the last publicist they replaced, at least they have them. Also, if they don't know anyone at a particular media outlet, someone in the cubicle next to them probably does.

OUTSIDE PUBLIC RELATIONS FIRMS

Authors hire outside publicists for a number of reasons. Professional (independent) publicists or public relations firms have the resources available to give your project more thought and attention than your own publishing house can give to you. They *do* work with the in-house publicists to see what their long-term plans are for you and your project, and offer help in any way they can. Professional publicists also keep the in-house publicists informed as to what they are doing on your behalf. (I'm using the word *professional* only to draw a distinction between in-house and outside publicists. In-house publicists are also professionals. No disrespect is intended.)

Independent publicists also have several other beneficial qualities, such as time, staff, and a wider range of media contacts. Having more time allows the professional publicist more breathing room to be creative and think the publicity plan through. Rushing into action without thinking things through usually leads to disaster. Public relations firms usually have a larger support staff to help with the necessary work and can get the job done more efficiently. Professional publicists also have a wider variety of media contacts, because they don't contact "book" media exclusively. With a wider selection of clients, publicists and publicity firms often have to contact nonbook editors and producers. Most media outlets have someone who specializes in working with authors. Professional publicists work not only with them, but also with other types of editors and producers. This gives a professional more options to "pitch" your book for a story. In short, they have more time to give you one-on-one professional attention.

It is not always professional attention. Not one of my clients, past or present, has gone through the publishing process without the need for a little TLC and some nonprofessional therapy. I'm not a psychiatrist, but I can make a pretty good guess as to why this happens. Throughout the writing process, the writer has had absolute control over what he is doing. She can kill off a character if she feels like it, with just the touch of the delete button. She can put another character on a plane and send him to Guam. She can make the underdog win.

Once the author turns in the manuscript to the mean old editor, she gives up a significant amount of that control. Her baby is now in the hands of a nanny she doesn't really know. Will the nanny drop the baby? Kill it? Rewrite it?!

Tequila shots start looking good by lunchtime ... for the editor.

Authors will be calling the editor 500 times a day, obsessing about some relatively trivial matter, driving everyone at the publishing house to distraction.

Then, once the book is actually printed, authors start worrying about book sales and whether the book will be successful. Then they hate what the publisher is doing with their books. Each author believes they're all out to get him and make this the biggest flop the publishing world has ever seen. "If they were going to do *this* to my book, why did they even buy it in the first place?!"

Once authors are all wound up, that's when they decide to hire an outside publicist. They think they're hiring a publicist for publicity, but the job soon morphs into psychological therapy and handholding. Oh, sure, they desperately want to be on *Oprah, tomorrow,* but they need to be told that everything is going to work out just fine *today!*

I had one insane writer who started out OK (they all do, by the way), but by the end of the second week, she was driving me nuts! I was getting 15 or 16 phone calls *a day* from this crazy person! She became so neurotic about the publishing of her book that she burned out all the synapses that carry *reasonable* thoughts through her brain and took to babbling for hours at a time about I-don't-know-what. I was getting calls on Saturday and Sunday—five- and six-hour conversations!—talking about how she wanted to fire her agent, buy the book back, and publish the darn thing herself. That she knew not the first thing about publishing a book was, apparently, not the point. And just what the hell was she paying me for anyway? I've had two weeks already, now when was she going to be on television?! Didn't I realize that it only took the Good Lord six days to create the whole universe?! (Yes, but at the time, He didn't have to deal with a crazy author, now did He!) And on and on ...

Loss of control equals some bad days ahead for publicists. But I digress.

So, in addition to doing the publicity work that has to be done, an outside public relations firm can also give authors more time, to help them maintain a proper perspective. That is just one more benefit of an outside publicist.

The downside is that it can cost a lot. If you can afford to hire an outside publicist, I strongly recommend that you do so. They can accomplish a lot for you in a shorter period of time because they have the expertise and staff to get the job done more quickly than any individual.

DOING YOUR OWN PUBLICITY

Your third option is doing publicity for your own book. It is relatively straightforward—not necessarily easy, but it can be done. You will need to learn some basic publicity concepts to get you started. That is what this book focuses on: getting you started. It's going to take time, money, patience, and a good sense of humor to do this, but you really can do it and be as effective as a professional publicist.

Because each book and each author is unique, it will be necessary for you to develop a creative, interesting, and effective multitiered plan that makes the greatest use of your background and the specific subject matter of your book. If your book deals with topical issues, it will be necessary to be reactive to news events of the day. If those avenues do not present themselves, you will have to be proactive and create the necessary openings.(More on that later.)

Generating interest in an unknown quantity is difficult, but not impossible. The key is to write a good book, learn how to create interesting and effective press materials, and develop extensive relationships with various local and national media as quickly as possible so that you gain direct access to those reporters and editors who make the decisions on whether to run a story.

Table 3-1 summarizes the considerations in choosing a publicist. Whether you're using an in-house publicist, a professional publicist, or doing it yourself, the goal is the same: to get your name out there to the media and to the consumer.

TABLE 3-1   MAKING THE RIGHT CHOICE: SIX CONSIDERATIONS

	Professional PR Firm	In-House Publicity	Do-It-Yourself PR
Experience	Most professional PR firms have a lot of experience creating and executing a publicity plan for a variety of books and other products and services. In other words, they have a wide scope of experience.	Some in-house publicists have a lot of literary publicity experience and some are new to the industry. Their experience level and personal ability varies tremendously.	Most authors have very little, if any, experience in creating and executing a literary publicity campaign.
News Judgment	Most professional PR firms work with a variety of media and know which story is right for a particular media outlet. They tend to have a wider scope of media contacts, from automotive to zoological publications.	Many in-house publicists have limited general knowledge about the media because the books they handle are similar in scope and tend to be covered by the same media over and over.	A new author has very little experience with the media and must learn this over time.

TABLE 3-1 (CONTINUED)

	Professional PR Firm	In-House Publicity	Do-It-Yourself PR
Creativity	Because of their wide range of experience, most professionals have a higher level of creativity, just through sheer practice.	Again, depending on their level of experience, you can have a publicist that is very creative or one who can't tie his own shoes.	If you are creative enough to write a book that is actually being distributed, chances are you have enough creativity to generate your own publicity campaign.
Writing Skills	Some professionals couldn't write their way out of a paper bag, others are brilliant. Ask for writing samples before you hire a professional.	The same applies to in-house publicists. Ask for samples. A lot of recent samples, specifically from the publicist who will be handling your book.	If you can grasp the "inverted pyramid" style of writing and learn how to write concisely, you can do this.
Cost	$10,000 to $30,000	No cost	Time and expenses
Time	4 months to 6 months	2 weeks to 4 weeks	Unlimited

CHAPTER 4

EVALUATING YOUR BOOK

You've decided that you want to do your own publicity. Good. Now, you have to have a plan.

Just as you're supposed to outline your book before you start writing it, you should have an outline for your publicity plan. And just like your book outline, once it is finished, you should stick to it. The only acceptable reason for going "off-plan" is the occurrence of an unexpected news event that ties in with the subject of your book or lies in your area of expertise. For example, one of my clients, a doctor who specializes in laser eye surgery, was part of the Food and Drug Administration (FDA) trials to determine the safety of a new laser eye procedure. We had a publicity plan all worked out—but then the FDA released its findings a few days earlier than we expected. We had to scrap our original plan and scramble to get media alerts (i.e., urgent, one-page information sheets faxed to major media outlets that explain why they should talk to an author) out to all media to let them know that one of the doctors who had participated in the clinical trials was available to be interviewed as an expert. It would have been foolish to stick to the plan just for the sake of sticking to the plan.

Just when we'd gotten everything back on track, Ken Starr decided to release the Monica Lewinsky transcripts. Remember him: the Javert of independent counsels? Remember her: the White House intern-turned-purse-maker? All of humanity, it seemed, was more interested in cigars than in corrective vision procedures. Disappointingly, we lost that battle. We were upset and so was the client, but there was really nothing we could do. Those ridiculous transcripts kept the media diverted from a lot of other good stories for months (years?). Instead of bashing our heads against a brick wall, we decided to go around it by focusing strictly on medical publications that would be more likely to run a laser eye surgery story. In short, the plan had to be completely revamped several times throughout the course of our contract.

There are four primary things to consider before you begin putting your plan together.

1. You must objectively evaluate your book as a media product.
2. You must objectively evaluate your resources.
3. You must create a budget.
4. You must set clearly defined goals and objectives for your public relations plan.

Each of these four areas has to be clearly defined before you can even start making your plan. The first two will be the most difficult, because it is always tricky to look at something objectively after you've spent months and months of your life creating it.

Once you've finished your book, you have to be able to look at it both from the media's perspective and from the consumer's perspective. Your book is now a product, like toothpaste, that you have to sell to editors and your next-door neighbor. You must be able to separate yourself emotionally from your book and look at it in a new way—which is easier for an in-house or outside publicist to do than it is for the author because we are not emotionally attached to what you have written.

I'll give you an example: A few years back a very funny woman sent me her manuscript to consult on a book/movie she had written about "the Goddess that everyone on Earth had forgotten about." It was very Mel Brooks, very funny, and "perfect for Whoopi," so she told me. So I read it. And I laughed. Then I started looking at it as a product to determine its media-friendliness. I concluded that it would be a tough sell to get the media to write about or "cover" the book, for several reasons. First, the book's thematic elements were a little too far out for the media and had no possibility for news tie-ins. Second, this lady was a first-time author with no previous track record. Third, she was not a doctorate-level expert on goddesses. Fourth, the title (which will remain a secret) was not very interesting. She had a great story that I could do nothing with, from a media perspective. Those are the heart-breakers for a publicist. I don't know what happened to this book/film, but I do hope she reworks it and gets it published.

That is an example of a book that was not very media friendly. Here's an example that was *perfectly* media friendly.

Glenn, a public relations executive, always wanted to be a professional writer, so he wrote a very good book. (*Glenn* is not a pseudonym for me, in case you were wondering. After writing this, I probably won't ever even *read* another book. I'm a much better talker than writer.)

So this man wrote the perfect story at the perfect time. He wrote a terrific novel that took place at the turn of the millennium. It was about a cable news team attempting to discover if a woman who appeared on Millennium Eve was, in fact, the Second Coming. Great book! The book came out right as millennium fever was just beginning. It had newsworthy angles like religion, media fairness, homosexuality, and so on. This was as close to a slam-dunk as a first-time author can hope for. The timing of the book's release was perfect. We ended up getting tons of regional interviews and a few national interviews. Strangely, though, we didn't get a few of the national interviews that we expected. I don't know if these programs were a little nervous talking about the "Second Coming" being a woman, or if they thought advertisers would pull out because of the controversial nature of the story, or if they were afraid of offending their Christian readers/viewers. I did receive a scathing e-mail from the head of some Catholic something-or-other saying they were going to boycott the book, yadda, yadda, yadda. I kept telling them that it was only a *novel* and not really happening. (I could write another entire book about the blurring of fantasy and reality in the minds of the public, but I won't.)

This is a good example of what is considered a media-friendly book.

The upshot of all this is that the first thing you have to do is evaluate the thematic elements of your book to see if they will be useful for publicity. If you are writing a book about a new diet or the proper way to raise children, you already have a strongly media-friendly theme. For fiction, you are going to have to dig deep to find those appropriate media-friendly thematic elements.

Here are six questions to ask yourself to help objectively evaluate and determine the media-friendliness of your book:

1. **After reading my book, what should the reader have learned about the human condition?** *Love truly conquers all. Perseverance will always get you what you want. The innocence of a child will always be corrupted by life. Power is everything.*

If you can't think of an answer to this question, you are going to have to rely on one or more of the next questions. All of the examples for point number one are strong enough to become your "lead" or headline for your press release, which we'll talk about a bit later. It is critically important to identify the theme of your book, particularly for writing your press release and for pitching, which we'll also discuss later.

2. **Am I an expert on the subject matter of my book?** *Do you have a Ph.D. in bio-medical science? A B.A. in social work? A masters in communications? Have you studied the subject, on your own, for 20 years? Have you ever written an article on your subject that was published in your local newspaper? Are you a self-professed expert on meditation?*

The media loves experts. Remember the O.J. trial? Every news broadcast and talk show had a plethora of "talking heads" discussing the daily wins and losses of the trial. Every time there is a school shooting, the media trot out scores of child psychologists, law enforcement officials, and politicians trying to figure out the unexplainable. But there they are, nonetheless. There are about 10 cable channels that have talk/discussion programs running 24 hours a day. That is a lot of time to fill and that is a lot of opportunities for talking heads.

On the morning and afternoon talk shows, there are always family counselors or drug treatment experts trying to save the world in a three-minute segment. "Look your wife in the eyes and tell her you love her. Go on! Look. Can you see the pain you've caused her? Now, stop doing that. Can you promise her in front of all these people that you will never do that again?" "Honey, you're a door mat! Until you learn how to empower yourself, you're always going to be a door mat!" Real helpful. Forget the fact that it has taken these emotionally damaged people years to get into their messes; and now some talk-show host and her "expert" are saying "get over it and move on!" I believe these "experts"—or at least this use of experts—are extremely dangerous, because of their superficiality and gross oversimplifications.

If you are an expert, make it clear that some things will take more than three minutes to understand or "fix." This may not do much to further your second career as a talk-show guest, but you'll still have been able to garner some publicity for your book and you will have done a professional service to the talk-show audience, too. That's all I'm going to say on the matter, because it gets me crazy when I think about this too much.

I have been asked why an author who has written a novel that is more literary should consider becoming an expert. Isn't that more for nonfiction? No. If you've written a more literary book, the chances are that you were influenced by many of the great writers of the past or present. You've probably read more literary works than the average person and you probably know more about the mechanics of writing than most authors. If a program is celebrating the birthday of Hemingway, for example, you may have a lot to say about his writing style, his life, and how he influenced you and other writers of today. The difficult part will be to persuade the media that you know what you're talking about. A simple way would be to send them a two- to three-page bullet-point list of the things about which you can speak with some authority. I would also send them your biographical information to help lend you credibility.

The same basic principles hold true for both fiction and nonfiction.

3. **What is happening in the news that might tie in with my book?** *Has a new study just been published that proves owning pets will help you live longer? Has a housewife just made it to the top of Mt. Everest through pure perseverance? Has a child just witnessed a shooting? Has a long-lost wife just returned to the husband who refused to get remarried?*

Becoming a news junkie is a *must* if you want your book to be noticed. You need to be able to react to a breaking news story the second it hits the airwaves. You also have to be up to speed on what the news agencies are covering and on trends in the news. For example, after the tragic shooting at Columbine High School, almost all the news agencies began running stories about parental responsibility, gun control, and teenage rage. This was a short-term trend. If your book contained, however remotely, any thematic element relating to any of these three topics, you could have sent a media alert to your local newspaper, radio, and television stations informing them that you just wrote a book about this very subject. Even if your book is fiction, you may get a chance to speak out on your theme.

One of my clients created a high-quality, expensive line of probiotic health food supplements. (It's like vitamins, only with beneficial bacteria.) Sounds real technical, but it's not really. One of the benefits of these probiotic supplements, according to the client, is that they can help older people and young children fight off the very nasty *E. coli* bacteria found in spoiled foods. There was an unfortunate outbreak of *E. coli* in northern New York state and a couple of people died from *E. coli* poisoning. I read about it on a "breaking news" Web site and immediately went into action.

We compiled a list of the local upstate New York news programs and newspapers and started calling them to offer our client as an expert. Several of these media outlets were extremely interested in learning about probiotics and how it related to the outbreak. Pay dirt! We were asked to contact them the next morning to make arrangements for interviews. We were sorry about the outbreak, but happy to get our client on television.

When we called the next day, we were informed that Hillary Clinton was making an unscheduled appearance in that city and everything about the outbreak was on hold. By the time Hillary's visit concluded, the outbreak story had significantly cooled. We ended up arranging background interviews with the local media, which wasn't perfect, but it was something.

You have to keep your eyes and ears open to everything that is being reported by the media so you can pounce on any opportunity that presents itself.

4. **Does my book have any unusual angles that might be useful to the media or to a specific group?** *Does your book show the effect cancer has on a family? If so, a national oncology group may want you to speak at its conference from a humanistic point of view. Is your book an inspiring story about a child overcoming a disability? If so, a parents' support group may want to hear what you have to say.*

You can use public speaking engagements to help publicize your book. The simple fact that you will be appearing at a seminar can get you into the "what's happening" section of the local paper, which could lead to an interview later on.

Ivy wrote a metaphysical book on empowering yourself and creating a positive spiritual path. It was well written, but didn't have a great media angle, or "hook." She is an extremely dynamic public speaker, though, so we arranged a few public speaking engagements for her (something a publicist doesn't normally do for clients) at various venues in Manhattan. She was very well received and ended up selling a couple hundred books. Not bad for an evening's work.

This would be a good time to give you a word of warning. If you try to add an element to your story that is not intrinsic to its plot, just because you think it would be good PR, you will be caught and most likely severely punished by the offended group or the media. In other words, don't give a character some horrible disease just so you can get on television or get a speaking engagement at a medical conference. Write your story. If it's good enough, you'll be able to figure out a workable publicity angle. In all my years, I have never seen this gambit work to an author's benefit. Don't do it.

5. **Is my title exciting enough, and does it accurately reflect the story?**

The title of this book was originally *Grassroots Public Relations for Writers.* The publisher, rightly so, thought the title was too dry and didn't accurately match what I had written. It just goes to show you that even a professional needs an objective opinion now and then. We then came up with its current title, *Literary Publicity: The Final Chapter.* It's much better and reflects the information contained herein. Another title was suggested, *Literary*

Publicity: How to Sell Yourself and Your Book. That one didn't work for me. It sounded too used-car-salesman-ish. I wouldn't mind a short phrase like that appearing on the cover, but not as part of the official title. (I won't know who won that battle until this is published.)

A title should, as I've said, clearly reflect the story, and it should be interesting. It should contain a clever play on words, paint an interesting visual image, be bold, or simply be clear. If you get too esoteric with your title, no one will know what the heck to do with it and you will end up wasting a lot of time just trying to explain what your title means. Save the major creativity for the text.

6. Is my jacket artwork interesting and appropriate to the story?

I'm not a fan of romance novels (so shoot me!), but when I look at their covers I know exactly what I'm going to get if I buy one. The characters on the cover always look like they're saying, *"Willow pummeled Dirk's massive chest with her pigeon-like fists shouting, 'No, Dirk. I love Brock!'"* Whatever. The point is that these jacket covers accurately reflect the story and the genre of the book. If your story takes place in London in the 1920s, you probably don't want to use a type font that looks like a computer printout. It doesn't match.

Jacket art is like the clothing the story wears. It is the media's and consumer's first impression. It's just like going to a formal dinner party: You would not want to wear blue jeans with a big rip in the knee and a halter top. (Especially if you are a man.) You would get noticed, but it would be the wrong type of "noticed." (Especially if you are a man.)

In the initial phase of developing your jacket art, don't limit yourself. Think about things you normally wouldn't think would work and whittle down the choices from there. What about bold geometric shapes? How about hot pink as the field color? A picture of a brooch that the main character always wears? A knife with a drop of blood on its tip and a six-inch stiletto heel reflected in the metal? (Very big with murder mysteries.) Sure, these wacky ideas will probably not work, but you may surprise yourself with a toned-down version of one of these ideas. Never say never.

I bring up jacket art because it will most certainly create an impact on the reporter or editor when they open the press materials for the first time. It is your calling card. Every reporter or editor receives thousands of things in the mail every day, so you want something that will freeze them in their tracks and make them think, "Humph, maybe I'll take a look at this over the weekend."

The jacket art for a book I recently worked on set the authors, me, the editor, and the graphic artist at each other's throats, dividing us into two camps. Me and the authors: "us"; "them": the editor and graphic artist. What began as a friendly discussion quickly turned into a verbal brawl. It was not pretty. I'd tell you the title of the book, but I'm still afraid I'll get sued. Anyway, the book is about the Vietnam War and "us" felt that a cool "rising sun" type graphic with the title in an Army stencil-like font would be great. They thought a pretty silk fabric in Army green with a military medal that's not even in the book would be greater. Yeah, I think of silk when I think of war. Right! And what's with this medal? Gee, I have a thought: How about we use the medal that we *do* have in the book? Wow, what a concept. The first shot was fired.

Well, we ultimately came up with a compromise that worked, but it was rough going for a few days. Take your time and think about the impact your artwork will have on the media and the consumer. It will really help your cause. (By the way, that war story was the first book from that publisher to make a best-seller list.)

CHAPTER 5

EVALUATING YOUR RESOURCES

The second part of planning your publicity strategy is evaluating your financial and human resources. Now that you have a handle on your book as a product, it is time to look at what resources you have available to put your publicity plan into action.

FINANCIAL RESOURCES

The biggest question to ask yourself at this point is: Can I afford to do this? In the next section we will discuss budgeting, but that's not what I mean here. You will need to know if the publisher is willing to give you some extra money to cover some of the expenses of publicity like travel, postage, copy costs, review copies, and so on. If they are willing (and bless them if they are!), you should get a hard figure of exactly how much they will allow you. *Exactly* how much. This way you will be able to make an informed decision as to how much you are willing to spend out of your own pocket. Are you willing to sacrifice your planned summer vacation money, or the piano lessons for your daughter, or the down payment on a new house? These are real questions that require some very serious discussions. Publicity is not an exact science and does not come with any—repeat, *any*—guarantees. You could spend all your savings and not get one interview.

When I say serious discussions, I really mean serious discussions. I learned this part the hard way and I don't wish this life lesson on anyone.

An older woman, Rose, sent me a manuscript for a book about a talking dog from Mexico that makes it big in Hollywood (this is years before the famous Taco Bell chihuahua). The author had worked in Hollywood for many years and this story was an extremely humorous way for her to satirize her real-life experiences deep in the trenches of LaLa Land. For me, having worked in television and film for a few years, I instantly fell in love with this hilarious book. It was, and still is, one of the most creative books I have ever read. Rose is one of the nicest people you could ever meet, which I could tell after about 30 seconds with her on the phone. She told me she was taking a big financial risk in hiring me, but she was absolutely committed to making this book a success. We discussed what we could do, how much expenses would probably be, which media outlets we would contact, and everything else we were supposed to. I explained to her that I felt confident we could get some great entertainment media coverage, because, after all, that's what the book was about. I also told her that I wouldn't be taking her money if I thought we wouldn't be able to get her something.

She trusted my judgment and agreed.

I think because I loved Rose and the book, I came up with what I still think is the most creative press materials I have ever designed. We had "quotes" from Lassie and other famous dogs—some positive, some scathing and bitchy. The press release quoted the fictitious dog. The whole nine yards. Everyone I showed it to laughed and thought it was great. So did Rose. I thought it couldn't miss.

I sent out around 300 of these press kits and began making the follow-up calls. I was stoked! Nearly all of the entertainment editors, producers, and reporters *loved* the materials.

But in four months of solid work, I only got three hits, and those in second-tiered media outlets (i.e,. smaller cities). Rose was crushed and I was beside myself. I did absolutely everything right for this book (and then some), and I still only got three interviews. I felt like a total creep. I still do. I worked for two additional months, on my own time, to try to make it up to Rose, but got nothing else. I asked everyone to whom I had sent the materials point-blank why they weren't going to cover this book. None of them could give me a good answer. I still don't know why it didn't work, but it didn't and Rose spent a lot of money and didn't see a lot of tangible results.

It's difficult to look on the brighter side of intangible results when something like this happens. Factoring in the cost of publicity is an important element in determining whether you can do a publicity campaign. You will need to be *very* realistic about the financial investment of doing your own publicity.

HUMAN RESOURCES, OR THE PEOPLE YOU KNOW

You will also have to take stock of the human resources at your disposal. In short, who do you know that might be able to help you? I'm always amazed at the reaction I get when I ask an author for what is sometimes called a "big-mouth list." A big-mouth list is simply a list of well-respected, well-connected people you know who could use their connections and their big mouths to talk up your book. The author almost always says, "But I don't know any high-falutin' people!" Not true, everyone knows someone who knows someone who might know someone ... . It's best to start with your immediate family and work your way out in concentric circles, from closest to farthest.

The objective here is to find people who would be willing to send an e-mail to everyone at their company letting them know about your great new book; or include it in their newsletter (even if your book's subject matter has nothing to do with the topic of the newsletter); or talk to 20 people at the PTA meeting; or tell their librarian friends to put in a good word for your book; or anything, no matter how crazy it sounds, to get the word out.

Let's look at each of these groups and see if you can fill in some names to go in each group. On a piece of paper or the computer, list the name and how you would like that person to help you. I bet you will surprise yourself with how many options you actually have.

Immediate Family

Let's start with your spouse or significant other. Does his job permit him to send company-wide e-mails to his co-workers? If so, keep it brief: "Dear All: My spouse has just finished writing a new book that I think is great. If you get a chance, pick up a copy and let me know what you think. We'd love to hear your comments!" That can get the ball rolling. You might even have him take a copy into the office and leave it in the waiting room or post a notice on the bulletin board in the lunchroom. Think creatively.

Your kids. Don't be afraid to use their contacts. Hey, you're picking up the tab for their food, clothing, and CDs, it's the least they can do! Are your kids in any sports that have an adult booster club? Let them know. Think about your daughter's 10 best girlfriends. Who are their parents, and can you contact them and ask them to help with some of these ideas? (I would send them a copy of the book before you ask them, so they can give it some thought.) Would your kids be willing to pass out flyers at the library, school, supermarket, and other places? If not, tell the little ingrates that they're out of the will! And mean it.

Extended Family

Let's think about Grandma and Grandpa. Was Grandpa in the military? Does he keep in touch with any of the guys in his unit? I was pleasantly surprised to learn that there is a huge military network that remains in place long after all of the wars. The Vietnam book I wrote about earlier got some much-needed "heat" from a retired general; seems that ex-military personnel still listen to their superiors.

Does Grandma volunteer at a day care center or a senior citizen's center? Does she still talk to her old girlfriends? Remember that for every Grandma there are at least 50 kids, grandkids, and great-grandkids. So offer to pay Grandma's phone bills and get her dialing!

What about your brothers and sisters? Who do they know and what do they do for a living? (If you are currently fighting with your siblings, apologize! Doesn't matter who's right or wrong at this point. You can always pick open the scab after your books are in the remainder bin.) Ask them for help. The key is to ask them to take responsibility for a specific task. Don't be general, like, "Could you help me do some word-of-mouth for my new book?" That's too general. Be specific, like, "Will you put flyers on the windshields of all the cars in your office parking lot?" This will allow them to make an informed decision as to whether they can really help you or not. They may also come up with some of their own better ideas.

What about your aunts and uncles? Their children and their children's friends? Keep going through the family tree on both sides and see what they can do for you. Run it like a well-oiled machine; assign specific tasks to specific people; get the younger kids in on the fun. Make your family work for you.

Friends

I would be really careful with this one. Remember, you don't choose your family, but you do choose your friends. The same applies to them. You need to pay careful attention to their individual situations. If your best friend is going through a divorce, you probably shouldn't ask him for a lot of help. He probably has enough on his plate. Conversely, this may be just the thing to take his mind off his troubles. You decide, but be aware of what is going on in your friends' lives. Also, if a friend of yours has four small toddlers, she may be too wiped out to be of real assistance. In addition, be aware that helping you will probably fall toward the bottom of your friends' priority lists if they should land a new account or one of the kids gets sick. In other words, they might not be as reliable as family members.

Experts

Using examples from earlier in this book, think about your story. Does it have a medical angle, like cancer or drug addiction? If so, contact the experts. Look in the phone book or call your doctor's office and see if they have any information on medical conferences taking place in your area, or if they have associations with newsletters. Oftentimes, these conferences are so incredibly dry that the attendees would drink a glass of sand to get out of there, so they might welcome a layperson to come in and jazz things up.

Also, most newsletters have a "What's New?" section that might be a perfect place to announce your book. Ask around and find out which professional organizations have meetings and newsletters. See if you can set up a table in the lobby and sell some books, or at least hand out some flyers for them to take home.

You don't need to have a specific "button" in your story. If your book is purely literary, the same thing about experts still holds true. The only difference is that you want the literary experts to discuss the literary merits of your book: the style, the structure, and the story itself. They may also be interested in having you speak about the writing process, or what it's like to go through the publishing process. Go to a college campus and ask the creative writing professors if they'll take a look at your book and recommend it to other teachers and their students as an example of a contemporary literature piece that has just been published. Offer to speak to their classes. As a former teacher, I can't tell you how exciting it is to have someone else carry the load for a day.

Ask about literary-centered groups on campus. Leave flyers in the student union of your local campus. Ask if you can speak on the campus radio station.

People in Big Buildings

Here's a fun one for you: people who work in big buildings. Seriously. I'm talking about schools, churches, libraries, government offices, supermarkets, malls, airports, hotels, movie theaters, car dealers, art galleries, NASA (I wonder if astronauts are allowed reading material?), and any other big buildings that come to mind. Inside each of these big buildings is a slew of people who work there or use their services. If the book has any educational value, talk to the librarians at all the schools in your area. Often librarians are asked to submit ideas to library trade publications which will, in turn, write a review. Free PR!

Look at my list of big buildings and think about specific subject matters that are appropriate to each of the buildings. Also, think about different church groups. Will your supermarket let you hand out flyers? I'm telling you, a big key is big buildings!

Time

It may seem odd to include *time* in the "evaluating your human resources" section, but it really is not. For this one, *you* are the human resource. You need to evaluate how much time you realistically have to execute your own publicity plan. This is going to take as much time as you can possibly give it. It is exhausting, frustrating, exhilarating, irritating, maddening, technical, and time-consuming. It's also a blast when you get the hang of it!

Go through your weekly schedule and figure out what days and times you can allot to working on your own publicity. Let's say you have a demanding full-time job, for starters. You have to get yourself ready for work. Maybe car-pool to the office, so you have to pick up four other people. Work for eight or nine hours. Drop your carpool people back off at their homes. Pick something up at the dry cleaners. Attend a business dinner (yuck!). Talk to your best friend on the phone for five minutes. Pay some bills and give your significant other at least 10 minutes of personal attention (except Saturday nights—that requires 15).

See, if you really break down your schedule, you may find that you don't have the time to do everything that must be done to make this work. That being said, don't get crazy yet. There are ways around some of these obstacles. I'll give you a quick set of examples now so you'll keep reading. Since we have not gotten to the part where we talk about the specifics of what's involved in publicity (like press kits, follow-up calls, etc.), just grasp the point that it *is* possible to cheat Father Time a little bit.

You can use your computer to send multiple faxes overnight when phone rates are cheaper and you're sleeping. You can leave voice messages for reporters when you get home from work and check your answering machine 50 times a day from work and call them back when the boss is not looking. You can prepare your mailings over the weekend after you send the kids and your spouse to a movie. Better yet, have your kids be the envelope-lickers and stamp-sticker-on-ers. Everyone is always complaining that parents don't spend enough quality time with their kids. If they're licking envelopes, at least you'll know where they are and maybe bond a little.

The point is, don't panic about the time issue just yet. You just need to know that a lot will have to be done in a short period of time, and plan according-ly. Your mantra during this time should be "This too shall pass." The publicity plan is not forever; it's just for a few months.

Some things you should plan *not* to do right in the middle of a publicity campaign: vacations, elective surgery, home remodeling, get pregnant (either you or your partner), start a new job, or anything that generally upsets your regular schedule. This will be stressful enough—you don't need to add to it.

This really happened. We were working with another doctor/author (I seem to work with them a lot) on a book about sports medicine. It was an inter-esting book, even though my idea of exercise is driving the one block to the convenience store to get cigarettes. Through all of our efforts, we managed to get this doctor on four national television programs, three national radio programs, two regional morning shows, and a partridge in a pear tree.

You can imagine how excited we were that his book and our pitch had worked. My account executive came running into my office to tell me the good news and I congratulated him and told him to call the client right away and spread the good news.

He came back ashen-faced a few minutes later and told me that the good doctor would be unable to do *any* of the interviews because he was going skiing with his family and that is "family time. No business allowed." He wouldn't even do the radio interviews via phone from his hotel! He could-n't give us 30 minutes for national exposure *from his hotel room*?! If he had been in my office, I would have wrapped my hands around his neck until I crushed his windpipe and watched him turn an ugly blue and drop dead right at my feet!

He never even told me he was going anywhere, for starters. Then, to have the nerve to decline *national interviews* was just beyond my comprehension. I called him back to explain the seriousness of this situation, but he didn't budge. We had to call all these journalists back and decline their interview offers. We looked like total jerks! Then, three weeks later, the author had the gall to send me an e-mail detailing how upset he was that we weren't get-ting him any interviews! Some people! This still makes me nuts and it hap-pened four years ago.

Make sure you have the time to do this, once you decide to proceed with a publicity plan, or I will personally hunt you down and hurt you. (I'm O.K. now, the medication just kicked in.)

For a full publicity plan, I usually allot about 25 to 35 hours per week, depending on the scope of the plan. If you are doing things locally, you can probably get along with about 20 hours per week. For a regional plan, think about 25 hours per week. For a national plan, allocate 35 to 40 hours per week.

CHAPTER 6

BUDGETING YOUR PLAN

The next phase in developing a publicity plan is budgeting. This is the most tedious part of the whole process, because there are a million little pieces of the puzzle to figure out so you can come up with a final dollar figure. If you take each element one at a time, you shouldn't have any problem. Please note that you are going to have to write all your collateral materials for the press kit *before* you go through some of these steps, so that you will know how many pieces of paper are in your press kit (for copies, etc.) and how heavy your press kit will be (for postage). Make sure you have a calculator and a pencil sharpener and lots and lots of paper, you'll need them.

TEN STEPS TOWARD AN ACCURATE BUDGET

Step 1: Count the Number of Media Outlets You Want to Contact

You will need an exact count of all the media you are going to contact. You can also work this backwards, too. You can decide that you are going to contact 50 media outlets per month and figure out which ones you'll contact as you go. The first way is a target-centered budget. You are more concerned with getting materials sent to the appropriate media than with the budget. The second way is a financial-centered budget, wherein cost is the primary consideration. We will discuss how you get the correct contact information for all of these media outlets in later chapters. Remember to include newspapers, magazines, television programs, and radio programs. Write down your final number on a separate piece of paper.

Step 2: Determine the Cost of Your Supplies

This includes all your basic office supplies, such as mailing labels (which are surprisingly expensive), envelopes, note pads, bulletin boards, a big calendar, stick-on notes, pens, paper, tape (oddly enough, you'll go through lots of tape), folders (again, very expensive), and so on. You are setting up a "war room," so think about everything you'll need. I suggest you get an office supply catalog and flip through it. You may be very surprised at how expensive all this stuff is. If you buy as you go, you'll blow your budget very quickly. Only get what you really need. (I'm like a kid in a candy store when it comes to office supplies. There's just something about a really cool stapler that I can't resist. I don't need it, but I want it. I'm a freak, what can I say?) Come up with your final number and write it down under your final media count.

Step 3: Copies

You are going to have to make copies of all the papers you will include in your press kit. Unless you can sneak copies from your job, you should plan on paying about 5 cents per copy. There are usually 9 or 10 pages in each press kit. I'll use 10 because it's easier to do the math. Let's say you're sending out 50 press kits. 50 press kits x 10 pages = 500 pages. 500 pages x $.05 = $25.00. This amount could be more if you are using fancy paper or colored paper. On most of our press kits, we have the jacket cover copied onto white card stock and cut to size. We then spray-mount that to the outside of the folder so it looks like it was printed. I recommend using white folders and white cardstock because it looks a bit more professional. The cover copies will run you about another $4.00 total. Always remember: bulk copying is cheaper.

There are literally thousands of variables for copies: You can use colored paper; just remember that dark colors do not copy well and do not fax well. Keep it light. You can have the contents cut to various sizes, although this adds a cutting cost charge from the copy center. You can use expensive folders or cheap folders. You can have letterhead printed by a professional print shop or generate it via your computer. Textured paper or regular bond, and on and on. Depending on your design, it can be more expensive or less; just know it will be expensive.

Step 4: Letterhead

Let's take a moment and discuss letterhead. You will need to put all the press materials, except the press clippings, on some type of letterhead. You will also need letterhead for follow-up memos to the media. Some of my clients provide me with their company letterhead. Otherwise, I usually create let-terhead for my authors, and I try to match the font used for the cover art as best as I can. This keeps things consistent and less confusing for the media. Another consideration is legibility. If I fax this, can the receiver read it? I always fax a piece to myself before I present it to the client for approval, just to make sure it's viable. Finally, does the letterhead look "clean"? Less com-plicated is better.

Most popular word-processing programs have a generous assortment of fonts and graphic stuff to help you create your own letterhead. I think cre-ating your own letterhead is tons of fun! It's also a lot cheaper than paying a printer a fortune to have it professionally designed and printed. You really don't need to waste your money on that. The computer letterhead should be just fine.

Step 5: Photographs

I have never met an author who likes to get her picture taken, but you're going to need a black-and-white photo, or "headshot." This is so the print media can include your photo with the article and for the television media to get a look at you to see if you are *"mediagenic"* (a word coined a few years back based, on "photogenic"). Basically, they want to make sure you don't have two heads. For your photo, you want to look your best. People are going to judge you by your photo. I know it's not fair, but life never is. I high-ly recommend working with an established professional photographer in your area to get the best shot possible. This can run anywhere from $150 to $500. Oftentimes, the publisher has already taken care of this for you. If that is so, ask the publisher for an original 8 x 10 glossy of the photo and take it to a photo duplicating company. Here in Los Angeles, with its flood of actors and wannabes, this is a big business. We have more photo companies than gas stations. You should be able to find a photo duplicating company in your local phone book. Go there and ask to see some of their past work, to see if they're any good. The duplicate photos should run about $100 for 500. The photos that you don't use make Great Holiday Gifts for Family and Friends!

Step 6: Postage

Don't forget to budget for postage. It adds up very quickly. Continuing with our example, if you are not going to include a copy of the book, but just send the press kit, the postage would be $1.21 x 50 = $60.50. If you are going to include the book, it will be $3.20 x 50 = $160.00. And that's at early-2001 rates! See what I mean? It adds up quickly. There is really no way to cut the cost on postage, because it is what it is. Don't forget that when you weigh the materials, you need to include the envelope and label, too. Sometimes this is just enough to push you into the next postage bracket. A little hint about postage: If you don't have a postage meter, I recommend you get the self-adhesive stamps. Fifty stamps is a lot of spit! That goes for mailing envelopes, too. Those bottles with the sponge on top always leak and make a big mess. Self-sealing envelopes cost a bit more, but they are worth it in time and saliva.

Step 7: Faxing

If you don't have a fax machine, get one. You can get a cheap one for about $100. Two more words: plain paper! Don't get one of those heat-sensitive fax machines. You'll have mounds of curling, scrolling fax paper all over the place. One trick I use is to load our fax machine with yellow bond paper. This way I can easily distinguish incoming faxes from outgoing. If it's yellow, it's incoming. If it's white, it's outgoing. You don't have to, of course, but it helps. You should also have a dedicated phone line just for the fax machine, or have the fax share your dedicated computer modem line. If you share the line, just remember that you can't receive faxes if you're surfing the Net.

Step 8: Overnight Delivery

Another big cost to consider. Most overnight delivery services have a Web site where you can plug in your Zip Code and the receiving Zip Code and they'll tell you how much it's going to cost. Sometimes you can use the cheaper two-day service and still track it. Sending a package across the country can sometimes cost more than $40.00! Look for the slowest (and thus cheapest) service you can possibly use, or you could be in debt before you know it.

You will probably need overnight delivery at one time or another, to respond quickly to a media request for another press kit or copy of your book. If a national publication needs this material right away, you will want to overnight it to them *pronto*. Do not try to save $10.00 and risk losing the interview by using snail mail. You also don't want to give them the time to change their minds.

Step 9: Messenger Services

Messenger services also use zone pricing. Use a messenger service only when it is absolutely necessary. One delivery can run you $25.00, depending on the zone, time, and speed of service.

Step 10: Phone Calls

Keep in mind that you may be making a lot of long-distance phone calls. Depending on how many media outlets you are calling and their locations, your phone bill can jump significantly from your pre-publicity bills. It could reach an additional $200 per month or more. If you make the calls during off-peak hours, you can save yourself some money.

OPTIONAL COSTS

The costs listed in the preceding section are prerequisite costs. There is really no way around those costs. There are other costs, though, that fall into the "optional" category. These are costs that you may incur if you want to do something extra to help publicize your book. Here are some additional costs to think about.

Travel

You may want to do a book signing or speaking engagement in another town; you may want to attend a convention; or you may book yourself for an interview in another state. Most television programs will not pay for your travel, so be sure to include hotel, car service, and meals in your travel budget.

Advance Copies of Your Book

Most publishers will give you a certain number of free copies as part of your deal. You will need to discuss publicity copies with your editor to determine if they will give you additional copies for promotional purposes. If you have a solid publicity plan, they will probably be more likely to give you an additional 100 copies to send to the media. If they won't give them to you, you will have to purchase them at the "author price," which is usually 25 to 40 percent off retail. For example, if your book is retailing for $24.99, subtracting 25 percent leaves your cost at $18.74 per copy. Multiply that by 50 copies and your cost is a whopping $937, plus shipping. Even if the publisher gives you 40 percent off, that is still $749.50. That is a lot of cash.

Special Events

Determining the cost of creating a special event is anyone's guess. It really depends on how fancy you make it. If it is a launch party for 100 people (from your big-mouth list), with cocktails and finger food, it can run you $500 to $1,000. Take great care, when creating a special event, to make sure that the benefits justify the expense.

Web Site Design and Maintenance

Almost every author has a Web site for her book(s). We'll get into the philosophical arguments about the Web and Web sites later. Should you choose to create a Web site, it will cost you $50.00 for a site setup fee and another $70.00 to register your Web site's name. Additionally, if you are not computer-savvy, you will need to hire someone to create the site for you. This can be very inexpensive if you get a high-school kid to do it for you, or it can be very expensive if you hire a professional. A professional can cost upward of $5,000. There are a lot of free programs offered on the Web that can help you create your own. If you do some research, you should be able to create a Web site without breaking the bank.

VNR/EPK

A video news release (VNR) or an electronic press kit (EPK) can be an effective way to reach a large segment of the media without leaving your home. Both are exactly what they sound like. They are also both expensive.

A **video news release** is the video version of a printed press release, with the addition of b-Roll, which is usually a video picture without sound or a direct interview. (For example, when a foreign dignitary visits the White House and does not grant an interview, the newscaster will tell the story with a voiceover while the viewers watch the video of the president and some Big Yaboo shaking hands.)

An **electronic press kit** will use video to explain all the items that are covered in the print press kit. Both attempt to entice the media into covering the subject on their programs. These methods are fairly expensive and thus are usually reserved for high-profile lawsuits or corporate launches.

The purpose of both VNRs and EPKs is to give television news programs videotape to run along with the spoken story. If you don't give them a direct interview, the benefit is that you, rather than the media, control the "sound bite." Most VNRs and EPKs are carefully constructed so that the media cannot take a statement out of context. Because television is a visual medium, they want moving pictures. If the only moving pictures they have are the ones that you supplied them, they're forced to use them.

Because of the expense, I have never used a VNR or EPK for authors, nor have I ever heard of any publishing house using them either. They use advertising, marketing, and publicity instead. It's cheaper and more effective. The only example I can give you to illustrate the benefits of using a VNR or EPK involves an entertainment lawsuit I worked on many years ago. At least it will give you an idea of how these work.

I worked on a lawsuit with a famous singer and her record company. A backup singer claimed that she sang co-lead vocals on several of the songs on an album, and she wanted to get paid for doing that. The media immediately went into "Milli Vanilli mode." (Remember the two guys who were caught lip-syncing on their award-winning album?)

We created a VNR for the media because it was the fastest way to get several key messages out to the media in the shortest period of time. We needed to clarify that the lawsuit was a contract dispute between the record company and the backup singer—*not* between the famous singer and the backup singer. That was step one. We also needed to clarify that this was a contract dispute and not a credit dispute. The plaintiff wanted the record sales money, not the glory. We also needed a visual picture of the famous singer saying, point-blank, "This is not true. This is my voice and my voice only on this record."

There was also an intangible point we had to make. Because we had the head of the recording company appear with our famous singer client at all times, it showed that the record company was behind their singer 100 percent and that they intended to go to trial and vindicate themselves and the reputation of the famous singer.

After we shot and edited the VNR, we sent it over a satellite feed that sends the pictures up to a satellite, from which television news programs could downlink (like downloading on a computer) the video and play it on their news programs. We made it available at about 3:30P.M. East Coast time so the East Coast news programs could run it on their 4:00P.M. news. We got amazing coverage, and by 11:00P.M. West Coast time, most major network news programs had changed their slant on the story, from "Famous singer is a fraud" to "A contract dispute between a backup singer and a record company is set to go to court in three days." The tone of the stories changed significantly from negative to positive for the record company and the famous singer.

We went to trial and presented the facts, and the jury threw out the case in less than 20 minutes—which is how long it takes to fill out all the jury forms! We won. As a side note, at trial, the record company presented the recording tapes, which I had a chance to listen to several times; the backup singer, in my opinion, was wrong. The record company spent hundreds of thousands of dollars on this lawsuit to protect its financial interests in one of its major recording stars. It was money well spent.

VNRs or EPKs are extremely costly. They can cost as much as $15,000 to $20,000 to create and send out. I highly recommend that if you're thinking of doing this, don't. Your money is better spent on hiring a professional publicist.

Book Signings and Parties

You will also have to decide if you want to try to do book signings or a launch party at your local bookstore. These two events fall in a gray area, as they are more promotional/marketing events than publicity vehicles. That being said, many newspapers and television news agencies in smaller towns may find a book signing by a local author worthy of coverage.

Events such as these can cut both ways. They can get you media coverage and they can also disappoint and frustrate you. Arranging a book signing is not all that difficult. It requires a lot of leg work and attention to detail, but you don't have to be a rocket scientist to set one up. The thing that concerns me the most about book signings is the psychological toll they can take if they don't go according to plan.

Chris wrote a great book on self-discovery and dealing with his own midlife crisis. Many men, during a midlife crisis, will trade in their wife of 30 years for a younger model, buy a sports car, and start wearing tacky jewelry. Not Chris. He decided to keep his family intact and, instead, build a sports car from a kit. The book uses the building of the car as a metaphor for Chris's own inner reconstruction. It's funny and poignant.

Chris lives on the East Coast, but was making a trip out to the Los Angeles area and wanted to have a book signing at a very popular bookstore on Sunset Boulevard. He arranged everything for the book signing and I made all the necessary preparations for media coverage. He was excited. I was very nervous. I'd been through book signings before with first-time authors, with mixed success.

Sure enough, no one showed for the book signing. I mean no one. No fans and no media. Chris was upset, but tried to take it all in stride and laugh it off. His feelings were hurt and he was starting to doubt his talent as a writer. The psychological toll this took on him lasted for three or four weeks. It took a phone call every day for me to finally talk him off the ledge. His expectations were too high and the results too disappointing. As his publicist, I should have tried harder to dissuade him from doing this, but his heart was set on it.

I've also seen friendships, not destroyed, but seriously altered by book signings. The author tells all his friends to come out to his book signing; some show up and are supportive and others do not. The author feels slighted by the no-shows and feels that these people are not really his friends and on and on. It can be a bigger mess than it's worth.

If you feel confident that this will work for you, I recommend that you contact the manager of your favorite local bookstore to see if she has any interest in allowing you to have an event at her store. You should also ask her if any past book signings have garnered any media attention. If she has never gotten the media to attend an event at her store, you may want to think twice before doing all the hard work of throwing one of these bashes.

If you get the green light, make sure you contact all the local media and make sure your newspaper includes the date in its "happenings" section.

Things you'll need to think about for a book signing:

- The location. At which bookstore do you want to have this?
- The day and time. Ask the store manager what is the heaviest traffic day at the store. Also find out what is the most effective time. Maybe a Thursday night is best, because the store has "open mic" night in its café. Maybe Saturday afternoon is best. Discuss this with the manager and work out the best day.
- Arrange this well in advance to allow the manager to include your book signing in the store's newsletter or any flyers it sends out to regular customers. This will also allow you to contact the appropriate local media to try to get the event covered.
- Location, location, location. Within the store itself, where will they set up your table? If it's way in the back, people may not even know you're there. Try to get a table set up in a heavy traffic area.
- Make sure you know where the coffee/water/bathrooms are. If you need any of the big three, you're going to have to make it quick. You don't want to lose potential sales while wandering around looking for one of these.

- If there are not a lot of people waiting in line, feel free to chat with the people when they're at your table. Taking a few minutes to give them some personal "face" time can get you three or four more book sales. They'll happily tell their friends and family about how nice you are and how interesting your chat was. They'll sell the book for you.

- Do not pull a diva thing. You are not a foreign dignitary or super-star. The people at the bookstore are trying to help you. Don't bite the hand that feeds. It is easy to get frustrated when things are not going perfectly and to lash out. Hold your tongue until you get home, then let it rip! Remember, you'll probably write another book and need the bookstore again.

- Try not to back your friends and family into a corner, demanding that they attend. This is your book, your business, and your respon-sibility—not theirs. Spouses are not required to attend. In fact, I recommend they don't. This should not be a shared experience. You are there to do a job, so do it. Spouses, I give you my full sup-port to stay home.

- Send out "save the date" invitations early (about five weeks) so people can do just that. Follow up with an official invitation about 10 days prior, as a reminder.

- Have no expectations and you will have complete fulfillment.

CHAPTER 7

SETTING REALISTIC GOALS

Well, you've evaluated your book, evaluated your resources, and determined a budget. Now you have to think about your goals—realistic goals. Now is the time to determine if you have the right book, enough help, and an accurate-enough budget to make this work. This is the scary part.

It is extremely important to set realistic goals for your publicity plan. You need to have a clear idea about what specifically you are trying to accomplish. Wanting your book to be wildly successful is not specific enough and not very helpful, from a practical point of view. What are your specific target goals? What do you hope to accomplish by the end of the publicity campaign?

Each author will have his own ideas about this. If you are a new author, you may not get on a national talk show, but you can speak at your local university, which will (you hope!) alert the local media to your speaking engagement. Same with your local libraries. They usually have an "in" with the local media and may get you some coverage. Even some of the popular bookstores have media contacts that may help get you some media coverage. Many non-profit organizations receive media coverage for some of their events. Keep your options open.

Smaller markets also mean less competition. If you live in a small town, you will probably find it easier to get media coverage, simply because the media have more time to devote to local people and issues. In contrast, in New York, there are more media opportunities than in a smaller town. However,

New York also has a lot more news to cover. Consumers in major metropolitan areas expect their news outlets to supply them with both local news coverage *and* national and international news coverage. The news outlets themselves want to be perceived as major players in the national and international scene. This can work against authors in general, and new authors in particular. More space may be given to world events and less to the literary world.

Established authors can reasonably expect more extensive media coverage than new authors, because they already have a track record. The media may already be familiar with their writing. These authors have also been through the process before and have learned shortcuts and more effective ways of gaining media coverage. In this case, experience does count.

Here are some questions you may find helpful in determining your specific goals. Keep in mind that the answers to these questions may change as you move through your publicity plan.

1. How many media outlets do you realistically want to cover your book? Come up with an exact number. How many newspapers? Magazines? Television programs? Radio shows? What led you to that number?

2. Combining the readership/listenership/viewership figures, how many people do you want to try to reach? Again, come up with an exact number.

3. What intangible goals do you want to accomplish? Make a specific list.

4. What will you have to accomplish to consider this a successful publicity campaign? Make a specific list.

5. What pitfalls can you anticipate? Make a specific list. Is there anything you can do before you begin your publicity plan to counteract the obstacles? What? Why do you think these will work?

If you know specifically what you are trying to accomplish, you will be better prepared to face the challenges that lay ahead. This will also help you determine what and how much you will need to do to succeed. It will also keep you sane during those insane times by helping you see more clearly that things really are going better than you might have thought. It will help you keep a proper perspective.

PSYCHOLOGICAL STRESS AND PUBLICITY

The psychological stress of executing a publicity plan, on you and those around you, can be enormous. Working full-time and trying to run a publicity campaign is, as I've said, exhausting. You may miss many of your son's Little League games, a family celebration or two, or an anniversary. Your employer may not be too happy about your outside activities, and your family may start to resent your absence. Add to that the worry about the success of the book and you have a lot of stress. By keeping your finger on the emotional pulse of your family and friends, you should be able to get through this just fine. I also believe that if you include your family and friends in this process, they'll be more understanding and help to alleviate some of the pressure.

If you thought all those rejection letters from publishers were difficult to handle, know that the media rejections can be even worse. Sometimes an editor will simply say, "Not interested," and hang up, before you even get a chance to finish your pitch. Or one may say, "Well, send it again, and I'll take a look at it," and then never return your phone call. Try not to take rejection from the media personally, even though that's very difficult. Keeping your perspective and a positive attitude can be exhausting.

Getting stressed out because you are not seeing great tangible results, and because you are spending more time and money than you anticipated, can really take its toll. If that starts to happen, reevaluate your plan. Can you slow down a little? Can you get more help? Can you revamp your plan into a more workable one? Try to move around the brick wall, not through it.

REALISTIC GOALS AND SUCCESS

Much of the stress related to publicity can be attributed to having unrealistic goals. The truth is, if you are a first-time author, you probably will not be on *Oprah.* You probably will not make the front page of the *New York Times.* You probably will not get a five-page full-color layout in *Vanity Fair.* And you probably won't get your own radio show. You might, but probably not.

If you are focusing on a local publicity campaign, you probably will get a little coverage in your local paper, maybe a shot on some of the local radio stations, and maybe a book signing or two. The more press kits you send out, the greater your chances of success. For a first-time author, if you can potentially reach 500,000 to 1,000,000 people, I would consider that a success. You may reach these numbers from 2 major media outlets, or you may reach them from 15 smaller outlets. It just depends.

Keep in mind that everyone has to start somewhere. For this book, you may get local coverage; on your next, you may get regional coverage; on your next, you may get national coverage. It is all a process and it all takes time. *You must have realistic expectations or you will be miserable.*

If you can answer "yes" to the following questions, you probably have a media-friendly book and reasonable expectations and should proceed with your publicity plan.

1. Is my book media friendly? Is the subject matter of interest to a wide spectrum of consumers?

2. As an author, will my story be of interest to the media and the consumer?

3. Are there news tie-ins that fit with my book?

4. At minimum, is there a specific group of people that would be interested in my book?

5. Do I have an accurate and interesting title? Is the artwork interesting?

6. Can I afford to do this? Can I afford to fail? Remember, you will probably never see this money again. It's like gambling in Las Vegas, where you only take as much as you can afford to lose.

7. Do I have enough people around to help me with some of the work? Can I do this all by myself if I have to?

8. Do I have the confidence to contact the right people in those big buildings?

9. Do I have the time to do this?

10. Do I have the ability/money/time to get the necessary contact information on the media and compile mailing lists?

11. Am I determined enough to see this through?

12. Can I overcome my fear about doing something I have never done before?

13. Do I have the support of my publisher?

14. Can I stay focused on my current responsibilities, like my family and my job, and still do this? (There is no point in doing this if it might cause you to lose your job or your significant other.)

15. Again, can I afford to fail?

CHAPTER 8

MEDIA—
AN OVERVIEW

Before I discuss all the different types of media, I think it is important to discuss media in general terms.

The New International Webster's Comprehensive Dictionary of the English Language (1996 edition) defines the term *media* as: "Means of disseminating information, entertainment, etc., such as books, newspapers, radio, television, motion pictures, and magazines." For the purposes of publicity and this book, it can also include the people who work in these areas.

It's important that you understand a few things about the media. The following are my opinions, jaded as they may be, about the media and are born of direct life experience. They are opinions based on how things actually are, as opposed to how they should be. Here are my random thoughts:

- The media do not owe you an interview. In fact, they don't owe you a darned thing. They don't owe you a return phone call. They don't owe you polite conversation. They don't owe you the time of day. They don't even owe you a good program. They owe their advertisers and their bosses. Period. If you don't like their product, don't watch it, don't listen to it, or don't read it.

- You need the media more than they need you. They have enough story ideas for a month of Sundays. Be nice to them even if they aren't very nice to you. They have the power—grovel accordingly.

- Reporters, editors, and producers are generally good people who often are stuck in a bad situation. They have a tough job trying to please network executives or editors-in-chief who, oftentimes, wouldn't know a good story if it bit them on the ankle.

- The budget constraints within which the media people have to work are often beyond belief. Budget cuts lower morale and tie the reporter's or producer's hands. Good stories are sometimes killed because of budget considerations. They are constantly frustrated.

- The media is rife with herd mentality. There is little difference among the different morning shows, local newscasts, or newspapers. You've seen one, you've seen 'em all. The same holds true for network prime-time television programs. Someone once said that there hasn't been an original idea in Hollywood in 50 years. The same is true of the news business, in my opinion. If you have something new for them, it will be that much harder to convince them to cover it.

- If you make an effort to understand what they do, they will make an effort to help you. If you give them attitude, they won't help you.

- Be succinct and don't waste their time; they like that.

- Many media people have a great sense of humor—at the right time in the right place.

- The media have a different perception of time than you do. You know how five minutes seems like forever when you're waiting in line at the bank or in your doctor's office? The bank teller or doctor thinks the day is flying by. You, in contrast, feel like you could have repainted your house by now. The same applies to the media. They're doing a million things all at once. You have to give them a chance to look over the material, have meetings about it, and free up some time to do something with your book. Two or three days for them is a drop in the bucket. Be patient.

WHERE STORIES COME FROM

Many people do not know where stories come from. Every few years some media outlet does a fun man-on-the-street interview, asking children and adults, "Where does hamburger come from?" The always-startling answer is invariably, "From the supermarket." Sad, really. If you ask the same people, "Where do media stories come from?" they would probably answer, "From the newspaper."

If you're keeping score, that would be wrong.

All of the stories you read or see everyday come from one of three places. First, journalists get the inside scoop from their own contacts that they have nurtured over the years; because of these relationships, they get information that's not otherwise generally available for their stories. When you see "Exclusive!" accompanying an article, chances are that the journalist has an informant who tipped her off. Second, journalists cannibalize stories from other journalists. This is the me-too school of journalism. If everyone else is talking about this, I should too! Again, it's the herd mentality. Third, they get stories from publicists. There is no way a journalist can keep abreast of all major news events. If he tried, he'd go insane (some have). This is where publicists are helpful. Publicists will contact a journalist whom they think would be interested in this little facet of our world. If the journalist likes it, he will write a story about it. We like this one the best.

Whichever way you slice this, all stories have to pass the "who cares?" test. The first thought to run through any journalist's mind will be, "Who is really going to care about this story?" If they come up with an answer that matches their demographic, they'll carefully consider the story. The next question they will ask themselves is, "So what?" Let's say your toys are going to be offered at three new national department stores. "*So what?!* So I'm happy for you, what do you want from me?" There is no real news story. If the addition of these three new stores makes your company the largest toy distributor in the United States, *now* you have a pretty good answer to "so what?"

CAN YOUR BOOK PASS THE "SO WHAT" TEST?

It is important that you develop the skill of being able to *honestly* put yourself in the shoes of the media. Whatever you wrote about may be frightfully important to you and how you view the world. That being said, you must allow for the fact that others will not share that view. Sometimes an ego-blasting "no" from the media can be explained and sometimes it can't. There is usually a compelling reason why they are not interested, you just can't see it—and sometimes you never will. Be honest with yourself. Ask yourself if this is really going to be of interest to a large majority of people. Notice I didn't say "should"; I said "is."

This is an honest-to-Pete true story. This particular writer happened to be a woman, but I've gotten equally bizarre concepts from men and women alike. This is not a gender-specific malady.

I was asked to speak at a writer's conference a few years back. After a general lecture, the audience broke down into smaller groups. The writers were told to give me a brief descriptions of their book so I could give them each a quick take on its media-friendliness.

One woman had written a book about how to incorporate old beer cans into articles of clothing (hats, vests, etc.) by knitting cut-out panels of aluminum beer cans together. I began to explain to this lady that her market was limited from a consumer point of view, and even more limited from a media point of view.

Although "being green" is a hot topic these days, I went out on a limb and told this author that I didn't think many people would be willing to take the time (and risk of personal injury) to cut out panels from their beer cans, much less know how to knit them into a sweater-vest. Let's face it, if you've got enough beer cans to make an entire ensemble, you probably shouldn't be playing with sharp objects.

More to the point, despite the odd recycling angle, the media are not going to be interested in this story. It's not something their readers/viewers/listeners are going to want to hear about. Some might, but not the majority. The majority always wins with the media. If their demographic won't be interested, the media will reject the idea.

Although the author felt very strongly about this, most people would find it a bit silly. She had the right idea (i.e., environmental concerns), she just went about expressing it in a less effective way than she might have. She's not wrong, by the way; she just picked a path that's less likely to succeed than, say, *"How to Start a Recycling Program in Your Home Town."* That would've gotten her some media coverage and sold some books.

To finish up this ugly moment in my life, the author went after me with both barrels. She was absolutely livid that I didn't "get" it. Who the hell was I to tell her what was going to work or not?! She then proceeded to string together a fabulous strand of obscenities that proved she really did have a way with words, she just needed a little guidance with her material.

I tell people all the time: Think about the public relations realities *before* you even start writing the outline for your book.

Think of this during the idea stage of the writing process:

- Who *really* is going to be interested in this?
- What media outlets will be interested in writing about your story?

Please do not waste a year of your life writing something no one except family and friends will ever read—unless that is your goal. Make sure your book passes the "so what?" test.

A DAY IN THE LIFE OF A PRODUCER

If you have a clear understanding of the day-to-day routine of the media, you will have a better chance of getting the materials to the right person at the right time, thereby increasing the likelihood of getting an interview. Media folks' routines are not like any routine you have ever experienced, so you may want to pay particularly close attention to this section. Now, of course, they all wake up, take a shower, brush their teeth (we hope!), and head out the door. That is where the similarities between your life and theirs end.

I'll base the next example on an associate producer friend of mine who worked on a popular afternoon talk show (no, not *Oprah,* and stop guessing because I'm not telling). As an associate producer, his job is to come up with ideas for shows, present them to his boss (the executive producer), and find guests to appear on the approved shows. It's a tough job and the hours are terrible. Every morning he would walk into the studio and be greeted by a wall of sound: arguing, phones ringing off the hook, fax machines beeping, copy machine noises, more arguing, and 200 phone calls all taking place at the same time. It was organized chaos.

Then he would go through the faxes that had come in overnight, grab a cup of coffee, and check his phone messages (using the speakerphone), while simultaneously checking his e-mail messages on his computer. Sometimes, he tells me, he had 35 to 40 faxes, 30 phone messages, and 60 to 70 e-mails—and he'd only been out of the office for 5 hours. He would sort and prioritize all this stuff and get started on the work that had to be done before that day's taping, as well as preparing for the next show. Invariably, one of his guests would get cold feet and he would have to spend 45 minutes talking them back into appearing (and answering e-mails at the same time). Once that was done, the phone calls started for the next day's show. Most days he started at 8A.M. and didn't leave until 10P.M. Sometimes more, sometimes less. It was fun, but he felt like he lived in a constant state of "fight-or-flight."

Producers are some of the most competitive people you'll ever meet. Every producer's goal is to get his segment on the air before anyone else. The office politics at a television talk show makes Congress look like a bunch of amateurs. I just caught a rebroadcast of a behind-the-scenes documentary about *60 Minutes.* If you want to witness competition, get a copy of that documentary. I've been told though, that *60 Minutes* was fairly civilized compared to other shows. The Discovery Channel, A&E, and

The Learning Channel often have behind-the-scenes programs that I highly recommend you watch, just to get a sense of the media world. Also, I started watching the White House briefings on C-SPAN. Quite an education.

Another suggestion: If you're ever in Atlanta, I recommend taking the tour of CNN. It is an impressive operation and you can catch a glimpse of the hard-news business in action. You can also call your local television stations and see if they offer guided tours. You never know who you will meet. The same holds true for newspapers and radio stations. The worst they can do is say "no."

Keep an eye on your local newspaper for any seminars being given by local or national media people. It's a great way to schmooze a media person in a less stressful environment. Most media people love to answer questions about what they do. Who doesn't? You just have to pick the right time and the right place. Be reasonable and don't stalk the poor people.

The bottom line is that you are going to have to understand the media so you know how to use them effectively.

DIFFERENT TYPES OF MEDIA

M edia can be broken down into two categories: print and electronic. Don't get nervous about the "electronic." That's just a fancy name for television and radio. I discuss the Internet in a separate section. First, I'm going to tell you about each of the media types and then, in Chapter 11, I'll tell you how to find them.

Whether they are print or electronic, all media have two things in common. One, they all have a defined lead time. A **lead time** is the amount of advance time they need to include a story about your book in their publication or on their program. It can range from a matter of minutes (for a breaking news story for television) to months (for a monthly print publication). Two, they are all concerned about their demographics, or who is watching their program, listening to their radio show, or reading their publication.

The following box contains a quick reference chart to help clarify some of this.

LEAD TIMES AND DEMOGRAPHICS

Every form of media has a lead time, which is how far they plan ahead to release their stories or publications to the public. Lead times vary from very long to very short, depending on the medium.

- Monthly magazines are considered long leads because they typically work three to six months in advance (sometimes explained as "working four months out").

continued

LEAD TIMES AND DEMOGRAPHICS (CONTINUED)

- Weekly magazines work about three or four weeks ahead.

- Newspapers, one to three days, unless it is breaking news.

- Weekly newspapers, about two weeks.

- Television talk shows, four to six weeks ahead.

- Morning shows, one to two weeks.

- Evening news magazines vary depending on the story, but generally about a month.

- Radio, generally about two weeks.

This means that you have to send your materials at the right time to make a particular medium's deadline if you want your stuff to appear at a specific time.

Demographics tallies the similarities among viewers/listeners/readers. The information generally concerns age, race, economic background, and habits.

If you know that the primary demographic of a magazine is young girls between the ages of 13 and 17, and your book is about retirement, you probably wouldn't want to send your materials to this magazine. There would be no point in wasting the stamp, because the magazine's demographics do not fit your material.

Knowing the demographic information can save you a lot of time and money.

Hint: You can call the ad sales department at any media outlet and request this information. They will also give you an editorial calendar that will alert you to special issues or subjects they plan to cover in the coming months.

PRINT MEDIA

As I stated earlier, media comes in two flavors: print and electronic. Print media include magazines and newspapers. One might also consider newsletters a part of the print media. That one is a little iffy only because newsletters do not have the checks and balances and the same journalistic standards as magazines and newspapers. They typically are generated by one main person or a select few who share the same editorial bent.

Let's begin our fascinating look into the bowels of media with magazines.

Magazines

There are several different types of magazines. They are distinguished not only by subject matter, but also by the frequency with which they are published.

- Some are monthly *(Cosmopolitan, Publish Magazine)*
- Some are quarterly; usually spring, summer, winter, and fall *(Reform Judaism, Real Estate Business)*
- Some come out eight times a year; I don't know why and I don't know what the technical name for "eight times a year" is *(The Crisis, BC Outdoors)*
- Others come out bimonthly *(Physical Therapy Products Review, Electronics Specifier)*
- Some come out weekly *(Time, Newsweek, Entertainment Weekly)*
- There are no daily magazines that I know of.

It's extremely important that you do your research before you start sending out press materials. You must plan ahead. *Most monthly magazines work three to four issues ahead.* That is really crucial to understand. If a magazine is going to publish an article about your book, they are going to want it in the issue that corresponds with the launch of your book.

In other words, if your book will be ready for the public in June, the magazines are going to want to include the corresponding articles in their June issues. For a monthly, that means sending them a review copy and your information in January or February! Many times the publishers don't even have a review copy available that early, which makes it more difficult to get a review or feature into a monthly magazine.

Sometimes you can get around this if you have a subject that is what we call "evergreen," and the magazine will fudge the deadline. For these evergreen stories, it doesn't matter what time of year it is. They can run these whenever they want to without it seeming out of place. They also love lists. Some examples are:

- 10 Ways to Lower Your Cholesterol!
- 7 Secrets to Firmer Buns!
- 5 Meals in 20 Minutes!
- 10 Way to Boss Your Boss—and Not Get Fired!

Here are some examples of subjects that are time-critical or season-dependent and would not be considered evergreen:

- Stocking Stuffers for under $10.
- Special Valentine's Ideas for Newlyweds.
- Tools to Buy for Father's Day.
- Yom Kippur—Creating a Tradition.

It would look strange to run the "Valentine's Ideas" in August, right? You get the point, I trust.

So, if you're going to try to buck the system, you have to know the right way to do it. Think before you send. Those are words to live by. They should go right next to "Never Drink and Type."

Another thing to think about regarding magazines is the magazine itself.

- Are you sending your materials to the appropriate magazine?
- Does this magazine have columnists who publish in each issue and who might be predisposed to write about your book?
- Does this magazine do special issues that focus on a subject appropriate to your book?

Learn as much as possible about where you're sending your materials. It wastes money and time sending materials to someone who is not likely to be interested.

Newspapers

The good news is that almost everything we've just discussed regarding magazines also applies to newspapers. The only difference is in lead times. Most daily or weekly newspapers have a short lead time; anywhere from a week to a matter of hours, depending on news events of the day and the subject matter of your book.

If you've written a book about the erosion of the congregation within the Catholic Church, keep your eyes peeled! As soon as you see a story in the paper about the Catholic Church (pro or con), call or fax (fax is better, in this case) the reporter who wrote the story or the appropriate editor and tell him that you've written a book that deals with a related subject and that you would make yourself available to them if they wanted to write a sidebar story about the erosion of the congregation within the Catholic Church. (A *sidebar* is a smaller story that takes one element of a major story and highlights an interesting point or explains something that most readers may not understand. It's a good way to get your foot in the door.) This is a proactive step. You have to do the legwork.

I read two or three major newspapers every day, subscribe to many magazines, watch local and national television news, and check the Internet several times a day. It's vital that you keep abreast of news events. It could be (and oftentimes is) the best way to get publicity about your book.

All the other principles apply. Send to the appropriate person at the appropriate time. You don't want your materials to get there too much before your book is ready. That's "letting the materials get cold." You *don't* want that. Too soon, and the materials will get shoved into a drawer; too late, and they won't be able to use them.

Also, don't forget the "local-boy-does-good" angle. Many smaller newspapers like that type of story. If you grew up in another city and have only recently moved, call your old paper anyway. Many of your old friends will be interested in your success.

Once you figure out all of this, the next question is: To whom do I send my book and press kit materials? Here is a very brief explanation of some of the job titles. Again, there are exceptions to all of these.

Publisher or General Manager

The publisher or general manager is the head honcho. She owns or has complete control of the overall operations of the publication or television station. She's generally most concerned with the financial aspects of the publication. Don't send stuff to the publisher/GM unless that's the only name you can find. Some smaller publications only list the publisher because the newspaper is a one-man band, so to speak, so you're sort of stuck. Call first to make sure there is no one else to send it to. If the person named is the only one, go ahead and send it. Magazines and newspapers use both of these titles; television uses only general manager.

Editor-In-Chief

While the publisher is jet-setting around the world, playing golf or suntanning in Aruba, the editor-in-chief is doing all the work. He is primarily responsible for all editorial content in the publication. Typically, he only meets with each department head and sets the tone or ground rules about the content each department is going to have to deliver for each issue. Still really high-up. Don't send stuff to the editor-in-chief unless absolutely necessary. This title is used by magazines and newspapers.

Managing Editor or Bureau Chief

This is the editor who directs the daily news operation. This is somewhat different from the editor-in-chief, in that the managing editor is most concerned with the hard news stories that will appear in the publication (as opposed to "fluff" pieces). A *bureau chief* is the director of the news operation in a location other than the originating city. For example, the *New York Times* has offices or "bureaus" in Washington, D.C., Chicago, and Europe, for several reasons. Legislation approved in Washington, D.C., can have a great impact on business practices in New York, as might a terrorist bombing in Europe. Having a local bureau allows news agencies to create relationships with the locals that can help them get the most accurate information in the fastest possible manner. I wouldn't send a managing editor or bureau chief anything unless absolutely necessary. These titles apply to certain employees of magazines, newspapers, and sometimes to television news programs. (Peter Jennings holds the title of managing editor of his nightly news broadcast.)

Senior Editor or Executive Editor

A senior or executive editor is like the chief of staff. He's the right-hand guy to the editor-in-chief or managing editor. Many publications have five or six of these editors, each handling specific areas or topics such as foreign, domestic, metro, high-tech, etc. This is a good person to send material to, *providing the publication doesn't have a specific editor for your topic.* The air is still rarified here, though. This title is used by magazines and newspapers.

Specific Senior Editor, Section Editor, Senior Writer, or Features Editor

Now we're talking! Most publications have departmental breakdowns within the overall infrastructure. This is where you want to send your stuff. Try to find the appropriate editor and address your correspondence to her. For example, if your book is fashion-related, you would send it to the Lifestyle or Fashion editor. You can usually find that person's name in the front of the magazine. If not, pick up the phone and ask the receptionist which editor handles whatever you are looking for. You may get the verbal equivalent of eye-rolling, but so what! It never hurts to ask. Be nice and polite and eventually you'll get the information you're looking for.

Assignment Editor or Line Editor

An assignment editor works directly with the reporters, developing story ideas. This is another good person to contact. These editors know the strengths and weaknesses of their reporters, as well as what the reporters are already working on, and can generally bend the ear of the editors above them—providing that they feel the story has merit. Magazines, newspapers, and local and national television news programs usually all have assignment editors.

City Desk Editor or Metro Editor

A city desk or metro editor is primarily concerned with local news stories, like city council meetings, local drive-by shootings, local school test scores, weather, local strikes, and so on. Again, she is more involved with hard news. If your press release angle fits this category, this is the person to contact. If you are trying to get a profile story or lifestyle trend story, this is not the person to contact.

Reporter or Correspondent

Reporters and correspondents are the people who write the stories. The difference between a reporter and a correspondent is that the reporter works out of the primary newsroom and the correspondent typically writes from a bureau or anywhere other than the primary newsroom. By the way, a freelance writer is a reporter hired on a per-story basis and is not an employee of the newspaper. Unless you personally know the freelancer and know that he has pull at the publication, don't send materials or pitch a story to that person. It's normally a waste of time and money. If you read a story in the newspaper that is related to your angle, jot down the reporter's name from the byline and send your materials to him. Reporters are found in all news media.

Columnist

If you read a columnist's column consistently, you can learn some personal details about her that may spark an idea for you. For example, if you know the columnist was in the Marine Corps, and your protagonist is a Marine, you may want to send the columnist a copy of your book with a personal note enclosed, telling him you thought he might like to read this. It can't hurt. You can find columnists in magazines and newspapers.

Copy Editor

This is another person to whom you do not want to send material. This is the person who works on stories *after* they have already been written. He does just what the job description says: edits the copy of the story. If you send your material to copy editors, they'll just throw it out. It's "not my union," as they say.

Book Reviewers

I purposely waited until now to discuss book reviewers. Getting a review copy of your book to book reviewers in local, national, and regional media outlets (which include print and electronic media) is usually the responsibility of the publisher. This is important for three reasons.

- First, it is extremely costly to send out a mass mailing to so many outlets. I strongly believe that this cost should be incurred by the publisher, *not* the author. These costs are factored into the equation by the publisher before it closes the deal with the author.

- Second, book reviewers expect to receive the latest books directly from the publishers. If they receive it directly from the author (or personal publicist), that sends up a red flag—intentional or not—that the publisher is not behind the book. An analogy can be drawn to the film industry: If the studio does not have a preopening screening for the media, that generally implies that the film is in trouble. That may be true or it may not be. However, the negative impression it creates is difficult to overcome.

- Finally, book reviewers are insulated. They don't like to speak directly with authors. They say it's to remain objective. I think it's probably more about getting hundreds of calls from authors and not having enough time to read the mountain of materials they get sent each month. If you send material to writers who are only book reviewers, don't contact them. Leave them alone. Just send them the book and move on. The only thing you can do is read the book review section each week and see if a review of your book appears there.

If you are self-publishing and are going to be responsible for contacting book reviewers, there are a couple of things to keep in mind. First, book reviews are done primarily from galleys. This means that you will have to have galley copies (or page proofs) ready according to the media lead times *prior to the actual publication date.* The sooner you have galleys ready, the better. Second, these don't have to be terribly pretty. You can go to your local copy center and have bound galleys made. Make sure you clearly mark the galleys as follows: "Uncorrected proof. Do not quote without prior permission." That way they won't print a typo or a section that you have already rewritten.

You have to be able to read when it comes to print media. Not so with electronic media. The beauty of electronic media is that you can multitask and learn about the world around you at the same time. You can lick stamps and watch the news at the same time. You can make pitch calls from your car phone and listen to the all-news radio program at the same time. Electronic media also reach more people than print media.

Bowing to peer pressure, I am also going to include a section on the Internet as an additional media genre. I also discuss why I'm not completely convinced of its usefulness as a publicity tool at this time.

ELECTRONIC MEDIA

Before I get into the nuts and bolts of electronic media, I must explain that there is a method to my madness. As we go through each of these types of media, remember that the process is *additive.* Many of the same points that applied to print media also apply to television and radio. Know your media outlet, find out who to send your stuff to, and follow up with phone calls and fax reminders. (More on that later.) Here I'm only going to discuss things that are particular to each type of electronic media outlet.

Local Television

Morning News Programs

Most metropolitan cities have their own morning news programs. In Los Angeles, for example, we have the *KTLA Morning News*. This is a wacky group of people who read the news and do some fun human-interest stories to break up the monotony of reporting that our world is going to hell in a handbasket. They may be interested in your personal story and, hence, your book. Send your material to an associate producer or segment producer. They are the people that pitch story ideas to the executive producer. They are generally easier to get to than the executive producer.

I don't recommend sending your material to the show hosts—they generally just read the news, but don't choose what they read. You'll also irritate the segment producers who are supposed to be coming up with brilliant stories. If the host pushes you and your book, the segment producer may be a bit frosty upon your arrival at the studio.

There is also the "Good Day *Whatever Your Town Name Is.*" If a television station in your area has one or more of these types of programs, go ahead and send your stuff there, *providing you feel strongly that it is something they would be interested in.*

The key is to watch all of these programs over the course of a month or so, to get the feel of what types of non-news stories they cover. Do they focus on local high school activities? The arts? Cars? Fashion? If you are going to give yourself a crash course on the local morning shows, you may want to keep a log or journal detailing the stories for that month. It'll help remind you later on when you're ready to send your press materials out. I think this is a good idea even for the national morning shows and afternoon talk shows.

Local Evening News

Your local evening news programs may also be interested in you and your book. If you can come up with an appropriate, newsworthy angle, they may interview you. For example, if you are a doctor and the first one in your area to perform a particular surgery, that would fall under the public interest or health category. The news program looks good by helping the community get healthier, and you get media exposure. Both of you win.

Unfortunately, if you've written a spy thriller, they may have a difficult time fitting you in. You should put yourself in the news director's shoes. She's got a thousand stories she can tell each day, no thanks to guns and car chases, and now you want her to talk about a *spy novel?* Very tough sell. Now, if you were a retired *real* spy who'd written a book ... now that might be something.

Also, don't forget about your local public affairs programs. Each local television station usually carries several hours of public service programming. They often run them at off-peak hours or on Sunday mornings. See if your book might be of interest to one of these programs.

TELEVISION SWEEP PERIODS

Three times a year, national and local television stations have a month-long "sweeps" period to determine new rates for advertising on their programs. This happens in November, February, and May of each year. This is typically when news programs run sexy or tabloid-like stories to entice viewers to watch their news broadcasts. This increases their ratings, and thus they can charge more for commercial time throughout the year. You can tell this is happening when you see news programs promoting "a special report on the latest bikini fashions for the summer," or when prime-time programs run "a very special episode."

If you can create a flashy angle for your book, this is the time to send it out to the news programs.

National Television

A word about national television. National television is the big leagues. It is the difference between television programs that may cost only tens of thousands of dollars (local) and those that cost multi-millions of dollars (national). The financial stakes are higher for the production entity and many more people are watching. You will not get a second chance with a national outlet. If you screw it up, that's it. They have memories like elephants. Contacting national media to book an interview requires a great deal of finesse.

The other thing to keep in mind is that (generally) your book will have to be available nationally—the Internet doesn't usually count, unless your story is of topical interest—if you want them to cover your book. This usually means New York, Chicago, and Los Angeles.

If you choose to take the big plunge and approach national television outlets, here are some things to keep in mind. First off, you would contact one of the producers or segment producers. If you call the general number of the program, someone can steer you to the right person. Don't bother with the executive producers; they have a million other things they're worrying about.

If you should get the correct producer on the phone, be brief and get to the point. Be very *very* brief. Producers are extremely busy, so you don't want to irritate them with the entire history of your project. Give them the concise version of your press release and let them decide if they want to know more. Be professional-friendly, not next-door-neighbor-friendly. There is a sample pitch script coming up later in the book to get you started in the right direction.

Remember to make sure that your stuff is appropriate for a national audience.

Network News

For network news programs, your subject must be timely *and* of interest to a majority of people on a national level. Period. If your book is not about government, politics, or international trade, you're probably out of luck. The only exception might be as a "person of the week." You'd have to save 60 small children from a burning building and put yourself in harm's way to win that one, but anything's possible.

Weekly News Magazines

Weekly TV news magazines, such as *Dateline* or *20/20,* want stories that have a beginning, a middle, and an end. Each story must also be personalized. What all this means is that if your book exposes local government corruption, you need to find Birtha Littlespoon, age 85, whose life savings were siphoned off by a corrupt government agency and now lives on dog food because of those bad old men. I'm exaggerating, but not by much. These programs have to be able to tell a complete mini-story in about 12 minutes. A happy ending doesn't hurt either. The final shot should be Birtha eating her first turkey dinner in 57 years with her family (who wouldn't give her a dime while she was knee-deep in dog food; you'd be surprised at how much people "care" when they're going to be on television).

Daytime Talk Shows

I'm going to go on a rant, here. You may want to head for the nearest bomb shelter.

Oprah. I lied when I told you that I wrote this book for only two reasons. If I can also get you to understand the whole "Oprah thing," I can die a happy man. You're not going to like what I'm about to write, but I swear it is the truth! (Not the politician kind of truth, but the real kind.)

There is very little *anyone* can do these days to get you or your book on *Oprah*.

Period.

I'm going to say it again and put it in a box for emphasis.

> There is very little *anyone* can do these days to get you or your book on *Oprah*.

Now I'll tell you why. You know those dumpsters they use at office buildings and apartment complexes? They're those big green or brown metal things with flaps for lids? Well, I've been told by a former employee that her book club has become so successful that Oprah receives about *11 of those dumpsters worth of new books each and every week*. Sometimes more! There are literally 11 dumpsters in the main lobby of Oprah's office building—not at the studio, at their offices—and these are filled to beyond-capacity each week.

Because of the overwhelming response and the constant arm-twisting from publicists and publishers, Oprah has decided that she will go to her *own* bookstores and pick her *own* books, thank you very much. Gail or Stedman may nudge her, but she's on her own. You can certainly send a copy there, but be aware that a staff person probably just snagged it and gave it to his mom as a birthday present. Your book will very likely NEVER BE TOUCHED BY THE GREAT ONE, HERSELF.

Can you tell that I've had this discussion with *every single author* I have every worked with?

I'm sorry, but it's true. Forget about Oprah. There are several other fish in the sea. Contact Jenny, Sally, Montel, Jerry, Leeza, Maury; what the heck, contact Judge Judy! Just don't bother with Oprah. If she wants you, she'll let you know.

I also want to tell you that at all of these programs, each segment producer has her own specialty. Some only work on celebrity guests, some on books, others only on women's issues, and so on. It's important to find out who does what *before* you send material. If you send it to the wrong person, they'll just throw it out. Call or research first.

Again, research the programs that seem the most likely to be interested in your subject, find the right contact person, and follow up with a phone call.

Radio

Radio. Specifically, talk radio. Every city and almost every town has talk radio. If yours doesn't, you're probably living in Antarctica. The same principles apply: Listen to and research the programs that seem the most likely to be interested in your subject, find the right contact person, and follow up with a phone call.

The best thing about doing radio is that you don't always have to be physically in the studio with the host. Most radio programs have the technology to do what is called a **phoner**. All that means is that if you are booked to appear at 5:00A.M., you can stay in your jammies and fuzzy slippers, have a cup of coffee, grab your phone, and be interviewed! No showering or Sunday clothes necessary. Radio talk shows are also great because you can do a million of these in one day. You don't have to drag yourself all over the country. You can give an interview for New York at 5:00A.M. and another interview for Dallas at 5:15A.M. and be back in bed by 5:30A.M. Just don't double-book a time slot, and take the answering machine off!

It is also important to note that a radio station may want you "in-studio," that is physically in the studio with the host. If that is the case, make sure you give yourself plenty of getting-lost time. Some studios are in out-of-the-way places and are not clearly marked. This is most likely so our brains won't fry from close proximity to broadcast energy fields, and to keep crazy people from showing up on their doorsteps.

Radio programs sometimes have multiple guests or phone-in callers. It is important that you stay on message. Don't get dragged into a philosophical argument with a crazy caller. Keep talking specifically about your book and keep saying the title. Remember that you are there to entice the audience to go buy the book, not tell them the whole story. A good rule of thumb is to say the title no more than three times within a seven-minute segment. The host will say it once to introduce you and another time to thank you for being on the program. That's enough. If the host doesn't, by all means repeat away!

Another thing to think about is that local radio programs change constantly. They are constantly moving shows around, cancelling them, or switching hosts. Keep up with those types of changes. It's embarrassing to contact a radio station and be told that that show went off the air two years ago.

INTERNET

I am still a bit ambivalent about the Internet as a publicity tool. I don't know if it is just that it is new and untested, or that it is so time-consuming and probably not worth the minimal payoff you'll probably get. The thoughts I am about to express are my personal opinions and gut reaction to what I have seen over the last two or three years. Keep in mind that I may change my mind about all of this next week. Things move rapidly in this electronic world, and no one knows what's going to happen next week with the Internet. If anyone tells you differently, they're lying.

The Internet is probably the most important marketing tool created in the 20th century—and now, the 21st century. Never before has the consumer been able to learn so much about the world just by sitting in a chair and staring at a screen. I have seen live television shots from the space shuttle looking back down on Earth, something my grandparents could never even have imagined. I have toured the art galleries of Paris, found medical information written so even *I* can understand it, gotten free legal advice, and done a million other things just sitting at my desk.

In addition, I have hundreds of thousands of choices if I want to buy a music CD, a video, or a book that's been out of print for 10 years. I can buy clothes, watches, canoes, dogs, and even a car online. I can talk to someone on the other side of the world and even see them, in real time. All these choices and abilities are a direct result of the Internet.

As a marketing tool, the Internet is fantastic! Being able to access goods and services that have never before been available to a lot of people is terrific. The problem is: How are they going to learn that these goods and services are available? You have to be fairly proficient at using search engines, and there is a lot of chaff mixed in with the wheat. (It's like trying to find the correct spelling in the dictionary when the reason you're looking the word up in the first place is because you don't know how to spell it. Does it start with a "c" or a "k"? Is it "i" or "e"?) It still takes time to search through all the results to find exactly what you are looking for.

Anyone with a computer can have the world at their fingertips. A great debate, which has been dubbed the "Digital Divide," has begun about just that: "Anyone with a computer." The problem is that not everyone has access to a computer or the Internet. There are several reasons for this, including cost, technological familiarity, physical location, and transmission access. All these obstacles directly relate to using the Internet as a publicity tool.

If you cannot afford a computer or the monthly access fees, you are not going to use the Internet. You may be able to use a computer at school or at your public library, but they often limit your time. If you only have 15 to 20 minutes online, you will probably focus on sending and receiving e-mail instead of surfing the Net to find out about a new book. If you have no computer experience or are not technically apt, computers may frighten you and you will not use the Internet. My parents, who are in their early 70s, would have no idea how to use a computer, even if I gave them one. Yes, they are intelligent enough to learn how to use one, but they did not grow up with computers as an integral part of their daily lives, so it is not important enough to them to take the time to learn. Extremely rural areas may not have access to reliable phone service and many older buildings are not wired for the Internet.

All these things, factored together, mean that the Internet caters to a specific type of person. The people who *do* use the Internet may not be the appropriate target audience for your book. An argument can be made that the people plugged into the Internet are the same people who buy books: educated and middle-to-upper income, generally speaking—but what about the businessperson who is constantly traveling? Or the house-bound caregiver with four children to look after? Or doctors who work 36 hours at a stretch? How often do they take the time to search the Internet to learn about new books? I don't know the answer to that and I suspect no one else does, either.

In addition to the uncertainties about Internet users and proper use of search engines, another obstacle to using the Internet for publicity is that some sites "repurpose" materials from the original sources. For example, some newspaper and magazine Web sites do not include original material or stories. They take a story as it appears in the actual physical newspaper or magazine and upload it to the Web site. They typically do not have reporters write new stories specifically for the Web site. They just "repurpose" (essentially, reuse) the print story material. This is beginning to change, but we'll have to wait and see how much original content they start adding.

It makes sense, when you think about it. If a story is good enough for the Web site, it should be good enough for the newspaper or magazine. The primary purpose of many Web sites is to generate consumer interest in subscribing to the print publication.

The same thing holds true for news programs. CNN's Web site is a natural extension of its broadcasting. If you don't have access to a television, you can go to its Web site to check out the latest news stories. Radio-program Web sites usually give you programming information and sound bites from past programs. Some also offer real-time audio of their programs.

Another thing that gives me pause about the Internet is experience. Traditional media have had the luxury of learning what works and what doesn't over a long period of time. Newspapers and magazines have been around in one form or another since before Moses brought down the tablets. Cave men were recording "the big wooly mammoth takedown" eons ago. Newspapers, books, and magazines have been around for a reasonable amount of time. We have come to expect a certain level of professionalism and integrity from them (warranted or not). The Internet has not been around long enough to fully trust, in my opinion. Are the people creating these Web sites seasoned journalists? Are they held to the same ethical standards as for traditional publications? Can they tell the difference between fact and opinion? I don't know, and that makes me nervous. Also, how can you determine circulation figures for a Web site? Does a meter reading that counts the number of "hits" a Web site gets translate into purchasing power? All publications can give you a fairly accurate circulation figure so you can determine whether it is worth your while to send them your materials.

The Internet seems to be run by younger people. In many ways, I think that's good: a fresh perspective and all that goes with it. However, a new reporter working for a traditional publication is mentored by a more seasoned editor. Checks and balances are built in so the young journalist doesn't shoot himself in the foot. Is someone doing that for the upstart news Web sites? I don't know, and that makes me nervous, too.

Here's a recap of why I'm not totally convinced that the Internet is an effective publicity tool:

1. Searching for the right site takes time, and I don't think most people have that long an attention span.
2. The target markets may not be appropriate for your book.
3. There is a lot of chaff mixed in with the wheat.
4. Repurposing of materials means that you may not get on it anyway, if you didn't break into the print medium.
5. Not everyone has access to the Internet or knows how to use it.

6. Some Web site operators lack experience and integrity.

7. There are few checks and balances with regard to either personnel or the information disseminated.

My friend Laurie, who owns a Web site development company, took issue with me about some of these concerns. She made many good points. She said, "You're looking at this from a *businessman's* point of view and that might not be right for new authors."

"Well, I *am* a businessman and I have to look at the cost-effectiveness of things," said I. "Time is money!"

"You gotta see it from the author's point of view. They want their book to be successful, however much time it takes. They're motivated for different reasons. If they want to take the time to search the Internet for the right Web sites, just tell them how to do it and let *them* decide. Sheesh!"

That being said, many of my concerns are being addressed by some very good Web sites and the people who run them. I also agree that, although it might not be the *best* publicity tool, it is an amazing research tool that can be very useful to an author.

Since you're probably not going to listen to me, I'll give you step-by step instructions on finding and contacting the Internet media in the research section, Chapter 11.

HOW THE MEDIA KEEP TRACK OF THEIR CONSUMERS

As you might guess, each particular category of media likes to keep track of who and how many people are reading, watching, or listening to their newspapers, magazines, television shows, or radio programs—and those of their competitors. With the huge influx of cash generated by advertising in all of these media, setting advertising rates based on the number of potential consumers has became big business. If a newspaper can tell a potential advertiser, "If you buy an ad with us, you can reach 100,000 more people than our competitor. Of course, it may cost you a bit more, but it's worth it," it can charge more for the ad.

Print and electronic media had to develop a way to prove their boasts. What marketing and public relations professionals soon realized is that this demographic and circulation information can be equally useful to them and their clients. Here is how they keep track of these financially important figures.

Television

Television uses the Nielsen Ratings system. They put these things that look like cable boxes in randomly selected homes across the country (supposedly a representative cross-section of Americans) to record what these households are watching, 7 days a week, 365 days a year. The information is sent electronically to a main facility where figures are extrapolated, and the results are made public either overnight or weekly. The "overnights" are the quick calculations (sort of the rough-draft figures), which may or may not change after the ratings folk have had a chance to do a more detailed study; that study is released once a week. They can break the figures down by day of the week, time of the day, regional or national, and by demographics.

Television stations use ratings not only for advertising purposes, but also to see which programs "beat" the competition. Many shows are cancelled because they have "low numbers," or, in English, attracted a low number of viewers according to the Nielsen company.

Publicists use these numbers to determine whether it would be useful to contact a television program. We also use this information to break a tie should we get two offers for interviews on competing programs. If one program has more people watching, we'll pick them instead of the program with lower numbers.

When a television station or program tells you its viewership figures, you should remember that these are estimated figures and not 100 percent accurate; it's more like an exit poll during an election. Also, the figures represent estimated *potential* viewership. That doesn't mean that Sally hasn't left her television on and gone out for a night with the girls. It is as accurate as they can get with the technology available today. Tomorrow, who knows? We may all get microchips implanted in our brains at birth to record all this stuff.

Keep in mind that we also factor in demographic information. We might choose a lower-rated program that has a demographic that's more complementary to our client's subject or product.

Radio

Radio uses Arbitron Ratings. The Arbitron company arrives at its figures primarily through questionnaires. They get demographic information and estimated listenership numbers by the quarter-hour. Not very exciting, but important for advertisers and publicists.

Print Media

Newspapers and magazines arrive at their audience figures through questionnaires and subscription figures. It is a lot easier to come up with a circulation figure for newspapers and magazines. All they have to do is call up their accounts receivable department and ask how many subscription bills they sent out last month.

What doesn't get factored into circulation figures is the "pass-around" figures. This is a number everyone tries to estimate to add on to the circulation figures. How many other people read the *same copy* of the publication? Think about it. You're in your dentist's office and there's a stack of hundred-year-old magazines sitting on the coffee table. The dentist is an hour behind schedule and you have to sit and wait until he's finished drilling someone's tooth. What do you do? Pick up one of those old magazines and start flipping through it. If you multiplied the number of dentist offices across America by the number of people who flipped through a magazine while waiting, you'd have a pretty big number. That would be your pass-around figure. How many people have passed a magazine on to someone else who consequently didn't buy a copy of his own? All those people with nothing to do but read old magazines—boggles the mind, doesn't it?

It ain't perfect, but it's the best means we've got to determine who and how many people are reading/watching/listening. The figures are not 100 percent accurate, but they are as close as the industries can get.

I hope I've supplied you with a just a little more impressive cocktail conversation for your next soirée. You're welcome.

PART 2

PRACTICAL
MATTERS

BRINGING THE ELEMENTS TOGETHER

In the preceding pages, we've been discussing necessary background information and theories about publicity, a publicity plan, and the media. Thus ends the discussion portion of our program. Now comes the interactive part. It's time for you to become the Charlton Heston of publicity. It's time for you to actually *do* all this stuff.

I will walk you through a step-by-step procedure that, by the end, will give you a publicity plan and the collateral materials you'll need to make this happen. Remember, **collateral materials** is just a fancy name for the written stuff that's included in a press kit.

The first piece of advice I can give you at this point is make sure you have a quiet place to work. It takes a lot of focus to make sure all the pieces flow together. You won't be able to do this on the fly, as it were. Send your family away for the weekend or check into a hotel room with room service, if you have to. Unplug your phone, lock your door, turn off your pager, shut off your television, and don't answer your e-mail. No distractions.

If you are the type of person who needs some sound floating around, I suggest some classical music or New-Age-type music. (I can't listen to any music with lyrics because I get too distracted by the words or unconsciously type to the beat of the music.)

Another suggestion is to clear off the table or desk at which you will be working. Don't be looking at work papers or the kid's homework; it will distract you. Start fresh and be organized. Believe it or not, I really do these things for every press kit I write. I'm doing it right now, as a matter of fact.

My desk is clear, no distractions—I'm hermetically sealed in my office and I'm not leaving until this puppy is done! I'm living on coffee and cigarettes.

Take one step at a time. Don't think about everything you're going to have to do or you'll probably freak out. Take this one step at a time. Complete step one. Then, and only then, go on to step two. And so on. It is easier than it may seem. It just takes concentration.

Here we go! Do these steps, be brilliant, and good luck!

After you have determined that you want to do this, that you have the right media-friendly book, and that you can work within your budget, here are the practical steps to execute your publicity plan. The list may look intimidating, but we'll go through it one step at a time.

YOUR TO-DO LIST

- ✓ Reread your book
- Jot down major plot points
- List news tie-ins
- ✓ Create a media shopping list
- ✓ Create a media database
- ✓ Create a headline for your press release
- ✓ Write the lead for your press release
- ✓ Write the body of your press release
- ✓ Proofread and format your press release
- Choose a photographer and get your picture taken
- ✓ Write your one-page biography
- ✓ Write a story synopsis for your book
- ✓ Make a list of 10 sample questions
- ✓ Make a list of potential "advance praise" writers
- Gather related articles or past media clippings
- Create your publicity timeline
- Put your press kits together
- Create mailing labels
- Determine the correct postage
- Mail out the press kit materials
- Keep a running status report and mail log sheet
- Begin follow-up calls/pitching
- Do it all over again for round two
- Be prepared for the unexpected
- Stay on top of your plan.

THE FIRST STEPS

Reread Your Book and Make Notes

This may seem like a strange first step, especially since you wrote the book in the first place, but it's not. Chances are you haven't read your book cover-to-cover in quite a while. Even if you have, you now have to read and look at it through "publicity eyes." You are not reading it for story, you're reading it to determine what things contained in your book will help you with your publicity plan. Plus it can't hurt to refresh your memory.

In Chapter 4, I discussed the five questions you should be able to answer when evaluating your book from a publicity perspective. As you read your book, make a list of topics contained in your book that might be of interest to the media. You may use some or all of these ideas for your press release later.

You don't have to be neat about it, or use perfect grammar, and spelling doesn't count. This list is for your use only. To help illustrate these points, I've created a make-believe book titled, *Life As We Know It,* by John Smith.

As I'm reading through my make-believe book, I'm jotting down some of the main subjects that are either major or minor elements of the plot. My list looks something like this:

MAJOR PLOT ELEMENTS	
chemical weapons	Louisiana
teenage angst	gambling/Las Vegas
stock market	Middle East religious conflict
political coverups	alcohol abuse
fly fishing	adoption
abortion	

See? It's not particularly pretty, but it's going to be useful later on. Yours might be longer or shorter, depending on your book. This applies to both fiction and nonfiction.

After you've finished reading and compiling your list, look through the list items and see if there are possible news tie-ins. Jot those ideas and some notes down. Using the examples from our hypothetical book's list, my notes look like this:

—Chemical weapons: possible tie-in to news story because UN peacekeeping forces have discovered 4 chemical weapons plants over the last 6 months: Serbia, Iran, North Korea, and China. Timely for newspapers/TV news/*Time/Newsweek.*

—Teenage angst: where it can lead—Columbine, suicide, joining gangs, drug use, smoking, communications breakdown with parents/family. How to help: open communication, be nonthreatening/nonjudgmental, etc.

—Stock market: plot in book parallels current market conditions, good tie-in for business editors or business mags. Protagonist has similarities to A. Greenspan.

—Political coverups: like Watergate—how long has it been, anniversary date? could be good sidebar story for Clinton troubles.

—Fly fishing: when are world championships? find out, good tie-in. if it's close enough, can hand out flyers. Women taking up sport in large numbers. Good article for fishing mags and TV shows—find out when they're on and watch.

—Abortion: too general and too many angles. Figure out two. think more about this.

—Louisiana: story takes place in L. great local media angle or travel mags.

—Gambling/Las Vegas: not much to use here, skip it unless can't think of anything better.

—Middle East conflict: media probably wants official experts, but might be good sidebar for some print media.

—Alcohol abuse: Wife of protagonist is a drunk. are there any new statistics out on women & alcoholism? research more—if yes, can I use?

—Adoption: little kid in story is orphan. He's lost in the system—how common is this? great for lifestyle sec of newspaper and maybe talk show circuit.

This should get your creative publicity juices flowing. It gets you to start thinking about your target media markets and your press materials. These first two lists will play a key role in your publicity plan throughout the entire process, so keep them handy.

Make a Market Classifications Shopping List

Using the lists you've created, start making a "shopping list" of media market classifications for each of the points you wrote down. Media **market classifications** are the general types of media you want to contact by subject category. It's like book genres. For example:

—Chemical weapons: chemical trade media, hard news media, political media, environmental media, military media

—Teenage angst: lifestyle, parent/child publications, teen mags, general interest, hard news (with proper current event tie-in), education/teacher publications, afternoon talk shows, teen-targeted radio programs

—Stock market: business media

—Political coverups: too many—have to narrow down the angle first

—Fly fishing: sports media, women's general-interest media

—Abortion: narrow down angle first. Check on future legislation at state level

I hope you're starting to get the idea.

Create a Media Contact List or Database

Using the research tools we will discuss later (in Chapter 11), you're going to start creating your own media contact list. If your computer has any type of a database program, you should probably learn how to use it. Most database programs let you merge and sort information contained within the database. This will help you create labels and personalized letters. It will save you tons of time in the long run.

Using your market classifications list, compile all the media markets that you listed. There's no need to record duplicates. Here's what it should look like (I put it in alphabetical order because it appeals to my sense of order; no other reason):

— afternoon talk shows	lifestyle
business	military media
chemical trade media	parent/child
education/teacher	political
environmental media	sports
— general interest	teen
hard news	women's general interest

Using your reference tools (i.e., *Bacon's Media Directory*, friends, the Internet, the Yellow Pages, directory assistance, etc.), begin to create a list organized by these market classifications. It helps if you divide each of the classifications into the subgroups of: Newspapers, Magazines, Radio, Internet, and Television. This will help you determine lead times and mailings. It's just a more organized way of keeping track.

You want to get the following information for your database:

1. Name of media outlet
2. Contact person and her title
3. Mailing address
4. General phone and fax numbers
5. Direct phone number, if possible (sometimes very hard to get)
6. E-mail address
7. Circulation/viewership/listenership numbers

You may want to make separate entries for first and last names of your contacts. This helps with merging names for personalized memos and letters. It allows you to write: "Dear Bob: Blah, blah, blah ..." It makes your correspondence less cold and impersonal.

Compiling this list may take some time. I suggest that you create your entire database before you begin mailing press materials out. You could run into trouble getting contact information for what is supposed to be your second round of mailing and that will throw off your entire timetable. This will also give you a specific count on the number of outlets you plan on contacting, which determines how many press kits, copies, and so forth you'll need.

If you find you have too many names, use the circulation/viewership/listenership figures to pare down the list. Send to the ones with the highest c/v/l numbers first. You can always do another mailing later to the ones you initially cut from the list.

Once you're done creating your contact lists, *back the lists up on a separate disk or tape and put it somewhere safe*. True story: I had a media database of more than 10,000 media contacts (I've been doing this for a while) that we used for all our clients. I spent a lot of time and money having the information entered and continuously updated in this thing—it is our lifeblood. A few months ago, I decided to be a hotshot and get more RAM for all our computers to help speed up this process.

I walked—nay, swaggared—into the staff office and announced proudly that "in just a few short days, our computers will be better, faster and stronger than ever before." The staff looked at me like, "Whatever," and went about their business. Undeterred, I went back into my office and daydreamed about computing at higher speeds.

The day finally arrived and I opened the packages containing the RAM. I'd done this before, so I knew how simple it is to pop these RAM cards into a computer. After about an hour or so, I announced that everyone could fire up their computers and get back to work.

Chest puffed with pride, I watched and waited as each worker turned on a computer. The first worker said, "Um, nothing's happening." Worker two, "Yeah, same here." I'd done mine first, and everything was fine with mine. Maybe they're not seated properly, I thought. I had the staff move aside and wiggled the things around a bit and told them to try again.

No luck.

I called the Internet company's help line and explained the situation. They had me read the part numbers on both of the RAM thingies. "Well, those are the wrong RAM cards for those computers. Sounds like you blew out your motherboards." If you know anything about computers, you know that the motherboard is the brain of your computer. Never, ever blow out your motherboard. It a very Bad Thing.

I got a touch upset with this poor kid on the other end of the phone who'd had nothing to do with selling me the wrong RAM. Very colorful language was used. That's all I'm going to say on that matter.

I hung up.

I threw up. (I'm not kidding.)

Twelve years and ten thousand names lost to fried microchips.

Two days later, we all had brand spanking new computers and no database. I had a company do a hard-drive recovery, but for some reason they couldn't get the database back. You might ask, did I have a backup disk? Of course I did. The only problem was that the last time I backed it up, I had brown hair. Everything's back to normal now. Thanks for asking.

The moral of the story is: Always back up your database. Frequently.

A friend reminded me of a low-tech way to create a media list: Note cards. Color-coded note cards! I'm almost convinced that this is the best way for you to keep your list, because you're not necessarily trying to keep 15 clients' media contacts straight. It's simple, accurate, easy to use, and you don't have to worry about backing them up—unless you lose them. (Try not to do that.) I feel like an angel came down and kissed my brain. My friend is very, very smart and I'm glad she's my friend. That, right there, is worth the price of the book!

At this point, you have a list of all the media you want to contact, on computer or your color-coded note cards, and a few basic angles for your press release. Now you have to write the press release.

A press release is the most important piece of paper you will include in your press kit. It is *not* a work of fiction! It is the make-or-break thing that entices the media person to read the rest of your press kit—and book. It is usually 1 to 1-1/2 pages long, 1-1/2-line or double-spaced, and always typed. It must contain the who, what, when, where, why, and how of your book. Most of your energy should be concentrated on writing this correctly. It may take you two or three days to get this just right. Don't send it out until you are sure it says exactly what you want it to say. It's like answering the question, "Honey, do I look fat to you?" Think very carefully before you react.

A press release is the first item you will have to create that you have to include with your collateral materials. Writing a press release is simple in concept, but difficult in execution. I will break it down into bite-sized bits and also discuss the other collateral materials you will have to create.

COLLATERAL MATERIALS

Writing all the collateral materials can be tedious and frustrating. Keeping in mind that these materials are going to make or break your publicity plan should help motivate you to get the job done. If you start to get frustrated, walk away from it for a while and clear your head. (It shouldn't be too much of a problem, seeing that you've already written a whole book.) This can take from two or three days to a couple of weeks. Be patient.

Create a Headline for Your Press Release

A headline is the thing you look at when you're scanning the newspapers over your first cup of coffee. It's the thing that grabs your attention and makes you want to read the article. Only in this case, its purpose is to make the journalist want to read your book.

The first step in creating an interesting headline is to fantasize. Picture yourself opening the newspaper one morning, turning a page, and seeing an article about you and your book on page 4. Now is your chance to play editor. What does the headline say?

Using our examples, here are some possible headlines:

———

Example 1: "Chemical weapons" possible headline:

AUTHOR JOHN SMITH TO RELEASE NEW INTERNATIONAL CHEMICAL WEAPONS NOVEL TITLED, *LIFE AS WE KNOW IT.*

———

Boring. Boring. Boring! You want to use active verbs, match the tone of the book, and keep it as short as possible (three lines at the most). This example uses a passive voice (boring), and doesn't sound international thriller-ish (boring), but it is short and sweet (but boring!). We need to jazz it up a bit.

———

COULD IT HAPPEN THIS WAY?

AUTHOR JOHN SMITH HAS PULSE ON INTERNATIONAL CHEMICAL WAR CRISIS IN RIPPED-FROM-THE-HEADLINES NEW THRILLER, *LIFE AS WE KNOW IT.*

———

It's a little histrionic, but it might work. It's a bit longer than our first example, but at least it's more interesting. This version is probably good for newspapers and other harder news outlets. I think the reporter or editor would at least take a look at the rest of the release—and that's exactly what a good headline is supposed to do.

Let's try another one.

———

Example 2: "Teenage angst" possible headline:

AUTHOR JOHN SMITH PENETRATES THE VEILED MIND OF A DISTURBED TEEN IN NEW THRILLER, *LIFE AS WE KNOW IT.*

—————

Not bad. *Penetrates* is a good word, so are *disturbed* and *veiled.* A little mystery and weirdness, they like that. I'd read it. (Maybe *I'll* write it when I'm done with this one.)

A couple more examples to help you out.

—————

Example 3: "Stock market" possible headline:

ALAN GREENSPAN'S GOT *NOTHING* ON JAKE BARLOW IN JOHN SMITH'S NEW NOVEL, *LIFE AS WE KNOW IT.*

—————

The good thing about this example is that every business reporter or editor snaps to attention at the mention of Alan Greenspan. It'll get their attention. *Keeping* it will be up to the next part of your press release, the lead paragraph. One potential problem with this example is the number of names floating around in the headline. It might get confusing. This one is a bit shaky, but could probably work.

—————

Example 4: "Political coverup" headline:

IF YOU CAN'T GET ENOUGH OF *"WHATEVER*-GATES," JOHN SMITH'S NEW NOVEL, *LIFE AS WE KNOW IT,* HAS A "-GATE" YOU'LL NEVER FORGET!

—————

I don't like the imbalance with all the italics on one side. It looks lopsided, but it's kind of clever and it just might work. If they get the Watergate, Travelgate, Filegate, etc., reference, we're home free. If not, we have to create another one. Again, the first full "text" paragraph (the lead) will help determine the viability of this headline.

When you're working on headlines, think up as many as you can and run them by your spouse, friends, or co-workers and ask them which one strikes their fancy. Most people are fairly intuitive when it comes to picking out something that interests them. Remember, a reporter is a spouse, friend, and co-worker too. They have the same likes and dislikes as anyone else you know.

Write the Lead

The **lead** is the first paragraph of the press release. It should contain all of the pertinent information: the who, what, when, where, why, how. Technically, proper grammar is not a requirement in this paragraph. Run-on sentences and funky punctuation are fine, as long as it makes sense. Don't try for flowery here. You have about two sentences to hook the reporter. Make them count. It must all be the truth. Don't embellish—it'll come back and bite you in the you-know-what later. Be extremely accurate.

When you begin writing, remember to tie your headline into your lead paragraph. That's good. If you don't, the headline will make no sense and you will confuse the reporter or editor. That's bad.

Here are some examples of leads based on the previous examples. I'm not going to use the first one, because it's not very good and I wouldn't use it anyway. I'll skip to example #2, just because.

———

Example 2: Teenage angst:

AUTHOR JOHN SMITH PENETRATES THE VEILED MIND OF A DISTURBED TEEN IN NEW THRILLER, *LIFE AS WE KNOW IT.*

Author **John Smith** has accomplished what few authors before him have done. He has convincingly penetrated the mind of a disturbed teenage killer in his latest novel, *Life as We Know It* (Publishing House Name, [release date]). Dismembered bodies of high-school girls are turning up all over the quiet town of St. Olaf and no one knows why. They all have one thing in common—they were all wearing headbands. As Detective Ty Jones races against time to find the killer and stop the killing, he is pulled into the terrifying vortex of a killer's mind that makes Norman Bates look like an amateur. You'll never wear a headband again.

———————

I like that one. Would you read that book? Would it at least pique your curiosity? That's all you're trying to accomplish with a press release.

Back to the regular order.

———————

Example 1: Chemical weapons:

COULD IT HAPPEN THIS WAY?
AUTHOR JOHN SMITH HAS PULSE ON INTERNATIONAL CHEMICAL WAR CRISIS IN RIPPED-FROM-THE-HEADLINES NEW NOVEL, *LIFE AS WE KNOW IT.*

Serbia, Iran, North Korea, China. UN peacekeeping forces have discovered four chemical weapons plants in these countries in the last six months. *That's real.* Author **John Smith** will make you believe the unbelievable in his new novel, *Life as We Know It* (Publishing House Name, [release date]). Using his expertise as a chemical engineer, Smith has blended fact and fiction so seamlessly, you won't know where one stops and the other starts. Chemical manufacturing magnate, Ty Jones, is out for his morning run in the new park in his affluent neighborhood, when he trips on something sticking out of the ground. On closer inspection, Jones discovers two things: One, there's a small pipe sticking out of the ground; and, two, a small whisper of smoke is coming out of it. He knows that smell only too well. Discovering what is at the other end of that pipe and who put it there will send Jones running for his life, taking him on a terrifying journey to Istanbul, Hawaii, and the Kremlin. If he is to survive, he must become what he is not: a killer.

———————

How's that? I've done three things with this release: (1) I've made it sound exciting; (2) I've tied it into a hard news event; and (3) I've introduced the fact that the author is an expert in chemical engineering. This third point sets up a potential "talking head" guest spot, should the United Nations forces discover another chemical weapons facility. (I'm always thinking ahead.)

I don't want to do this next example! I don't *know* anything about the stock market and I don't *care* about the stock market. I hate this example. You may hate some of your choices, too, but you can't ignore a major market like the business media, so you and I are just going to have to tough it out! Too bad for me. Cross your fingers.

———————

Example 3: Stock market:

ALAN GREENSPAN'S GOT *NOTHING* ON JAKE BARLOW IN JOHN SMITH'S NEW NOVEL, *LIFE AS WE KNOW IT.*

Alan Greenspan catches a cold and global markets and interest rates tumble. He has *that* power. Jake Barlow, the protagonist in **John Smith's** new novel, *Life as We Know It* (Publishing House, [release date]), has a whole lot *more*. Inflation is rampant, a depression is imminent, and the President of the United States secretly signs Executive Order GF5874, granting Barlow unlimited—and unprecedented—power over all government financial institutions. By the time the Senate Oversight Committee on Economic Affairs discovers the Executive Order, it's too late to stop Barlow from ruining the world's financial infrastructure and bringing the G8 to its knees. Only one man can stop him: Ty Jones, the brilliant financial savant who retired in disgrace seven years ago. His very public crucifixion was orchestrated by none other than Barlow. It's payback time!

———————

Well, it ain't great, but it does fit the bill. It matches the headline and would probably be of interest to the business media. It would bore me to death. I'd rather string popcorn, but that's just me. This example serves as a reminder that you can't always write about what *you* want to write about. Often you have to write about what you think *they* want to read. Them's the breaks.

———————

Example 4: Political coverup:

IF YOU CAN'T GET ENOUGH OF *"WHATEVER-GATES,"* JOHN SMITH'S NEW NOVEL, *LIFE AS WE KNOW IT,* HAS A "-GATE" YOU'LL NEVER FORGET!

Watergate, Travelgate, Filegate, Zippergate. Would you believe Melongate? **John Smith's** uproarious new satiric novel, *Life as We Know It* (Publishing House, [release date]), drops ace reporter, Ty Jones, into the squishy underworld of, well, the melon industry. Melon production is at dangerously low levels due to a mysterious plague affecting melons all over the world. Prices for melons are skyrocketing and Jones thinks he knows just who is behind it. Going undercover as a melon taster, Jones and his beautiful sidekick, Kanta Lowpe, set out to get the story of their lives! Life as We Know It takes a satiric look at government corruption, media frenzies, and the public's insatiable appetite for political coverups. Will Jones get to taste a sweet cantaloupe? You'll have to read page 134 to find out.

––––––

I'm having a little fun here, but if your book is funny, you have to match the tone of the press release to the tone of your book. I think this release is kind of funny, and if the book really does take a satiric look at the more serious issues of government corruption, media frenzies, and the public's appetite for scandal, why not? The business media have to wade through all sorts of dry stuff. This might go over really well. Most media people do have a good sense of humor, from time to time. Give it a shot. You would probably want to have a more serious backup release, though, just in case you get some strong negative responses from the media.

So far, so good. You've determined which media you want to contact; you've come up with an angle, which you turned into a headline; and that headline helped you write your lead paragraph. Not bad for a couple of days' work. Sit back for a few minutes, have a soda, and admire your work. You've earned it!

O.K. Time's up. Back to work. Wasn't that refreshing?

Write the Body of the Press Release

I will be hard-pressed to give you examples for this part of the press release, because every book is different in scope, tone, style, and genre. That being said, there are some guidelines that I think will help you get started on the body of your press release. Just keep matching the tone of the headline and lead, and you'll be fine.

Once you get on a roll with the lead, the body of the press release will probably start to flow naturally. It is an extension of the lead paragraph. Your *second paragraph* should cover why you decided to write this book, from a philosophical perspective, and how you got the idea for the story itself. Include a short quote near the top of the second paragraph, if possible.

The *third paragraph* should expound on the underlying theme of the book and be tied into, for example, chemical warfare, teenage angst, financial questions, or politics. This paragraph is typically a bit more straightforward and less "clever" than the headline, lead, or second paragraph.

The *fourth paragraph* can give more details regarding the plot of the story or the ideas contained in a nonfiction book. Here is where you would include statistics, if your book warranted it.

The *fifth paragraph* is the boilerplate biography that will appear on all other versions of press releases and must correlate to the full one-page biography that we'll write later.

The final sentence (note that I didn't say paragraph) is always the same: **For more information or a review copy, or to arrange an interview, please contact Your Name at (000) 555-1212.**

That never changes—unless you change your phone number.

Helpful Hint

If you are using your home phone number, please remember to record a professional outgoing message like, "You've reached the phone of Jane Smith. I'm sorry I'm not available to take your call right now. Please leave your name, phone number, the time you called, and a brief message, and I'll return your call as soon as possible."

For the love of Mike, do not keep the outgoing message with little Sally and Billy giggling about waiting for the beep! The media will hang up on you faster than you can say "remainder bin"!

Proofread What You've Written

I hope I don't have to tell you why.

Still, there are some tricks that might help you proofread more effectively.

- To check your spelling, read your press release *backward.* Someone told me once that if you do this, your brain can't automatically fill in the blank if a word or letter is missing. By reading it backward, you take each word individually. I don't know if there is any scientific proof of this, but when I do it I always catch misspellings.

- Read your press release out loud. I would wait until you have the house to yourself, so they don't get two doctors' signatures and put you away, but read it out loud. You will find jumps in logic and poorly written sentences this way.

- Have someone you trust read it, too. A fresh set of eyes can spot mistakes better than you can because they don't know what to expect, so they're paying closer attention.

- Put it down for a day or two. This is for the same reasons as before—fresh eyes and all that. You may also discover that the release doesn't "play" as well as you thought when you were writing at 3:00 A.M.

Put the Release in the Correct Format

You'll need to include some traditional pieces of information at the top of your press release such as the phrase, "For Immediate Release," the date, and contact information. The press release is always and forever on your letterhead. No exceptions. Ever.

Here's an example:

LIFE AS WE KNOW IT, by John Smith

For Immediate Release   Contact: John Smith
September 4, 2001   (000) 555-1212

Author, John Smith, Penetrates the Veiled Mind of a Disturbed Teen in New Thriller, *Life as We Know It.*

Author, **John Smith** has accomplished what few authors before him have done. He has convincingly penetrated the mind of a disturbed teenage killer in his latest novel, *Life as We Know It* (Publishing House Name, [Release date]). Dismembered bodies of high-school girls are turning up all over the quiet town of St. Olaf and no one knows why. They all have one thing in common—they were all wearing headbands. As Detective Ty Jones races against time to find the killer and stop the killing, he is pulled into the terrifying vortex of a killer's mind that makes Norman Bates look like an amateur. You'll never wear a headband again.

Paragraph two.

Paragraph three.

Paragraph four.

Paragraph five.

For more information or a review copy, or to arrange an interview, please contact John Smith at (000) 555-1212.

###

Notice that the phrase "For Immediate Release" is bolded and underlined, whereas the contact information and date are not. Also, the last line is bolded. I do that because it reminds the media about an interview and reiterates the phone number. The three "#" symbols indicate that this is the end of the press release. It used to be "-30-" a long time ago. This signal had to do with typesetting machines, and was gradually replaced by the three pound signs. If you use the "thirty dash" today, they'd probably think you had a 30-page press release!

All press releases are written using the Times Roman font (or the closest thing you've got). Do not try to be cutesy with the fonts. First, it will irritate the media. Second, fonts "sans serif," or without serifs, are difficult to read. *Serifs* are those little lines that project out from the ends of letters, just like you're reading right now. Here's a sentence using the Arial font, which does not contain serifs. Those little lines help your eyes stay in a straight line and make large quantities of text easier to read.

Finally, if you can get your press release on one page, that's good. If you can't, don't worry. You can have up to 1-2/3 pages, double-spaced. It's just faster to fax—and read—if you have it on one page. Mine are usually about one and a half pages. Any longer than that, you might as well send them the book.

So far you have completed the following:

1. You've determined that you want to do the publicity for your own book.
2. You've determined that your book is media-friendly.
3. You've reread your book.
4. You've listed the major and minor plot subjects in your book.
5. You've listed the media market classifications that you think will be interested in your book.
6. You've created a database of media contact information.
7. You've written possible headlines for your press release.
8. You've written a strong lead paragraph for your press release.
9. You've written the body of your release, including the boiler-plate and contact information.
10. You've proofread your press release to death.
11. You've formatted your release properly.

Now set the press release aside.

Choose a Photographer

I suggest that you choose a photographer at this point, for a couple of reasons. First, you need time to digest all the work you've been doing. Second, it's going to take some time to get a photographer and get the copies of your headshot made. Third, it will give you time to do them over again if you hate how they turn out.

As I stated earlier, your headshot serves two purposes. The print media will either use a headshot or a picture of your jacket art to go along with a review or a feature article. Sometimes they'll use both. You want to be ready for them and not give them an excuse to "push" the article to a later date. A book review or a features article is pretty boring without some kind of artwork accompanying it. Remember, a photo is the first impression the media—and the public—gets of you.

We've all looked at photos in the newspaper or family albums and instantly decided whether we like the person or not. *He looks like a jerk. She looks like a floozie. He looks like such a nice young man. I bet she's a little devil.* Your eyes truly are the windows to your soul. A picture creates an immediate impression about a person, so make sure you do this right.

The television media want a headshot to make sure, well, that you don't have two heads. It is superficial but very important to them that you have the right "look." If you look like you should be on *Jerry Springer,* the *Today Show* will be much more hesitant to have you as a guest. This does *not* mean you have to look like a starlet (especially if you are a man), but you should look professional and presentable. Leave the hot pants and six-inch stilettos at home—and that includes you women out there, too.

You may think you don't have enough money to be messing around with a professional photographer, but this is one expense that you can't get around. You really do get what you pay for.

You can find a professional photographer in several different ways. You can use the good old Yellow Pages; look under "photography," and start making phone calls. You can ask friends if they know a good photographer (not Uncle Bernie "who's really good!"). If you are in a major metropolitan city, you can call the local chapter of Actor's Equity and ask them for referrals. Actor's Equity is the union for stage actors, and since all actors need headshots, they know who to go to—and for cheap!

Once you've got a bead on a photographer, you should arrange to meet the photographer and ask him to bring a portfolio. You wouldn't buy a car without kicking the tires, would you? The same applies here. Some photographers seem to be better at "glam shots" than generic headshots. A **glam shot** is a glamour shot, a highly dramatic photo style, like the cover of a major fashion magazine. You don't want that. You want a headshot that accurately reflects your personality and is somewhat conservative. You want the photo to be taken in the studio, no location shooting, please.

Quick story. I worked with an author a couple of years ago who wrote a great book on the millennium. Before I agreed to take him on, I asked him for a copy of the finished book, which he gladly sent me. When I got the book, the first thing I did was look at his jacket photo, because we'd only been speaking via the phone. His picture made my heart sink. His publisher had used a photograph of the author in *fishing gear!* This was a end-of-millennium thriller and they use fishing gear?!

Keep it simple: traditional studio headshot and no fishing gear. Light gray background.

What you should wear depends on your personality and your look. You don't want to wear something that will make you feel very uncomfortable, because that will show on your face in your photo. If you are a woman, a dark crew-neck sweater (no cowls, they make it look like your head's in a bowl) or a dark business suit with a plain light-colored shell underneath. Something simple and professional. Tell your photographer what the photos will be used for and she'll be able to help you with your wardrobe.

If you are a man, a dark suit and tie are always safe. If it looks good, you can do the dark sport coat and polo shirt thing. Again, ask your photographer; he may suggest that you bring several choices to the photo shoot and take a few pictures in different outfits.

The one thing you *cannot* wear is pure white—cream is O.K., but not pure white. When newspapers reproduce your photo, pure white "burns out." That means you can't see any shadows or gradations of gray and you lose that three-dimensional feeling.

You've found a photographer, looked through his portfolio and picked out your wardrobe. Now you actually have to get the picture taken. I know, I know, stop whining. It'll be over before you know it.

Here are some dos and don'ts for your big day:

1. Get as much sleep as possible the night before your photo shoot. You don't want to look all puffy with bags under your eyes.

2. Don't drink a lot of alcohol the day before; it makes you puffy.

3. The top models, both men and women, will fill up the bathroom sink with water and add tons of ice. They will then dunk their faces underwater for as long as they can hold their breath and repeat the process until the morning puffiness goes away.

4. Shave as close as possible without cutting yourself—men, too. (A little humor.) The studio lights will show your stubble more than in regular lighting.

5. Don't get your hair cut the day before and don't try a new style, either; it could look terrible and then you're up a creek without a paddle. Make it look as good as possible. Women, no really big hair. You know what I'm talking about! The photo editor at the newspapers will crop it out anyway and it may look weird. You can set your hair, just don't rat it out like Phyllis Diller.

6. To smile or not to smile? Some people look better not smiling. Ask your family, they'll tell you the truth.

After you've gotten your picture taken, it will take a few days to get the proof sheets back from the photographer. A **proof sheet** is an 8-1/2 x 11 glossy sheet of photo paper with rows of developed film printed right on the page. You use this to pick out the photos you want made into your 8 x 10. Because the pictures are only about one-inch square, you need a loupe, like a magnifying glass, to look at them up close. Some fancy photographers use digital equipment that lets you see your photos on-the-spot on a computer screen. I would still get a print made to see how it looks in real life.

Working with the photographer, pick out three or four photos you both like and have the photographer make enlargements. Sometimes it's difficult to see minor flaws in the small versions, but they will become glaringly obvious at full size.

Once you've picked out the best one, take the enlargement to a photo duplicating shop and ask them to make as many as you'll need, based upon your media contact list. Be sure to ask about special pricing deals. Strangely, at the photo shop we use, it's cheaper to get 500 than it is to get 250. Why? I don't have a clue. That's just the way it is. Be sure to ask.

If you don't have to, don't tell them to put it on a "rush." That means they'll do it quicker, but it can double your costs. No sense wasting good money if you don't have to.

Now, set the photos aside.

Write Your Biography

I've never met an author who didn't hate to do this. I can't do this for them because, usually, I've just met them. I don't know anything about their lives and I certainly can't make it up! A written biography (or **bio**) is used by the media as potential background information for their stories. For you, it can spark some creative ideas for market classifications.

Many years ago, I worked with an attorney/author who was in his late forties and had just written a legal thriller. As I looked over the rough draft of his bio, I was struck by the fact that he was an avid surfer. Who would've guessed? Just for the fun of it, I contacted a surfing magazine, and wouldn't you know it, we got a two-page, four-color article about "the surfer that wrote a book." You just never know.

I agonized over this next part for a long time, because there are so many variables when deciding what to include in a bio and what to leave out. I guess it's because of my years of experience, but I just intuitively know what's going to help and what's not. I think the best way to proceed is to keep it simple and let you decide how creative you want the bio to be.

You definitely want to match the tone of your bio with the tone of the book and the press release. That I'm sure about.

Here's a way to get started with the bio; you can polish it after you get this part written. Use the old standbys: who, what, when, where, why, and how.

1. Who are you? Include your name, of course, but also include your current job if writing is not your primary job. Are you a first-time author, doctor, lawyer, student, stay-at-home-dad, a construction worker, a shoe salesman, etc.?

2. What were you trying to accomplish with this book? Were you trying to bring the plight of the poor to national attention? Trying simply to entertain? Trying to share your love of cooking? Those types of things.

3. When did you write this book? Did you write it on the weekends? Did you write it while on vacation? How long did it take you to write (only if your answer is extraordinary)? Did you write this when you were pregnant? In between court cases or surgery? Put the time in context.

4. Where are you from? This is helpful for "local-boy-does-good" stories. Did you grow up overseas? Are you an Army brat? A cowboy? Los Angeles, Colorado, New York, Atlanta? And include an interesting brief anecdote.

5. Why did you write this book? That's self-explanatory: What drove you to write this particular story?

6. How? How did the idea for the book come about? How does this affect the outside world?

Important thing! This is in paragraph form, *not* in résumé format. You're not looking for a job, you're looking for media coverage.

Once you have this exactly how you want it, set it aside.

Write a Synopsis

A **synopsis** is a brief outline or overview of your book. This is incredibly helpful to the media. It gives them a chance to decide quickly whether this is something they are interested in, so you'd better write it well!

Unless you're self-published, you've probably already done something similar for your publishing house. If not, think about "The Beverly Hillbillies" theme song. It tells you, in 30 seconds, the *whole* story about that poor mountaineer who barely kept his family fed. Another good way to get some ideas about writing a synopsis is to read the jacket copy on several books. Some will be good and some will be terrible. The more you read, the easier it will be to tell good jacket copy from bad.

The only other requirement is to make sure that your synopsis is double-spaced and only one page. That's it. Don't try to tell every little plot point in the story, just the basics.

Make a List of 10 Sample Questions

Sample questions give the media an idea of where you're coming from, as we used to say in the 1960s. It lets them know the types of questions you're prepared for and what you're probably going to focus on in an interview.

It's also a great safety net for the media in case a guest doesn't show up and they have to replace him with you. The host may not have time to read your book before this last-minute guest appearance, and it will give her a good 10 minutes of talk until she can figure out just what the heck your book is about.

It helps you, too. Knowing the answers before they ask the questions is very empowering. It helps with stage fright and jitters. At *least* you'll know the answers to 10 questions. It's like cheating on a test, only legal.

Think about what you want to say when you get interviewed and come up with a question for your answer. Do you want to talk about the thematic elements in your book? What about a social issue that directly pertains to your story? Being an author/job title? Any interesting questions—actually, interesting responses—you can think of. Come up with a lot of them and whittle it down from those. Ask people you know if they would want to know this about you or your book.

Double-space your questions. Do not include your *answers,* because the media may not like your answers, and then they won't interview you. Keep your cards close to your vest. Let them book you for an interview first, then give them your answers.

Make a List of People You Know for Possible Advance Praise

"Advance praise" is a nice bonus for an author to include in a press kit—and for the back of your book jacket. It adds to your credibility, plain and simple. This is also a one-page addition to your press kit. Contact experts or high-visibility people *you know,* and ask them to read your manuscript and write out a couple of sentences about how great they think it is.

Only ask people that make sense. If your book is medically based, don't ask a lawyer for a blurb. You'll have the media thinking you're a goofball. The exception would be if you know Johnny Cochran. He's high visibility—nosebleed visibility. If you know him personally, ask him.

Do not send your manuscript to famous A-list authors for a blurb. You will not get a blurb. Never. Ever. Ever. The blurbs you see them write for other books are usually arranged by the in-house publicist at the publishing house on a barter basis. "I'll give you a blurb, if you give me one." Or they have a personal relationship with the author that goes way back. Most A-list authors hate doing this. They have to stop what they're doing, actually read the whole book, and write the perfect blurb. Not fun.

It wastes the author's time and the time of people like me. I have to try to decipher the return address, throw it in an envelope, weigh it, get the postage right, stick it back in the mail, and answer 50 phone messages that say: "Did he have time to read it? I just *know* he'll really like it. If you could just give it to him, I know he'll just love it." No A-list author will love it. Sorry. They won't. Don't waste your time or money. Don't waste everyone else's either.

If you can find appropriate people to write blurbs for you, use them. If not, don't worry about it. Maybe next time. And don't ask Uncle Harry—no one cares what he thinks unless he's famous.

Type these up and set them aside.

Gather Related Articles or Past Media Clips

If your book deals with a complex issue, it is always helpful to do some of the legwork for the busy reporter. The purpose of including related articles or past media clippings is to lend credibility to your story and show that it is newsworthy. From our examples, I might include the news stories about the UN's discovery of the chemical weapons plants; five stories about teen murders from different corners of the United States; health stories about Alan Greenspan; articles that have headlines with any kind of "-gate"; or maybe even headlines about how the media "killed" Princess Diana.

Make sure the materials you choose are topical and relevant.

If you've written articles for your local newspaper, a professional journal, or a magazine, by all means, include those as well.

Make sure you have nice clean copies of all of these. Your local copy center has loads of tricks to make old newspaper clippings look great.

Gather everything you want to include and set them aside.

Assemble Your Collection

Don't forget to pick up your photos. Just thought I'd remind you.

As of right now, you should have all your collateral materials ready to go. Everything you are going to include in the press kit is done! Here s a checklist, just to make sure:

- ☒ Your press release
- ☒ Your photo (I hope they turned out great!)
- ☒ Your biography
- ☒ The synopsis
- ☒ List of 10 sample questions
- ☒ Blurbs from appropriate people
- ☒ Any background materials that you think are appropriate
- ☒ Press clippings, which are added to the press kit as they become available.

Stick all of the originals in a folder and put them away safely. We still have a few more things to do before we do something with them and you don't want to lose them.

Decide on the Order You Will Send Your Press Materials

Earlier, you made a list of media, arranged by media classification, that you think will be interested in your book. Now you have to decide in which order you will contact them (i.e., send them your press kit). There are three ways to organize this: one, by lead time; two, by circulation/viewership/listenership figures (highest to lowest); three, by the subject they cover. There are good reasons to use each of these three.

The lead-time means of organization, probably makes the most sense. Knowing (as you now do) that monthly magazines have the longest lead times, you'll want to get the materials to them first, because it takes them the longest to decide whether they want to use your book for an article. The sooner they receive the materials, the earlier they can publish the story. Remember, with long leads, that they want the story in the issue that corresponds to your publishing date (e.g., if you have a September publishing date, they want the story in their September issue).

Next would be the television programs, then radio, then weekly magazines, then newspapers, and finally, the Internet. This is a typical order based on lead times.

The second means of organization by circulation/viewership/listenership figures, is beneficial if you are nervous about running out of money. It's best to send to the media that will give you the most bang for your buck. If you have limited resources, sending to media outlets that can reach more than 100,000 people is better than sending to those that reach less than 50,000. After all, postage costs the same no matter who you're sending a kit to.

The third means, by the subject the media cover, is helpful because you can use the same spiel, or pitch angle, for one grouping, without switching gears for every phone call. Particularly when you tell them why this subject would be of interest to their consumers.

Deciding how you want to proceed is necessary for the next step, which is creating your timeline or calendar. You need to plan when you are going to mail and call the media and in what order.

Create Your Timeline

Your timeline is extremely important. It is your schedule of when you're supposed to be doing what. Mine looks like a calendar. Yours can look however you want it to, whatever is the easiest for you. You can even buy a special daily planner just for your publicity. I do recommend that you keep your publicity calendar separate from your real-life calendar. There is too great a chance that you will mix things up otherwise.

I'll use the "teenage angst" example and create a timeline so you can see what this should look like. I'm going to use a publishing date of September 15, 2001. Also, to simplify things, I'm going to use a maximum lead time of about three months.

I've got clean monthly calendars for June, July, August, and September in front of me and I've pulled out the target media list that we created earlier (see, I told you it would come in handy!). For the first draft, I'm going to use pencil in case I have to move things around. For the final draft, I'll use color-coding and different fonts. Figure 10-1 shows what it looks like.

According to my calendar, the first thing I need to get started on is developing the Web site. We'll talk more about that in detail later. The point is, if your Web site is going to be of any use to the media, you have to have it ready before you start to send out your materials. You'll include your Web site address on your press release and you don't want to tell the media to go look at something that's not there. As you'll see in Part III, this may take some time to design and get up and running, so plan ahead.

Also, as we learned earlier, you have to mail out galleys early so the reviewers have time to read your manuscript, decide that they want to write about it, and schedule it to run. These can be official bound galleys from your publisher or they can be bound by your local copy center. Remember to make sure you mark them "Uncorrected Proof" so nobody quotes something incorrectly.

The next step that I've scheduled is to do all the preliminary legwork. That's rereading your book, making all your notes, and so on. You'll also notice that I've scheduled a meeting with a photographer. Remember, you should get the headshots done early enough to redo if they don't come out so well.

Next, start creating your media database or contact list cards. As you can see, I've scheduled almost an entire week to do this. It could take you longer, depending on what sources you use to compile the list.

Then the biggie, creating the press release. I've scheduled three days to do this. Remember that you want enough time to look at it with fresh eyes.

June 2001

FIGURE 10-1

Sunday	Monday	Tuesday	Wednesday	Thursday	Friday	Saturday
Last and This Week: Develop Web Site 27	Mail Out Galleys 28	29	30	31	Read Book Make Media Notes 1	Read Book Make Media Notes 2
Finish Media Notes 3	Meet w/Photog. Arrange Shoot ASAP 4	Begin Media Database 5	Continue Media dB 6	Continue Media dB 7	Continue Media dB 8	Continue Media dB 9
Finalize Media dB 10	Create Press Release 11	Continue PR 12	Complete RP 13	Make Sure Web Site Is Up and Running! 14	Write Synopsis 15	Write Sample ?'s Praise List Gather Clips 16
17	Put Press Kits together and check postage 18	Label and stuff envelopes for Round #1 Media 19	Create mail log Mail Round #1 Magazines 20	Create Status Log 21	Prep Round #2 Media 22	23
Create Timeline Must have photos 24	25	Round One of Pitch Calls 26	Pitch #1 con't Mail Round #2 Radio 27	Pitch #1 con't 28	Update status 29	30
	Write Out Pitch 25					

Don't rush this part. This is also a good time to double-check and make sure the Web site is up and running. If it's not, rework your timeline. Don't send anything out until your Web site is ready—if you're going to have one. You don't *have* to have one, in case I did not made that clear earlier. It's optional. If you don't want to do it, don't. It will not make or break your book.

The next week or so is consumed with completing the other collateral materials needed for the press kit. Take one step at a time and you'll get it all done. Never panic. No one can write well when they feel backed into a corner. Take your time.

The day finally arrives when it's time to mail to the first round of media (i.e., long-lead magazines). This now means it's all real. There is no turning back. This should be a fun and nerve-wracking day. Remember when you're doing this to keep your mail log sheets up to date. It's a royal pain to try to recreate them later on. Also, create your status log.

You have two tasks to accomplish after you've mailed out your first round of materials. The first is to begin working on your phone pitch and actually start calling the media. The second is prepping for your next round of mailings.

And that's just the first month.

The second month is the "row, row, row your boat" part of the plan (see Figure 10-2). As you can see it's a matter of making pitch calls, prepping for the next mailing and more pitch calls, and so on. It is in this second month that you write and distribute a couple of fax blasts. These are one-sheet reminders that you fax to the media. It's like a shorter version of your press release without all the detail to the format of a press release. In a pinch, you can use the actual press release and scribble a little note like, "Bob, hope you've had a chance to take a look at the materials. Best, Joe." You hope that Bob actually gets it and thinks, "Oh, yeah! I gotta remember to take that home with me this weekend."

I have also scheduled a day to go around and talk to bookstore owners or managers to see if I can have a book signing or launch party. Remember, I'm not a huge fan of these, but many other publicists think they're a good idea. I'll let you decide for yourself.

The rest is just doing the work.

Month three is more of the same, with the addition of mailing out invitations to the big mouth list of people for a book signing (see Figure 10-3). Later in the month you should also send out a quick reminder, in case they've forgotten about it.

July 2001

FIGURE 10-2

Sunday	Monday	Tuesday	Wednesday	Thursday	Friday	Saturday
1	2	3 Begin Pitch #2	4 Holiday – No Pitch	5 Pitch #2 con't	6 Update Status	7
8	9	10 Pitch #1 Follow-Up	11 Pitch #1 Follow-Up	12 Write Fax Blast #1 For Round 1 Media	13 Update Status	14
15	16 Meet w/Mgrs. of Bookstores	17 Fax Blast Media 1 Magazines	18 Pitch #2 Follow-Up	19 Pitch #2 Follow-Up	20 Update Status	21
22	23 Mail Round #3 Television	24 Pitch #1 Follow-Up	25 Pitch #1 Follow-Up Write Fax Blast #2	26 Fax Blast Media 2 Radio	27 Update Status	28
29	30 Mail Invites to Book Signings	31 Pitch #2 Follow-Up	1 Pitch #2 Follow-Up	2 Begin Round #3 Pitch	3 Update status	4

August 2001

Sunday	Monday	Tuesday	Wednesday	Thursday	Friday	Saturday
29	**30** Mail Invites to Book Signings	**31** Pitch #2 Follow-Up	**1** Pitch #2 Follow-Up	**2** Begin Round #3 Pitch	**3** Update Status	**4**
5	**6** Pitch #3 con't	**7** Pitch #3 con't	**8** Pitch #1 Follow-Up	**9** Pitch #2 Follow-Up	**10** Update Status	**11**
12	**13** Pitch #3 Follow-Up	**14** Pitch #3 Follow-Up	**15** Pitch #3 Follow-Up	**16** Write Fax Blast #3 for Television	**17** Update Status	**18**
19	**20** Fax Blast #3 Television	**21** Prep for Mailing #4 Newspapers	**22** Pitch #1 and #2 Follow-Up Mail #4/Newspapers	**23** Pitch #3 Follow-Up	**24** Update Status	**25**
26	**27**	**28** Pitch #4 Follow-Up	**29** Pitch #4 Follow-Up	**30** Pitch #4 Follow-Up	**31** Mail Out Book Signing Reminder Update Status	**1**

This is the point when many of you may begin to feel discouraged. Maybe the media isn't calling you back or whatever. Don't be. Many times it won't happen until the very last minute. Make sure you don't sound panicked or angry. Stay calm and try another angle. Maybe you chose the wrong angle for that media type. Come up with something else and fax-blast them. Change your pitch around, make it fresh. If you've tried the same pitch a few times with no results, try a new angle. Keep plugging away.

The big month is here (see Figure 10-4). I can feel your stomach knotting. Relax! At this point it's either going to work or it's not. Worrying about it will not change anything. However, it will start to get a little hairy about now. Panic, regret, and worry will probably have taken control of your normally sane brain. This is normal. Just try to breathe through it. Keep doing the work and get more exercise than normal to keep your head clear and your mind from freaking out.

It's time to make sure all of the preparations for your book signing are in order, make a few phone calls to the big-mouth people, and start thinking about local media coverage for your event. If you'll notice, the day before the event is the time to start contacting the local television and newspaper people to see if they'll cover your event. This would be the time to send out a media alert. I'll show you an example in Part III.

One thing to keep in mind: If your book signing is on a weekend, you have to wait until the weekend assignment editor gets into the office. That is usually after 2:00 or 3:00 P.M. on Friday. If you call earlier in the day, you will speak to the regular assignment editor, who has no authority over how the media's resources will be used during the weekend. You have to wait for the right person. You should also call the desk early in the morning on the day of your event to see if they're going to show up.

After the official book launch, it's just a matter of continuing to follow up all your media leads. Four weeks after the launch date is probably a good time to start slowing down. By then, if they haven't covered your book, they probably won't.

That's how the timeline works. It's a lot of work, but so was writing the book in the first place.

September 2001

FIGURE 10-4

Sunday	Monday	Tuesday	Wednesday	Thursday	Friday	Saturday
26	27	28 Pitch #4 Follow-Up	29 Pitch #4 Follow-Up	30 Pitch #4 Follow-Up	31 Mail out Book Signing Reminder Update Status	1
2	3 Holiday – No Pitch	4 Fax Blast #4 Newspapers	5 Pitch #1,2,3 Follow-Up	6 Pitch #1,2,3 Follow-Up	7 Update Status	8
9	10 Pitch #2,3,4	11 Pitch #2,3,4	12 Pitch #2,3,4	13 Pitch #2,3,4	14 Call weekend assign. ed. @ local TV re: Book Signing on Sun.	15 OFFICIAL LAUNCH DATE!!!
16 Book Signings Call local TV in AM	17 Entire Week: Pitch #2,3,4	18	19	20	21	22
23	24 Entire Week: Pitch #2,3,4	25	26	27	28	29
30	1 Entire Week: Pitch #2,3,4	2	3	4 Continue Pub. Plan	5	6

Put Your Press Kits Together

You've decided on the order in which you will contact the media and have come up with a plan. You also know how many press kits you are going to need. Now you have to start putting all these elements together. There's nothing magical about putting a press kit together, but there are some logical things to keep in mind when you do. Here's what I would do:

1. Using some type of spray mount, affix the cardstock copy of your book cover to the outside of your two-pocket folder (see Figure 10-5). I would do all of these at one time. It's kind of messy, so wear old clothes and do it out in the garage. The mist from the spray mount tends to fly all over. If you get adhesive on your hands (which you will), you can take it off with nail polish remover. Better yet, use a nontoxic cleaner (like De-Solv-It) made from citrus oil. Your hands will smell citrus-y sweet!

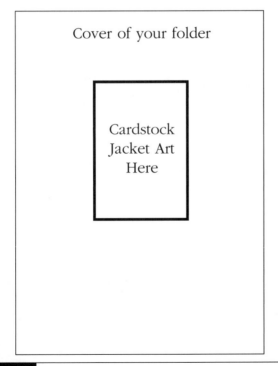

Cover of your folder

Cardstock
Jacket Art
Here

FIGURE 10-5

2. If you have professional business cards (that match your letter-head), pop one in the little holder slots on the inside pocket of the folder. Because this is very tedious, I now officially give you permission to turn on the television and watch some news programs. Multitask. Do all of these at once.

3. Now you have to put all the papers you've written into the folders. This is how I do it: In the left pocket, I put all the papers that talk about the book and background materials. From front to back: the synopsis, any blurbs or advance praise quotes, and background information/press clippings. On the right, I put everything about the author. From front to back: the press release, one-page bio, and sample questions. Finally, I put the 8 x 10 photo in on top of all the papers in the right pocket (see Figure 10-6). Feel free to do it however it makes sense to you, as long as you get everything in there.

You now have a complete press kit. Congratulations! Make as many as you will need all at once. I would also make up an additional 15 to 20 extra full press kits. The media tend to "mis-place" press materials—a lot!

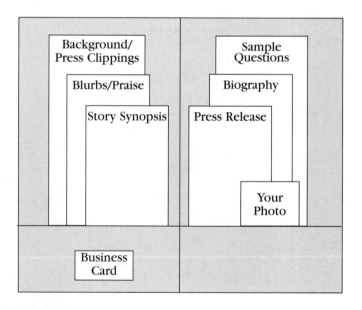

FIGURE 10-6

112 ■ LITERARY PUBLICITY *The Final Chapter*

Create Mailing Labels for Your First Round of Media

Feel free to hand-address (neatly) all the mailing labels. But—if I may be so bold as to remind you of the handcramps you get during the holiday season when you address all of those holiday cards to your friends and relatives— you may want to rethink the hand-written option.

A better way would be to use your computer's word-processing program and generate mailing labels with your computer. They are neater and easier to read. It is also helpful when you send additional information to the same media outlets. When that happens, all you have to do is print out another page of labels and you're ready to rock-and-roll.

As Grandma would say, "To each his own, honey."

Weigh and Stuff Your Mailing Envelopes

This step is really important.

If you do not have a scale made specifically for mail, take an envelope and a press kit and go to the post office and ask them how much it will cost to mail this first-class (regular mail). One missing press release or one absent photo can give you an incorrect scale reading, and you could get 100 press kits sent back to you marked "insufficient postage." This is very bad.

One time we had three mailings all going out on the same day, so I hired a temp to speed up the process. How hard could it be to stuff an envelope and put on the postage? Apparently, it's more difficult than one would think. When she said she knew how to read a postage scale she was lying. She was four cents short on *all* of the postage for the millions of press kits we mailed out that day. Every single one of them came back three days later! I ended up eating the cost of all the wrong postage, the envelopes, and the mailing labels. That mistake cost me $431.18 and three days' work. Believe me, I'll never forget it. Be accurate.

Stuff All Your Envelopes and Put the Postage on

After you're sure you have the right amount of postage, gather the family and friends and have a stuffing party. Have someone slap the mailing label on the envelope, another shove the press kit inside the envelope, another seal the envelope, and another stick on the postage, while you check off the completed envelopes on your master mailing list.

Make a Postage/Mailing Log Sheet

You are going to need to keep track of when you mailed materials to the media and when you made your follow-up calls. You are going to be extremely busy with all of this and it is vital that you don't mix up your dates. Keeping track of 500 pieces of mail and 3,000 phone calls is a tricky business.

Your mailing log can serve two purposes. The first, obvious one is to keep track of when (and if) you sent the materials. The second, less obvious, purpose is that a good mailing log can help you with tax writeoffs. We love this. You can prove to Uncle Sam how much you spent on this project and take the business writeoff. Here's how your log should look:

DATE	MEDIA OUTLET NAME	NUMBER OF PIECES MAILED	POSTAGE
5/1/2001	New York Times	1	$3.27

Create a Media Status Report

As I said earlier, keeping track of hundreds of phone calls can make you nuts. It is a good idea to create a media status report that tells you who you sent materials to, when, to whom, and what they had to say when you called them to pitch your book. Your ongoing status report should look something like this:

NEW YORK TIMES (CIRCULATION 1,074,471)
Contact: John Smith, Lifestyle Editor

5/1 Mailed press materials

5/5 Left voice mail with John

5/7 John called and said "not right for his section." He forwarded materials to Jane Johnson, Features Editor.

5/8 Called Jane, left voice mail

You can do the same thing if you're using note cards instead of your computer.

Since John Smith "passed," or declined, you should also change the contact name on the status report to "Jane Johnson, Features Editor." There's no sense in keeping a name that's not going to do you any good.

A mailing log and status report should keep you on the right track and help you avoid mailing things twice or calling the wrong person. Again, it also helps you with tax writeoffs.

Note: *Please contact a professional tax person to make sure you are following the requirements of state and federal tax laws!*

"ROW, ROW, ROW YOUR BOAT."

Now it's just a matter of mailing; calling, calling, calling; mailing; calling, calling, calling; mailing; and so on. Mail out the materials to your first group of media. Record your results. Wait four days, then mail to the next group (group 2), and start calling group 1. Record your results. Wait four days, mail to group 3, begin calling group 2, make another round of calls to group 1. Record your results. Lather, rinse, repeat. If this is confusing, look again at the timeline; you'll get the hang of it.

Some Things That May Happen

Nothing ever goes completely according to plan. Murphy was right: Whatever can go wrong, will. Don't get thrown. Here are some troubleshooting ideas.

1. They haven't received the materials by the time you get them on the phone. Simply tell them you will give it another few days and call them back. "When is the least intrusive time to contact you?"

2. They haven't had time to look at the materials yet. Assure them that that is just fine and you'll contact them later in the week or early next week.

3. The press kit gets sent back to you with no forwarding address. Research the new address and resend. Make a note of it on your master media contact list.

4. The person you sent the materials to is dead. Out of the 1,500 "regulars" we work with, at least 3 media people die every year. (I swear!) If this happens, apologize and gently inquire as to who has taken over that person's responsibilities.

5. They ask you to fax over "some materials." Do *not* fax over the entire press kit. Only send the press release, synopsis, and your bio. Nothing else! <u>Resend a full press kit, via mail, to back up the</u> fax.

Managing Your Publicity Campaign

Once you've come up with your plan, you really need to stick to it. Every part of your plan is interconnected. If you skip one mailing, it's going to throw off the rest of your plan, like tumbling dominoes. If you can't commit completely, don't bother to even start. Keep in mind that this is only for a few months, not forever. If your friends or family are not being supportive, get new friends or a new family. This is too important and you've worked too hard to mess things up at this stage of the game. The more the people around you feel a part of the process, the fewer hassles you'll have to deal with.

Also, as I've pointed out earlier, you need to be adaptive, to a point, particularly when it comes to breaking news stories. Don't panic; just do the work and pick up where you left off on the plan.

The Dreaded Pitch Calls

Follow-up calls are what separate the professional from the amateur. I don't think anyone can teach you through a book how to handle this with finesse and grace. A *pitch call* is when you call the media person directly and try to get her interested in you and your book. This takes practice, so I would pick 5 to 10 media outlets that are less important to you and start with them. That way, if you mess up it's not such a big deal. You don't want to screw up and embarrass yourself with Jane Pauley or some other big-time reporter. Practice on your family and friends. You have about 17 seconds to hook them or lose them! Trial-and-error is the name of this game. See the sample "scripts" in Part III to get you started. The key is to be clear, concise, and quick. Remember, these people are under an ungodly amount of stress and working under terrible deadlines.

If anyone you're calling says, "I'm on deadline," immediately say, "All right, I'll contact you tomorrow," and HANG UP! The golden rule of media is: they never, *ever* say they're on deadline unless they really mean it! If they miss the deadline, they could lose a big story and possibly get fired. Do not attempt to engage them in conversation, even "for just a minute," when they are on deadline! There is never, ever an exception to this rule. Ever.

Media Alerts and Fax Blasts

A **media alert** is a one-sheet document that is typically faxed to the media as a reminder to cover an event. I use what I call a "fax blast." I'm not sure if other publicists use this term or not, but it does serve its purpose. A **fax blast** is just that: we are blasting all of the appropriate media on our lists with a fax regarding our client/author. We do this when something timely has happened in the news and we think our author would make a great "talking head" or pundit to comment about the subject at hand.

The media alert/fax blast literally includes who, what, when, where, why, and how. No flowery language, just down-to-the-bone information. See the sample in Part III.

These can be extremely effective if you get your timing just right. Often the media forget that you're out there. This is a great way to reestablish contact.

RESEARCH TOOLS

B y now you've read the preceeding materials and have a firm grasp on all that is involved in creating and executing your publicity plan. As promised, here are some research tools to help you with some of the things about which you may be unfamiliar.

The first thing you have to do is gather information. Specifically, you have to find out about the different types of media and how to contact them. Here are some ways to find out who is where and how to get hold of them.

1. The best and most complete reference books that I've ever used are published by Bacon's Information Inc. You can call them at (312) 922-2400 or go to their Web site at www.baconsinfo.com. These are the publicist's bibles. They come in several volumes. There is one for magazines, one for radio, one for television, another for print, and a new one for the Internet. They are very expensive. A whole set will probably cost you about $1,200. You can buy each volume separately if you want. Each is bigger than a library dictionary, and about as exciting, but they help a lot. These books give you contact information, circulation figures/market shares, phone and fax numbers, some e-mail addresses, and so on. If you can afford them, they're very helpful.

2. Go to your local public library. There are several types of reference books that include contact information. Ask your reference librarian for help. (Because you're a writer, you are probably already on a first-name basis with them!)

3. Go to a bookstore that has lot of magazines and newspapers and start copying down the contact information from the front of each magazine. Tedious, but always the most accurate. They list the most current editor, and other information. People in this industry tend to move around a lot. Also, watch the programs you're thinking of sending your materials to and jot down the names of some seg-

ment producers as the credits roll at the end of the program. The same applies to newspapers. Find a reporter that you think might be open to looking at your book and send it to him.

4. Radio is a tougher nut to crack. Use your phone book and get the general phone number of the radio station. The downside is that most receptionists are unfamiliar with the staff for each program. It's not their fault. Radio programs get cancelled all the time. It's difficult to keep track of what's on and what's not. Sometimes even the people working at the radio station don't know. Be patient. Keep trying.

5. Finally, ask your friends and co-workers if they know anyone in the media. I am constantly surprised by who my friends know, and most of my friends are not in this business. Someone always has an uncle, cousin, best-friend's-husband or someone who knows someone who knows the producer of something. I'll bet that someone you know knows at least one media person. If you schmooze them right, they might even give you other people to contact.

6. Use the Internet. As discussed earlier, use a variety of search engines to look for traditional media contact information and for online Web sites or publications. You can also use the Internet to discover media outlets you never knew existed. Also, Web sites for popular television shows, magazines, or newspapers often have a "how to contact us" Web page where you can get phone numbers, mailing addresses and fax numbers. There are also a lot of Yellow Pages or White Pages Web sites where you can type in a person's name or the name of the show/magazine/newspaper you're looking for and have the site search engine find it for you. It's like directory assistance, only for the Internet.

7. There are a few other books that I've either just flipped through or only heard about. I can't vouch for their accuracy or helpfulness because I've never used them, but they may help you nonetheless.

   - *Broadcasting & Cable Yearbook.* This covers radio and television.

   - *Standard Rate and Data.* This is primarily for advertisers and comes in separate volumes for each of the media types.

   - *Working Press of the Nation.* This covers all types of media in three volumes.

   - *Media Map.* This is primarily geared to business and finance print media.

- **Burrelle's.** This company started out as a clipping service and has expanded into media contact books. Comes in three volumes.

- **Editor & Publisher Year Book.** Daily and weekly newspapers only.

- **Gale Research.** A three-volume set covering all media.

- **Parrot Communications.** This also covers all media.

Again, the primary publication I use is Bacon's media directories. You will have to decide which is most appropriate to your needs and your budget.

THE INTERNET—
AN INTRODUCTION

A s promised, here's more about the Internet; I'll show you how to do this, and then you feel free to give it a shot. I'm going to do a bare-bones explanation right now, but I'll give you a full example in Part III when I show you a complete publicity plan.

There are only a few basic things to know about the Internet that can get you started. As you surf the Net you'll begin to understand the Web's finer points. In this short chapter, I briefly discuss:

1. Defining your search.
2. Using a search engine.
3. Understanding a Web site.
4. Contacting media through the Web site.
5. E-mail etiquette.
6. Attachments.

Alrighty, then. First, you have to define your search. What exactly are you looking for? A computer does not take well to "fuzzy logic," and it's not psychic. In other words, it doesn't know what you're thinking. You have to type exactly what you mean and mean what you type. If you are looking for a list of New York newspapers, you have to tell the search engine/computer exactly that. If you are too general (like just "newspapers"), you will get a list of thousands of inappropriate Web sites and have to sit there and sift through all of them. Type: "new york daily newspapers." This will narrow the search down to just New York. Note that capitalization usually doesn't count. Every search engine has some sort of advanced search section where it will prompt you for more specific information. If you're new to this, you may want to start directly there.

USING A SEARCH ENGINE

A **search engine** is the means of sorting through the tons of information running around on the information superhighway. It's like the old IBM key punching machines, only a lot faster. There's a slew of different search engines and each sorts information in a slightly different way. This means that if you used the exact same words on three different search engines, you could get three completely different lists of results, so it is always a good idea to try a couple of different search engines when you're looking for something on the Internet.

The search engine with which most people are probably most familiar with is "Yahoo!" Let's take a look at the main page and I'll point out a few things that might help when you're surfing the Web (Figure 12-1).

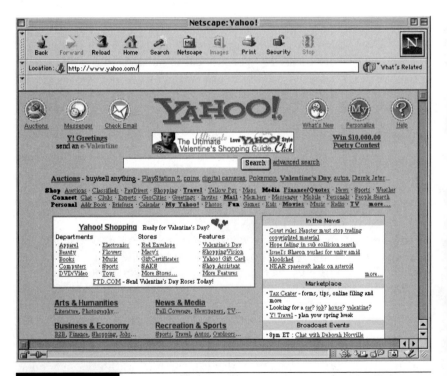

FIGURE 12-1   Reproduced with permission of Yahoo! Inc. ©2000 and Netscape Communications Corporation ©1999.

1. Right near the top of the page, just under the Yahoo! logo, there's a blank box with a button marked "Search" and then "advanced search." You type in the words that describe what you're looking for and click on "Search." At the speed of light, the Yahoo engine runs around its database, which catalogs a hefty proportion of the sites on the Web, finds all of the Internet sites that most closely match your request, and spits out a list for you to see. If you click on any one of the results, it will take you directly to that Web site.

2. Another cool thing on some of these engines is subcategories that will focus your search from the get-go. If it's a medically based Web site, it won't bother to look in the business and economy parts of the Internet. It can save you a little time and increase the number of relevant returns. Check out each of the subcategories—they may give you other ideas for publicity that you may not previously have thought about.

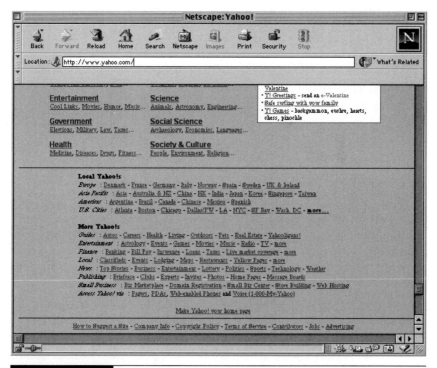

FIGURE 12-2   Reproduced with permission of Yahoo! Inc. ©2000 and Netscape Communications Corporation ©1999.

3. At the bottom of the page, you will see "Local Yahoo!s and More Yahoo!s" (see Figure 12-2). These two areas can also be of great help. The "Local Yahoo!" can focus your search to a specific geographic area, which is great if you are looking for media in Atlanta only. You would click on "Atlanta" and then do your search as you normally would.

4. "More Yahoo!s" are other places (pre-chosen by the site coordinator) in which you may be interested, like astrology, top news stories, or tax information. These can also be inspirational for publicity ideas.

5. Don't pass up "fan sites" just because they don't carry not a recognizable news name. There are millions of Web sites created by people just like you who are interested in, for example, the Civil War. If your story takes place during the Civil War, you should definitely send your materials to the person running the Civil War Web site. You should also send him a book. You would be amazed at how many people with similar interests check these sites out. They usually all know each other from bumping into each other in online chat rooms.

That's all there really is to doing a search on the Internet. As I've said earlier, you are going to have to sift through a lot of results that are inappropriate for what you need, but it is still fairly simple.

UNDERSTANDING A WEB SITE

Most Web sites have a main page and some kind of navigation system to get you to different pages within the Web site. The main or "home" page, sometimes called the "welcome page," is like the table of contents for a book. It gives you a brief idea of what the Web site is all about and then some buttons to get you to specific areas of the site.

On the Web site for Marich Communications Inc., I have a very brief main page and then several buttons across the top that you click on to get you to the page that has the information you are interested in. Any Web site could be only one page, but it would be like that roll of heat-sensitive fax paper. Who wants to scroll down 50 pages to get to where they want to go? It's a matter of convenience and cuts down on the download time. It's more like pages or chapters in a book.

ANATOMY OF A WEB SITE: MARICH COMMUNICATIONS WEB PAGES

Figure 12-3 shows the home page for my company, Marich Communications Inc. As you can see at the top, there is a header with the company name on it. Every Web site has this. It lets you know that you're at the right place. You can also tell if you've hit the right place by checking the URL up at the top of your screen. URL, by the way, stands for *uniform resource locator*—a fancy name for the Web site address. The URL for my site is: **http://www.marich-communications.com**. This will take you to the first page of my Web site, also known as the home page. Keep in mind that you must type in all the dots, dashes, slashes, and underscores for any Web site address or you could wind up at another site. For those of you who aren't particularly computer-savvy, if you ever want to go back to a home page without retyping the URL—which gets real old real fast—go to the top of your screen and look for "bookmarks" or "favorites." Click on one of those

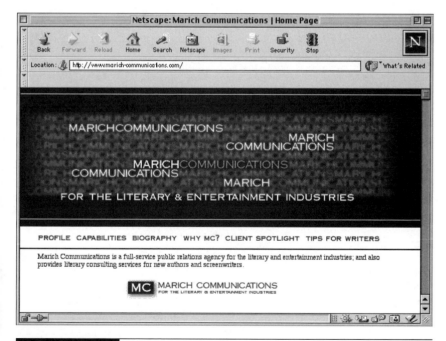

| FIGURE 12-3 | *Netscape Communicator browser window © 1999 Netscape Communications Corporation. Used with permission.* |

words and a little box will pop up and say something like, "Add Bookmark" or "Save as Favorite." Just click on that and the next time you want to go back, all you have to do is open your Bookmark or Favorite file and click on the place you want to go.

Just underneath that is the navigation bar. That's the part that says, "Profile, Capabilities, Biography, Why MC?, Client Spotlight, Tips For Writers." If you click on any one of those words, it will take you to another page that has that information on it. You can tell if a word will take you somewhere else by watching for the little arrow to turn into a little hand. How that came about is anyone's guess. If you don't get the little hand, you ain't going anywhere. For example, if you clicked on "Profile," you would see the page shown in Figure 12-4.

This page has some general information about my company on it. Because there's more text than fits on the one screen, there is a scroll bar at the vertical right side of the screen. If you click on the triangle pointing up, the page will scroll up. If you click on the triangle pointing down, you will scroll down the page. This is so you can see everything on that particular page. Also notice the addition to the URL. After the main address, it also says: "/pro-

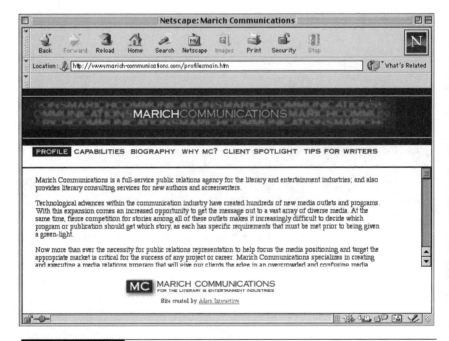

FIGURE 12-4   *Netscape Communicator browser window © 1999 Netscape Communications Corporation. Used with permission.*

file.htm." This is the URL, or address, for this specific page. You can also add this page to your bookmark or favorites list. You may want to do this on occasion if it took you a gazillion steps to get to the page you need and you don't want to go through all that again.

We'll look at one more page of this Web site. Clicking on "Capabilities" will make the page shown in Figure 12-5 pop up on your screen.

This page gives people more specific information as to what Marich Communications Inc. can do for our clients. It also includes special pricing plans, and a few other goodies. It is pretty much what the word implies: what we are capable of doing for our clients. Most items listed on the navigation bar will be worded in such a way that you can figure out what information the page is going to contain.

I want to point out a couple more things using this page as an example. If you look at the bottom of the screen, you will see the Marich Communications logo. If you click on that, an e-mail box will pop up and you can send me an e-mail. Most Web sites will have something like this, or they will have a separate button on the navigation bar that says, "Contact us." If you don't see that, try clicking on the company logo.

FIGURE 12-5   *Netscape Communicator browser window © 1999 Netscape Communications Corporation. Used with permission.*

Almost all Web sites that have been professionally produced tell you who designed the site. This is for two reasons. First, it gives the Web site designer free publicity. You can click on their logo to get to their Web site, where you can see other examples of their work. This is in case you like the site design so much that you want to hire them to do yours.

The other reason is that if you notice something is not working properly, you can be the nice person that you are and contact them to tell them to get busy and fix the problem.

If the information on that page is not what you were looking for, you can click on the "Back" button at the top of your screen. Sometimes it will be in words, as in my examples; sometimes it will just be a picture of two arrows, one pointing west and the other east (go back or go forward). You don't have to keep clicking on the navigation bar if you want to look at the preceding page.

Many Web sites will have different, smaller, less complicated headers than the one on the main page. This is just to give you more space to read what's on the page. They figure you already know where you are, so they don't need to impress you with their main-page header graphic again.

If you've found the page and the information you were looking for, you can also print the page by clicking on the "Print" button or the little printer icon at the top of your screen. Depending on how the Web site was designed, you may not be able to print all of the stuff on that page. Also keep in mind that the more graphics there are on a page, the longer it's going to take you to print.

If the page gets stuck and it won't let you click on anything, try clicking on the "Reload" or "Refresh" button at the top of your screen. Sometimes things just get jammed up; sometimes you encounter a Web site that wasn't designed properly, so you have to reload the information to "unstick" the page. Most of the time this will solve your problem. It's not unlike when your computer freezes up. Sometimes the only way to fix that is to restart your computer. "Reload" is the Web site version of a restart.

Once you check out a few sites, you'll get the hang of using them. The best piece of advice I can give you is not to be afraid that you'll ruin something. The beauty of Web sites is that you can't hurt them. Everything on a Web site is "locked in" so that you can't add or delete anything on it even if you want to. If you make a mistake, just hit the "Back" button at the top of the screen and start again.

CONTACTING THE MEDIA THROUGH A WEB SITE

Once you find the Web site you're looking for and determine that it would be a great place to send your publicity materials, you have to figure out how to send your stuff to them. There is usually a button marked "Contact us" somewhere on the main page or at the bottom of one of the other pages.

If you click on that, an e-mail box will probably pop up. Fill in the subject box with something short and sweet like, "*Book Title* information." Then go into the text box and type a very short, one-paragraph note—something like:

"My name is Joe Marich and I have just published a how-to book on doing your own publicity, specifically geared to authors. Since your Web site is all about writing, I thought you and your web-visitors might be interested in hearing more about this new book. I've attached a few pieces of information in WordPerfect9.0 format that I thought might help explain a little bit more about my book. If you have any questions, or would like additional information, please do not hesitate to contact me at 310-555-1212. Best regards, Joe Marich."

And you're done.

It's not always that easy. If you can't find the "Contact us" box, you may have to use the trial-and-error system. Many Web sites, especially those of the major news organizations, use their names in their e-mail addresses. For example, let's say you wanted to send materials to a fictional newspaper we'll call the *Anynews Tribune*. Its Web-site address might be: www.anynewstrib.com. This can give you a clue as to a reporter's e-mail address. Here are four ways I would try to contact reporter Bob Smith at *Anynews Tribune*.

> bsmith@anynewstrib.com (or .net)
>
> Bob.Smith@anynewstrib.com
>
> Bob_Smith@anynews.com
>
> B_Smith@anynews.com

It's usually something like one of these. If it's wrong, the e-mail will bounce back to you so you can try another variation. *Do not try all four at once!* The reporter may have two separate e-mail addresses, one for interoffice e-mails and another for outside e-mail. You will really tick Mr. Bob off if you send him the same stuff twice!

On some news Web sites, the reporter's name in the byline is in blue. This is a hyperlink that will take you directly to her e-mail address. This makes life very simple. Click on the blue hyperlink and fill in the subject box, write your note, and hit "Send." One down and a million more to go!

E-Mail Etiquette

First, be clear and concise. Don't ramble on and don't try to teach your contactees everything there is to know about your book. You just want to whet their appetite and find out if they want more information.

Don't gush. If it's a news agency, they're very busy. Be professional and get to the point. They don't know you, so they probably don't care a whole lot about your opinion of them. If you thought they were stupid, you wouldn't be asking them to write an article about you in the first place.

If they send you an e-mail indicating that they're upset that you contacted them this way instead of by traditional snail mail, take them out of your computer address book right away. If you get them mad, they'll never write about your book.

Attachments

I like to tell the contactees in the body of the brief note which format my attachment is in. It helps them figure out how to open it, or if they can't, how to resolve the problem.

Also, I wouldn't sent the entire press kit as an attachment. Just send them the latest press release, a one-page synopsis of your book, and your one-page bio. That should be enough information for them to decide whether they want to go to the next level.

More and more reference books are appearing that list Web sites by category or area of interest. However, keep in mind that many of the listings are out of date by the time these books are published. Nevertheless, they should get you started. These resources can help you target your "mailing" to the appropriate Web sites—providing they accept new materials. For instance, if you're looking to send press materials to Web sites that cater to women, they will list those all in one place and probably give you a little information about what types of materials each one will accept. This dramatically reduces the time you need to spend doing your own searches for the right Internet outlets.

The other good news is that there are literally hundreds of thousands of Web sites that may write about your book. Compare this to tens of thousands of traditional media outlets—your odds are dramatically increased. Of these hundreds of thousands of Web sites, most are not general-interest, but target-specific Web sites. They are targeted to their niche markets. This means that you can send materials to sites that are being used by your particular targeted consumer.

I have come to believe that there are many very useful Web sites run by experienced, professional, established companies and people. The difficulty for me concerns the amount of time it takes to determine which are trustworthy and which are not.

If you are well-versed in Internet workings, you should absolutely use the Internet to your advantage. If you are not, you may want to stick to the traditional media, at least in the beginning.

CREATING YOUR OWN WEB SITE

A Web site dedicated to your book can be helpful for the media, particularly if they have misplaced the collateral material you've already sent them. You can also put the Web site address on your press releases to alert the media to any updates about the book, upcoming book signings, and so on.

There are a lot of programs available that walk you through the Web site design process step-by-step. Consult your local computer store to determine the best program for your needs.

You should include the following information on your Web site:

1. A picture of your jacket art, at a resolution of at least 300 dpi. This high-resolution picture can be downloaded directly by the media to be used in a story.

2. A synopsis of the book. Keep it brief. Remember, you are not trying to tell the whole story, you're just enticing them.

3. Your bio.

4. Important dates. This will inform the media as to where you will be giving book signings or readings so they can attend if they want to. If you have to go to another city on business, you could even include the dates you will be traveling and to where. (You

don't have to get into *why* you will be in Peoria, just that you will be there on such-and-such date.)

5. You can have a "Reviews" page or section. Please keep in mind that you will need permission from the publication if you are planning on reprinting a review. **You do not own the rights to that material—the publication does!** Just because they talk about you does not mean you have free use of the review. Many publications require a reprint fee, which can be as much as $10,000 for a year or free if you fill out a release form supplied by the publication.

6. Don't try to put too much information on each page. Also, make sure the really important information is toward the top. Many people will not scroll down.

7. As with reviews, most photos are not free for use. You have to pay for them. Do not scan, for example, a photo from *Time* magazine. You cannot do that without permission, and most major publications will not give them to you for free. If you feel the need for graphics, either create your own or buy a CD-ROM with clip art. Most clip-art CD's are free-use, but read the packaging before you use any. Also remember that too many graphics will slow down the download process. Use only what you need. And *please,* no family pictures or snapshots. Keep this professional!

8. Use the copyright symbol at the end of each page. This way other people have to get permission from you before they use anything found on your Web site.

9. Don't center all your text. This screams "amateur hour!" You can center major headings if you want, but not the body of the text. If you have a lot of text, use a white background and a sans-serif font. It's easier to read onscreen. It is the exact opposite of the printed text that you use for your book or press-kit materials. I don't know why, but it just is. If you are going to use a lot of photos, they will look better on a dark background.

10. Make sure you have a navigation bar at both the top and bottom of each page, or one on the side of the screen.

11. Use your name as a domain name (the address) for your Web site. First, it will be easier to guarantee that the address is available. Second, you may write another book, and if you use the book title you'll have to go through the registration process all over

again. Contact a company called Network Solutions, at www.net-worksolutions.com, to register your domain name. This company is responsible for making sure, through its registration process, that no two Web sites have exactly the same name. It's about $70.00 to do this, and it's well worth the cost. If at all possible, don't use one of those "three free Web pages" offers from your Internet service provider. The address will be too complicated and it will appear amateurish.

12. Keep updating your Web site and keep it fresh.

A PULL-OUT SECTION

I've crammed a lot of information into a small amount of space at this point, so I wanted to create a pull-out section that you can keep nearby as you are gathering all the press-kit and other materials together. This may be redundant, but I think a quick checklist is always helpful. Here's what you need to do:

1. Create your collateral material and put it all in folders. **Collateral materials** is a fancy name for all the stuff you're going to put in your press kit. Don't forget to include:

   - The press release.

   - A black-and-white photo: either 5 x 7 or 8 x 10 is fine.

   - A one-page bio about yourself; don't worry if it's longer, just make it interesting.

   - A story synopsis.

   - A list of 10 sample questions.

   - Any "advance praise" quotes, if you can get any.

   - Any press clippings or related articles.

   - Anything else you think will help clarify things for the media person.

   I like to divide the contents of the folder in a logical manner. I prefer all of the information regarding the author in the right pocket of the folder, and all of the information about the book and background materials on the left. It's just a quirk of mine.

   Actually, there is a logic to it, but I'm not sure how to explain it. When the folder is opened, I like my client's face and info to be the first thing the media sees. After all, my clients are paying my bills. Also, when you close the folder, the photo slides around all over the place if it's in the left pocket, and it just gets annoying. But you do whatever you think is best; no one has ever been denied an interview because a photo was in the "wrong" pocket.

2. Research your media. Figure out who you want to contact and when you're going to have to get the materials to them (lead time). Get their correct addresses, phone numbers, fax numbers, and, if appropriate, e-mail addresses.

3. Address your envelopes. I think you'll find that 10 x 13 envelopes work best. They can handle the press kit folder and a review copy of the book, too. If you have a postage machine, figure out the postage first and run the empty envelope through the machine— *then* stuff all the material inside. You should figure about $1.43 in postage for just a press kit and about $3.20 in postage if you include a book. Do the math before you start on all of this, because it can get a bit costly, as you can see.

4. Mail your envelopes only to those you know you will be able to call within the next five days or so. Don't send out a thousand press kits at one time. You'll *never* be able to make all those phone calls and keep your sanity in five days. Give the mailing about three or four days to get to its destination and then make follow-up calls.

5. *Follow-up calls are what separate the professional from the amateur.* I don't think anyone can teach you through a book how to handle this with finesse and grace. You have about 17 seconds to hook them or lose them! Trial-and-error is the name of this game. I strongly recommend that you start making follow-up calls to the least important media outlets first, just to get the hang of it. The key is to be clear, concise, and quick. Remember, these people are under an astonishing amount of stress, working under terrible deadlines.

   If anyone you're calling says, "I'm on deadline," immediately say, "All right, I'll contact you tomorrow," and *hang up!* The golden rule of media is: they never ever say they're on deadline unless they really mean it. Do not attempt to engage them in conversation, even "for just a minute," when they are on deadline! There is never, ever an exception to this rule.

6. Make detailed list of who you've called. Keep track of each time you've called them and what they had to say (e.g., "I'll take a look at it next week."). This way you'll know how long to wait to call

back. Also, if you get an answering machine, leave your pitch message (see the script in Part III). If you've been trying over a matter of weeks, and they have not responded, they are not interested. Chalk that one up as "passed" and stop calling them.

This also is a good time to remind you not to get "pissy" if you keep getting a contactee's voice mail or machine. Do not get, or at least sound, frustrated when leaving a message. That is the kiss of death. Don't burn bridges!

7. Repeat the process until you've contacted all of your media.

8. Kick back, have a cup of coffee, and have a good laugh.

GIVING A GOOD INTERVIEW

Y ou've done everything we've talked about and you actually got your-self an interview! Congratulations! Now you have to learn what to do after you get the booking. This is the really fun part!

Here are some specific questions to ask once a reporter or producer agrees to an interview with you. Notice that there are slightly different questions to ask, depending on the medium.

IF THE INTERVIEW IS GOING TO TAKE PLACE ON TELEVISION:

When do they want to do the interview?

How long will the interview last?

What is the angle of the interview?

If the television studio is out of town, will they provide transportation?

If the television studio is out of town, can they do this via satellite?

If not a live interview, when will it air?

Do they need to do a pre-interview?

Do they need any additional information prior to the interview?

Will they do hair and makeup for you at the studio? (This applies to men, too.)

Do they need artwork for a bumper card?

A **bumper card** is a frozen image that flashes on the screen when the station is coming back from a commercial break or cutting to a commercial.

Often they will put up a copy of the book jacket cover and a phone number where viewers can order the book.

Always take two extra copies of your book with you when you do a television interview. Ask that the host hold up a copy of the book or that one be displayed on a desk or table on the set. These extra copies always come in handy.

IF THE INTERVIEW IS GOING TO TAKE PLACE ON RADIO:

When do they want to do the interview?

How long will the interview last?

What is the angle of the interview?

Is the interview going to take place in the studio or via phone? (Commonly called a **phoner**.)

Will there be audience call-in?

Do they need to do a pre-interview?

Will this be pretaped or live? If taped, when will it run?

What is the name of the host?

What is the "hot-line" number?

The **hot-line number** is a phone number most radio programs have specially designated for guests to call in on, which bypasses the main switchboard. It generally goes right into the control room. They will almost always call you—let them pay for the call. In the event that they don't contact you at the assigned time, this number acts as a backup so you can get to them.

Very important: Only give a phoner for radio on a dedicated phone land line. That means NO CALL WAITING! It also means no cell phones or portable phones. Spend eight bucks and get yourself an old-fashioned plug-in phone with a cord. If you have call waiting, turn it off before the interview. The radio people will be furious if you get "beeped" in the middle of an interview! In the past, I've used my modem or fax line and just plugged in a spare phone. Those lines are usually dedicated, with no call-waiting features. Also, ask if you can receive a tape of the interview for your files.

IF THE INTERVIEW IS FOR A PRINT PUBLICATION:

When do they want to do the interview?

How long will the interview last? (No interview should take longer than 45 minutes.)

What is the angle of the story?

In what section of the newspaper or magazine will the interview run?

Will the interview be face-to-face or a phoner?

Will they be bringing a photographer?

Do they need photos?

When will the interview run, in what issue?

Do they need any additional information prior to the interview?

The second point bears additional explanation. You need to control the time allotted for the interview. If it runs more than about 45 minutes, the reporter is going to start to get into more personal issues. He's already asked a million questions about the book, so there's nothing else to ask but personal questions. <u>Keep in mind that you want to sell books, not your life story.</u> By controlling the time, you force the reporter to stay within the topic at hand—namely, your book.

SOME WARNINGS FOR INTERVIEWS

1. Be aware of what you are saying at all times. The interview begins *the moment you step foot in the studio or greet the reporter.* No matter what they say, *nothing* is off the record. Stay on guard. If you're doing a television interview, pretend the camera is on you from the moment you step into the studio until you are in your car driving home. A lot of people have gotten caught off-guard because they didn't heed this warning.

2. Be aware of "ummmm"-ing a lot. It sounds unprofessional and is irritating to watch/listen to. It's a common habit of people when they're nervous. Be aware.

3. Avoid flippant or sarcastic remarks. They absolutely do not translate to print and you can come off looking like a real jerk. *And* sell no books. Avoid them for television and radio, as well. Why take the chance of being misunderstood?

4. You should already know the angle of the interview, but keep a bullet-point cheat sheet handy—for phoners only. Do not write out big, long-winded thoughts. Just jot down some of the things you want to remember to talk about. Think chapter titles. This is

also where your sample questions will help you get started feeling comfortable with interviews.

5. Dress and behave professionally. Be pleasant but not too goofy. They're doing their jobs, you do yours. This is not the time to get into any personal discussions about how bad your day has been, or how awful traffic was, or any other irrelevant matters. Pretend you're going into a business meeting and act accordingly: friendly, but professional.

   More on how to dress. A good key for television is to observe how the host dresses. Ladies, wear a suit or a pants suit. Always wear hosiery. Avoid sandals, if possible. This is no time for the "earth mother" thing. Avoid clangy jewelry, or the sound guys will be unhappy. Stick with tasteful, small, simple jewelry. Wear something comfortable that has clean lines. I'm not a fan of big bows on blouses, but I'll leave that up to you. A simple shell under a jacket always works. If you don't trust your taste, go to a good department store and ask a salesperson to help you pick out a nice outfit.

   Gentlemen, wear a suit. I know they can be uncomfortable, but you will look much better on camera. A suit forces you to sit and stand differently than jeans and a t-shirt, just because of its construction. Wear an off-white, light gray, or light blue shirt (*not* a denim shirt!).

   Wearing white: Don't. On camera, something pure white will burn out. If you've ever seen a photograph that contains too much contrast between white and black, you know what this is. It can leave a light trail whenever you move. Be safe and stay away from pure white.

   Patterns: If you wear a patterned suit with small checks or houndstooth, or if your tie has little checks, or tiny repeating images, the image can "jitter" or look like it's vibrating. The technical term is *line interpolation*. The camera gets confused as to which lines it should be recording and it can look like your tie is alive. It is very distracting. You can always be safe by taking a selection of ties with you and asking the producer which one will look best. Also, both ladies or gentlemen should also take a back-up outfit to the studio. You never know when some klutz is going to spill coffee on you right before you're supposed to go on. If you don't use it, no harm done. Feel free to ask the producer that is setting this up what you should wear.

6. Know your stuff. Reread your own book before an interview. The better prepared you are, the calmer you'll be. Don't obsess, just be yourself. Have fun!

HELPFUL HINTS FOR AUTHORS

I think it's time to take a short breather, with some helpful hints about writing books that I have discovered over the years. Some hints are appearing here for the first time; others I have already incorporated in the preceding text. A reminder never hurts, though!

SOME HELPFUL HINTS FOR WRITING:

- Think about the marketability and media-friendliness of your book *before* you begin work on a project. Is this story one the publishers want to print, the media want to write about, and people want to see/read? I know I'm beating a dead horse with this, but it is critically important.

- Outline your novel or screenplay. There are several reasons why this is crucial to successful writing.

  — First, you will need this to get an agent and/or publisher. Often you can sell your story while it is still in outline form. Agents sometimes use the outline to sell the screen rights. It's a lot harder to outline after you've already written the book. Do this first.

  — Second, you will be able to tell if your story flows and troubleshoot problems with the plot *before* you spend a year writing a full manuscript or screenplay.

  — Start with a one-page treatment. Graduate to a five-page treatment, then a fifteen-page treatment. Follow that with two sample chapters. Get the contract signed and your advance check cashed. *Then* write the full manuscript.

- Cruise bookstores. See what is out there. See what major chains are selling. See what people are buying. Look for trends. Check out the best-seller lists in the newspaper. *Then* start thinking of book ideas.

- Don't fall in love with anything you've written. Rigidity will make your manuscript/screenplay a great holiday gift for friends and family. It will not make your writing a reality. *Everyone* gets rewritten. *Everyone.*

- Make sure your agent knows your long-term goals. If you plan on making this a career, sometimes a smaller advance and a multiple-book deal will advance your goals faster than a high advance for just one book.

- Don't sign anything with an agent or publisher without having a lawyer look it over. As with any contract, each party is trying to get the most out of the deal. The agent or publisher may try to slip something into the contract that you don't want, and that only a lawyer experienced with publishing contracts is able to spot. Most agents and publishers are honest, but it is best to be safe.

- If you don't understand something about your contract, don't be afraid to ask point-blank questions, again before you sign anything. It is your responsibility to ask and their responsibility to answer. Keep asking until you fully understand the terms of the contract.

- Ask your publisher what your exact responsibilities are when turning in your manuscript drafts. I've just learned this the hard way for this book. I didn't realize I would have to separate all the graphics, insert computer codes, and edit and proofread my own manuscript. I'm sure they told me, but I didn't really hear them or understand what that meant at the time. I've had to put in a lot of extra time to learn these things and figure out how to do them.

- The reverse also holds true. Ask your publisher what its exact responsibilities are. What are they going to do for you and your book? Get it hashed out before you sign anything. This way everybody knows what they have to do and when. Because this is what they do for a living every day, I think they assume that every first-time writer knows all this. *(We don't!)* The people I'm working with are very nice and have been very helpful in guiding me through the process, by the by.

- If your publisher, like mine, sends drafts out for peer review, take the reviewers' comments to heart. The people who have commented on this manuscript have given me loads of valuable ideas and have helped keep me on track. It is always beneficial to have a fresh pair of objective eyes look at your manuscript. After all, these people are the start of positive word-of-mouth for your book. This also applies to editors.

- If you disagree with your peer reviewers or your editor, don't be afraid to stand up and say something. Just be sure you can back up your point of view. One peer reviewer for this book wanted me to write a book on marketing a book. That is not the book I wanted to write, nor, as I said a million times in the beginning of this book, is it a book I am able to write. He felt that a book on marketing would be more helpful than a book on literary publicity. He may be right, but I don't know how to do that. I explained this to my editor and she basically told me to stick to my guns.

- Creating a book takes time. If you started creating a book/screenplay today, it may not hit the shelves for up to a year and a half. This is not going to happen overnight.

- Give agents/publishers time to read your manuscript/screenplay. It can take up to three months to get a response. Be patient. Don't bug them.

- Don't ever be afraid to ask questions. No one can know everything about everything.

- Keep your sense of humor, as I've said before. We're not saving the whales, we're entertaining and (maybe) educating our audience.

PART 3

A SAMPLE
PUBLICITY
PLAN

A REAL-LIFE PUBLICITY PLAN

B y now, you know the differences between advertising, marketing, and publicity; you know how to think about your book as a product; you have written all your press materials; you have compiled your media lists; you know the proper etiquette for contacting the media; you know what makes a media-friendly book; you understand how much this is going to cost; and you're committed to doing this on your own.

Throughout the first two parts of this book, I tried to use examples based on a novel. I thought it would be helpful if you also saw the development of a publicity campaign, from start to finish, for a nonfiction book: namely, this one. I thought I would kill two birds with one stone, since I'm going to have to do this anyway, and you will get to see all the things I've been talking about in action—a final product out of all this hard work.

I will try to include snippets of my thought process along the way. I hope this helps to illustrate all of the concepts outlined throughout this book.

EVALUATING YOUR BOOK

1. **After reading my book, what should the reader have learned about the human condition (fiction) or the primary subject of the book (nonfiction)?**

After reading my book, authors should have gained practical knowledge about the art of publicity and how it works. They should also have greater insight into the world of the media. They should be able to create and execute a dynamic publicity plan, using the step-by-step instructions contained herein. This includes the concept of writing a media-friendly book, choosing the right target media, writing all the collateral materials, determining a budget, creating a timeline, and executing the publicity campaign for their own books.

They should also have gained an understanding of the emotional demands they can expect while executing their own publicity campaigns. Tangentially, this includes accepting the realities of media coverage for a first-time author.

2. Am I an expert on the subject matter contained in my book?

Yes. I have worked in the entertainment industry for 16 years, and in public relations for nearly 10 years, working with corporate clients, as well as both first-time authors and established authors.

3. What is happening in the news that might tie in with my book?

Nothing. Currently, there are no breaking news stories about publicity, per se. However, should there be another event like the O.J. trial, there could be sidebar stories concerning the media coverage of a high-profile trial for which my area of expertise might be of interest. Also, there might be an opportunity to discuss the proliferation of quickly written books about high-profile subjects and how the media and publishing houses use publicity for their own needs.

4. Does my book have any unusual angles that might be useful to the media or to a specific group?

Yes. Regarding media angles, there are a few. The uniqueness of a how-to book specifically on literary publicity might be of interest to the media. Both print and electronic media cover the literary industry and many different types of books. They might be interested in "list"-type stories such as "5 simple ways to publicize your book," or "5 reasons why publicity is necessary to make a book a best-seller." A feature story, such as "Why you should do your own book publicity," might also be of interest, specifically to the literary trade media.

Several specific groups might find this book of sufficient interest to extend an offer of speaking engagements. These include writers' conferences, university creative writing courses, and communications courses. Because understanding publicity and the media is critical to a successful book, and this book is specifically targeted to these groups, it is logical to expect some level of interest in having me introduce this material in an oral presentation.

5. Is my title exciting enough and does it accurately reflect the story?

Yes. You can't get more accurate than "Literary Publicity," and the subtitle, "The Final Chapter," is a fun play on words.

6. Is my jacket artwork interesting and appropriate to the story?

Not known. As of this writing, no discussion has taken place with the publisher regarding style and format for jacket artwork.

EVALUATING YOUR RESOURCES

Can I afford to do this?

Yes. My contract with the publisher includes a specified amount to go toward publicity for this book. Although this amount will only cover approximately 5 percent of the total expected costs, I have the means to supplement this amount to create and execute a full publicity campaign for this book.

Human resources available to me.

Because this is what I do for a living, I do not require immediate or extended family involvement in executing this campaign. From my years of experience, I already have a generous amount of media contacts and a support staff that will serve this campaign well.

For those of you reading this book, this is where you would compile your lists of family and friends and the specific jobs you would like them to be responsible for.

Also, because this is what I do for a living, I have the required amount of time to execute this publicity campaign. I also have much experience in estimating the amount of time each facet of this campaign will require.

Budget

MEDIA OUTLETS (total: 255 — Total press kits: 293):

I've just gone through my media database and come up with the following media lists. I made several decisions during this process. I decided to contact the publishing trade magazines, for obvious reasons. I think they might be interested in a how-to and reference book that writers can use to help them become successful. I'm expecting either a book review or a small feature story.

Publishing Trade

American Libraries	Publishers Weekly
Analog: Science Fiction and Fact	Rapport: The Modern Guide
BookPage	Realms of Fantasy
Fantasy & Science Fiction	Romantic Times
Fiction Writer	Science Fiction Age
Mary Higgins Clark Mystery	The Writer
New Mystery	Writer's Digest
The New York Review of Books	Writers' Journal
Poets & Writers	Writing

Magazines

I chose the following magazines for a variety of reasons. Most of them were chosen because I know they have book review sections or "what's new" columns; others, like *Chicago* magazine, because that is where I was born and raised, for a "local-boy-does-good" story. I also eliminated the smaller-circulation magazines because I want to get the most bang for my buck (especially since most of those bucks will be mine!). Some of these also made it to the list because I have long-standing relationships with several reporters and editors that I figure might give me a break. Also note that I may add some media outlets and cut some of these from the list. This is just a basic list to get me started.

The Atlantic Monthly	Marie Claire
Bikini	Maxim
Chicago	McCall's Magazine
Chicago USA	Men's Journal
Complete Woman	Mirabella
Cosmopolitan	National Enquirer
Details	New Times Los Angeles
Easy Living Magazine	New Woman
Elle	Newsweek
Entertainment Weekly	P.O.V.
Family Circle	People
GQ: Gentlemen's Quarterly	Reader's Digest
Interview	Real Woman
jane	Redbook
Ladies' Home Journal	Star Magazine
Los Angeles Magazine	Time
Mademoiselle	Us Magazine

USA Today Magazine
Utne Reader
Vogue

Woman's Day
Working Woman

Early Morning News/Talk Shows

The early morning news/talk shows listed here were chosen because I know many of the executive producers and segment producers and because their demographics fit with my book. The Los Angeles morning shows were chosen because this is where I currently live; again, "local-boy-does-good" might work. All of these programs are produced in the top 10 metropolitan media markets.

ABC 7 News Sunday Morning WLS -TV
Daybreak WPXA-TV
Eye Opener WCVB-TV
Eyewitness News This Morning
Eyewitness News This Morning WABC-TV
Fox Morning News
Good Day Atlanta WAGA-TV
Good Day LA KTTV-TV
Good Day New York WNYW-TV
Good Day New York Sunday WNYW-TV
Good Day New York Wake Up WNYW-TV
Good Day Street Talk WNYW-TV
Good Morning America
Good Morning America Sunday
Good Morning Washington WJLA-TV
Greta Kreuz WJLA -TV
KGO Sunday Morning News

KTLA Morning News KTLA-TV
Morning News WGN -TV
Morning News Early Edition WGN-TV
Mornings on Two KTVU-TV
NBC 5 Morning News WMAQ-TV
News 2 Chicago at 11:00 AM WBBM-TV
News 4 This Morning WBZ -TV
Saturday Today in New York WNBC-TV
Sunday Today in New York WNBC-TV
Sunrise KDFW-TV
This Morning
The Today Show
The Today Show—Weekend Edition
Today in L.A. KNBC-TV
Today in New York WNBC-TV
WGN Morning News

Talk Shows—General Interest

I know, I know. I told you not to send to *Oprah,* but I know a lot of people there, so for me this falls under the "send to who you know" category. I know I don't stand a snowball's chance in hell of getting on there, but maybe my personal contacts will give me an edge. I'm sending to the other shows mostly because I want them to know what I'm up to with the writing. I don't expect to actually book many (if any) interviews on these shows. It's really not their thing. I might be able to come up with an angle after I think about it for a while.

Jenny Jones Show
John King Variety Talk Show
Lifetime Live
Live with Regis
Montel Williams Show

New Maury Show
Oprah Winfrey Show
Ricki Lake Show
Sally Jessy Raphael Show
The View

Top 10 Markets—Newspapers

Every city across the country has a local newspaper. Most of those have a small circulation. For financial reasons, I'm only starting with newspapers in the top 10 media markets. These markets, in order of size, are: New York; Los Angeles; Chicago; Philadelphia; San Francisco; Boston; Washington, D.C.; Dallas; Detroit; and Atlanta. I will send to the book review editor and the features editor.

DESIGNATED MARKET AREAS (DMA)

You may want to tailor your publicity plan to only the top designated market areas (or DMAs). These are primarily chosen by population factors. There are 211 DMAs in the United States. Here is a list of the top 20 DMA markets:

1. New York, NY
2. Los Angeles, CA
3. Chicago, IL
4. Philadelphia, PA
5. San Francisco, CA
6. Boston, MA
7. Washington, D.C.
8. Dallas–Ft. Worth, TX
9. Detroit, MI
10. Atlanta, GA
11. Houston, TX
12. Seattle–Tacoma, WA
13. Cleveland, OH
14. Minneapolis–St. Paul, MN
15. Tampa–St. Petersburg, FL
16. Miami–Ft. Lauderdale, FL
17. Phoenix, AZ
18. Denver, CO
19. Pittsburgh, PA
20. Sacramento, CA

Army Times Publishing Service
Asbury Park Press
Atlanta Journal-Constitution
Baltimore Sun
Boston Herald
Chicago Sun-Times
Chicago Tribune

The Current
Daily News
The Dallas Morning News
Detroit Free Press
Detroit News
Fort Worth Star-Telegram
The Journal Newspapers

Greenwich Times
Los Angeles Times
The Morning Call
New York Post
The New York Times
The News Journal
Newsday
The Orange County Register
Parade
Philadelphia Daily News
Philadelphia Inquirer
The Press-Enterprise

The Record
Salt Lake City Tribune
San Francisco Chronicle
San Francisco Examiner
San Jose Mercury News
The Star-Ledger
St. Louis Dispatch
USA Today
USA Weekend
Washington Post
Washington Times

Radio Programs

All of these radio programs are talk radio, which is exactly what I want to do—talk about publicity, writing, and the media. By the time I mail press materials to these radio programs, I may or may not cut this down considerably, but for now, this is how the list stands:

A Woman's View
A Second Cup of Coffee
Access
All Things Considered
Amazon Country
America This Week
An Exceptional Woman
At Your Service
Barry Farber Show
Bay Area Woman
Bay View
Bernie Ward Show
Big Picture
The Bill Handel Show
Bill Wattenburg Show
Booktalk
Brian Copeland Show
C-Trends
Casper Citron
Chris Clarke Show
Conversation with Cele
Crosstalk
Dateline: Washington

The David Dinkins Show
The Derek McGinty Show
Dialogue 101
Double Take
Dr. Joy Browne Show
Dr. Nancy Snyderman Show
Dreamland
Ed Koch Show
Family Talk
FemiNazi Radio
Feminist Magazine
First Light
For Women Only
Forum
Free Forum
Freund's Forum
The Geoff Metcalf Show
Georgetown University Forum
Impact with Frank Sontag
In Depth
Issues
Jack Christy Show

The Jim Eason Show
The Kathy & Judy Show
KGO Afternoon News
KGO Noon News
L.A. Chicks
The Lee Mirabal Show
Left to Right
Lesli Baldacci Show
Lite Life Magazine
Live with Lou & Georgene
Liz Maita Show
Lynn Samuels Show
Mall of America Show
Markey & O'Malley
Mary Matalin Show
Michael Savage's Savage Nation
Morning Edition
Myrna Ochs Show
News at 11
Newstalk Network
Newstalk With...
Newsweek on the Air

Noon News
Not for Women Only
Open Air
Pat Thurston Show
Paul Harvey News
Point of View
Portfolio
Private Lives
Roe Conn & Gary Meier Show
The Ronn Owens Show
Sisters Times
Something You Should Know
Sound Off
Spectrum

Spotlight
SundayMagazine/Update
Talk America Radio Network
Talk of the Nation
Time For Women
Today's Issues
Today's World
Tom Hall
Tom Joyner Morning Show
The Tom Leykis Show
The Tracey Miller Show
UPI Roundtable
We The People
Weekend News Magazine
Weekend Headliner

Weekend Saturday
Weekend Sunday
While We're on the Subject
Wishing You Well
Woman to Woman
Womankind
Women at the Crossroads
Women Forum
The Women's Center
Women's Focus
Working Woman
Working Mom on the Run
The World Tonight
Your Health Matters

Cost of Supplies

I know I won't have to buy any new equipment or general office supplies, because I already have all I need. I will have to buy all of the press kit "fixin's." Here's how the supply budget looks:

Total number of press kits needed: 293

Total number of folders needed: 293

> The folders are sold 10 to a pack.
> I'll need 30 packs.
> Each pack costs $8.39.
> **Total cost: $251.70**

Total number of envelopes needed: 293

> The envelopes are sold in boxes of 100.
> I'll need 3 boxes.
> Each box costs $6.99.
> **Total cost: $20.97**

Total number of mailing labels needed: 293

> Labels are sold by the box.
> Each box costs $23.99 (on sale).
> **Total cost: $23.99**

Grand total for supplies (excluding office supplies): $296.66

Copy Costs

Total number of press kits: 293

Total number of pages in each press kit: 6

> Press release: 2
> Bio: 1
> Sample questions: 1
> Synopsis: 1
> Advance praise: 1

Total number of copy pages: 1,758 @ 5 cents per page:

> **Total for standard copies: $87.90**

Card stock covers: 147 (I'm going to put 2 on each page) @ 10 cents per page:

> **Total card stock copies: $14.70**

Grand total for copies: $102.60

Cost of Letterhead

Because I'm going to generate my letterhead directly in the computer, I will be able to print out master press kit copies directly onto my computer-generated letterhead and take those to the copy center. I can also print out all of my fax cover sheets and memos directly from my computer. This means I will have no additional costs regarding letterhead!

Cost of Photos

Total number of photos needed: 293

> Photographer cost: $175
> Photo duplication cost: $75 (I had to get 500 because they only do 250 or 500 at a time)

Grand total for photos: $250.00

Postage

Initial mailings will not include a copy of the book; I will send them out as requested.

Total number of envelopes being sent: 293
Postage cost for one full envelope: $1.27

Total for press kit postage: $372.11

When I send out copies of the book:
Total number of books to mail: 75
Postage per book: $2.31

Total for book postage: $173.25

Grand total postage: $545.36

Faxing

No cost.

Overnight Delivery

This is nothing more than an educated guess. I'm estimating that I will need to send out 20 press kits or books via overnight delivery over the course of the campaign. I'm using an average cost of $15 per delivery.

Grand total (estimate) for overnight delivery: $300.00

Messenger Service

Again, I'm going to estimate my costs. I will probably only have to messenger something to three or four media outlets. The average delivery cost in my area is about $10.00.

Grand total (estimate) for messenger service: $40.00

Phone Calls

From past experience, I know that my phone bills will be about $250 a month. Depending on your phone plan, yours could be a little more or a little less.

Grand total (estimate) phone calls: $250.00

Let's take a look at my fixed costs up to this point:

Grand total for supplies (excluding office supplies): $296.66	
Grand total for copies:	$102.60
Grand total for photos:	$250.00
Grand total for postage:	$545.36
Grand total (estimate) for overnight delivery:	$300.00
Grand total (estimate) for messenger services:	$40.00
Grand total (estimate) phone calls:	$250.00
Grant total:	**$1,784.62**

Optional Costs

Remember earlier in the book, when I discussed optional costs? Here is an estimated budget for these optional costs. Keep in mind that they may end up being more or even less than I anticipate.

TRAVEL

At the moment, I do not anticipate any travel on behalf of this book. If I get an interview outside of California, I will have to decide if the benefits outweigh the costs. I will have to take this on a case-by-case basis.

ADVANCE COPIES OF BOOK

According to my contract, I am allotted five books. I intend to keep these for my personal collection and probably give one to each of my family members. They're already gone and I haven't even finished writing this yet!

I'm sure that if I talk real nice to my editor, she may give me 40 or 50 books to use for publicity purposes. At least I hope so.

SPECIAL EVENTS

As God is my witness, I will not do any type of special event. Who has the time! Forget about the financial considerations, I just don't have the time to do this.

WEB-SITE DESIGN AND MAINTENANCE

I've designed my own Web site that I intend to add to my company's Web site at no additional charge.

VNR/EPK

Creating a VNR or EPK is not appropriate for this type of project. The media are either going to cover the book or they are not. A VNR/EPK would not be cost-effective.

Some Final Thoughts about Budget

There are no additional costs that I can plan for in advance at this point. The grand total stands at $1,784.62. I always factor in a 20 percent "oops-I-forgot" figure. There is always *something* that comes up unexpectedly, so I think it is important to include this contingency figure. In this case that would be $356.92; let's just say $375 and call it a day. My new total is $2,159.62.

Also keep in mind that your supplies budget will probably hover somewhere around $300 to $500, and maybe more if you don't have a fax machine or laser printer.

A final note: I've kept the number of media outlets to a bare minimum. If you were going to hire a professional, they would probably be sending to double or triple the number of media outlets, thereby tripling your costs. They would also have to factor in overhead like office rent, payroll, taxes, etc., putting your cost in the $2,500 to $5,000-per-month range.

All told, if my company was going to do a major national, regional, and local publicity campaign, I would charge $4,000 per month plus expenses for a minimum of 6 months. We'd be looking at $24,000 plus expenses. See how much money I'm saving you? I don't want to hear any complaining about the cost of this book.

I hate doing the budget! I'm mind-numbingly bored, so let's move on. Please!

SETTING REALISTIC GOALS

I have decided that I want to do my own publicity; I've evaluated my book and I think it's media-friendly; I can afford to do this; and now I have to set some realistic goals. If you remember this section from earlier, I had you ask yourself those 15 questions, like "is my book media-friendly? Do I have time to do this? Do I have the support of my publisher?" I've gone through those questions again and, happily, I was able to answer "yes" to all of them. Now I can continue through the process. My book also passed the "so what?" test. (I'm very proud!)

Psychological Stress

I am well aware of the psychological stress created by doing my own publicity. As I thrive on adrenaline, this should suit me just fine!

Media

I have a clear understanding about the media. If I didn't, I wouldn't be writing this book, so I think I'm good to go here.

THE NUTS AND BOLTS OF MY PUBLICITY PLAN

I'm going to take this step-by-step, just like I said in Part II. Here's what I did.

Reread Your book

Done. In this section I asked you to make a list of major plot elements that might be useful for your press release. In my case, the book is a single-subject book. I don't have any subplots or characters that do different jobs or talk about a variety of subjects. This is fairly typical of a nonfiction book. I used fiction in the early part of the book so you could see an example of that, and now I'm using this book as an example for nonfiction. (Hope it helps.)

Because this is a nonfiction, single-subject book, my list is fairly short:

- literary publicity
- the media
- writing tips

That's it!

The next step is to add some news tie-ins or story ideas. Again, this will be a little different for this type of how-to book. I need to come up with more feature story ideas, rather than hard-news tie-ins. Here's my list:

- Literary publicity: behind the scenes of a literary publicity campaign; 5 elements that make a media-friendly book; how to become a "talking head"; why you need publicity to make a book successful; it ain't easy: war stories from the publicity front; writing as big business; managing your media expectations; being on the other side: a publicist turns writer. Many of these will work only for trade publications. Some newspapers and general-interest magazines may like the behind-the-scenes or "tips" stories. War stories are good for radio/television interviews.

- The media: who are they and what do they do?, 5 tips for an effective interview; how a media story is born; the media as a business. Mostly for writing trade publications. Television may like the effective-interview angle.

- Writing tips: 5 tips for a successful book; making sure your book passes the "so what" test; long-term versus short-terms goals for writers. These are stories primarily of interest to writing trade publications.

Make a Market Classifications Shopping List

- Literary publicity: Magazines: writing trade, educations trade, entertainment, general-interest, women's and men's general-interest. Newspapers: book review editors, lifestyle editors. Radio: general-interest talk radio. Television: local/regional morning news/talk shows, national morning news shows, national afternoon talk shows.

- The media: Magazines: writing trade. Newspapers: lifestyle editors and Sunday magazine supplements. Radio: general-interest talk radio. Television: cable news discussion/issue programs, local community discussion programs.

- Writing tips: Magazines: writing trade, education trade. Newspapers: none. Radio: none. Television: none.

Create a Media Contact List or Database

Done.

Create Collateral Materials for the Press Kit

Since I have several ideas to choose from, I'm going to write a general press release that can work for several different media outlets. This will be my introductory press release that I'll use for my first round of mailing. If I think it will help later on, I will make different target-specific variations for the later rounds. These variations will have different headlines and lead paragraphs, but everything else will remain substantially the same.

— — — — —

LITERARY PUBLICITY: THE FINAL CHAPTER

JOSEPH MARICH JR., PUBLIC RELATIONS EXPERT, REVEALS THE SECRETS TO CREATING AN EFFECTIVE PUBLICITY CAMPAIGN FOR ASPIRING AUTHORS

— — — — —

or maybe this one:

— — — — —

SO YOU WANT TO WRITE A BEST-SELLER?

JOSEPH MARICH JR., PUBLIC RELATIONS EXPERT, SHOWS YOU HOW TO DO IT IN HIS NEW BOOK, *LITERARY PUBLICITY: THE FINAL CHAPTER.*

— — — — —

I like the first one because it's cleaner and more balanced. That being said, it is a bit dry and lacks some punch. I've used "reveals," "effective," and "aspiring," which are fairly active, but I think those words are overused. I like the book title standing by itself at the top, but I like the rhetorical question of the second headline, too. The first one is a little too "on the nose." The second one is a bit more creative. Maybe I can combine the two:

— — — — —

LITERARY PUBLICITY: THE FINAL CHAPTER

IF YOU WANT YOUR BOOK TO BE A BEST-SELLER, JOSEPH MARICH JR., PUBLIC RELATIONS EXPERT, SHOWS YOU HOW IN *LITERARY PUBLICITY: THE FINAL CHAPTER.*

———

It's a bit wordy, but I can live with that. I've got the title in there, twice in fact. I've got my name in there and the fact that I am an expert in this field. I've also communicated that this is a how-to book, so the media knows it is nonfiction without me having to say it directly.

I think I'm going to go with the last example.

Now I have to write the lead. Let's see how this goes:

———

LITERARY PUBLICITY: THE FINAL CHAPTER

IF YOU WANT YOUR BOOK TO BE A BEST-SELLER, JOSEPH MARICH JR., PUBLIC RELATIONS EXPERT, SHOWS YOU HOW IN *LITERARY PUBLICITY: THE FINAL CHAPTER.*

You finally finished writing the final chapter of your book and you think you're done, right? Wrong! You've really only just begun. You have one more chapter, and it is called Literary Publicity. *That* is your final chapter. With over 10 years of professional public relations experience, **Joseph Marich Jr.** shows new authors how to create their own "publicity machine" and get media attention for their books in his new book, *Literary Publicity: The Final Chapter* (Delmar, March 2001). In this easy-to-read, step-by-step book, authors will learn how to target the right media, develop an effective publicity plan, create an interesting and informative press kit—and "do-it-yourself!"

"I wanted to create a book that would help aspiring authors, who may not be able to afford a professional publicist, do their own publicity," says Marich. "I wanted to give them a practical tool, like a dictionary, that they can keep on their desk and refer to whenever the need arises." With the thousands of books written every year, it is vital that authors understand the publicity process—the media can make or break a book, no matter how well-written it is. Understanding this process will give new authors an edge.

The process of creating an effective publicity plan is no great secret. It just takes a basic understanding of some publicity principles, some writing skills, a lot of time, and an unlimited supply of determination. A little cash doesn't hurt, either. *Literary Publicity* is equally useful to novice and more established authors. The process is the same—only the media changes. New authors may start by getting local media coverage for their book, while more established authors may move up to national coverage.

Literary Publicity: The Final Chapter takes the author through the entire publicity process, from concept to reality. It includes writing the most media-friendly book, targeting the right media, writing a press release, and contacting the media in the most effective manner. There are no other books like this on the market. There are many great marketing books, but few (if any) publicity books specifically designed for authors.

Marich has over 10 years' experience working for major public relations firms. His clients have included many corporations, product lines and services, film and television productions, and even more authors. Marich is the president of Marich Communications Inc., located in Beverly Hills, California, where his firm specializes in literary, entertainment, and consumer public relations.

If you would like more information or a review copy, or would like to arrange an interview, please contact NAME at 000-555-1212, or via email at jmarich@pacbell.net.

— — — — —

There. That wasn't so hard.

I've proofread my release and now I'm going to put it in the correct format.

Here's how it looks:

—————

LITERARY PUBLICITY: THE FINAL CHAPTER

by Joseph Marich Jr.

FOR IMMEDIATE RELEASE   Contact: Name
February XX, 2001   310-555-1212

LITERARY PUBLICITY:
THE FINAL CHAPTER

IF YOU WANT YOUR BOOK TO BE A BEST-SELLER, JOSEPH MARICH JR., PUBLIC RELATIONS EXPERT, SHOWS YOU HOW IN *LITERARY PUBLICITY: THE FINAL CHAPTER*.

You finally finished writing the final chapter of your book and you think you're done, right? Wrong! You've really only just begun. You have one more chapter, and it is called Literary Publicity. *That* is your final chapter. With over 10 years of professional public relations experience, **Joseph Marich Jr.** shows new authors how to create their own "publicity machine" and get media attention for their books in his new book, *Literary Publicity: The Final Chapter* (Delmar, March 2001). In this easy-to-read, step-by-step book, authors will learn how to target the right media, develop an effective publicity plan, create an interesting and informative press kit— and "do-it-yourself!"

"I wanted to create a book that would help aspiring authors, who may not be able to afford a professional publicist, do their own publicity," says Marich. "I wanted to give them a practical tool, like a dictionary, that they can keep on their desk and refer to whenever the need arises." With the thousands of books written every year, it is vital that authors understand the publicity process—the media can make or break a book, no matter how well-written it is. Understanding this process will give new authors an edge.

The process of creating an effective publicity plan is no great secret. It just takes a basic understanding of some publicity principles, some writing skills, a lot of time, and an unlimited supply of determination. A little cash doesn't hurt, either. *Literary Publicity* is equally useful to novice and more established authors.

(MORE)

The process is the same—only the media changes. New authors may start by getting local media coverage for their book, while more established authors may move up to national coverage.

Literary Publicity: The Final Chapter takes the author through the entire publicity process, from concept to reality. It includes writing the most media-friendly book, targeting the right media, writing a press release, and contacting the media in the most effective manner. There are no other books like this on the market. There are many great marketing books, but few (if any) publicity books specifically designed for authors.

Marich has over 10 years' experience working for major public relations firms. His clients have included many corporations, product lines and services, film and television productions, and even more authors. Marich is the president of Marich Communications Inc., located in Beverly Hills, California, where his firm specializes in literary, entertainment, and consumer public relations.

If you would like more information or a review copy, or would like to arrange an interview, please contact NAME at 000-555-1212, or via e-mail at jmarich@pacbell.net.

#

————

Now the photographer:

A friend of mine, who happens to be a former professional photographer, has agreed to take my photograph. I just have to take her out to a nice dinner and let her drink herself under the table. I think I can do that. My nose looks like it should have its own Zip Code and my hair looks terrible, but she didn't have much to work with. The fault lies with my genetic pool and not with her. If you get a copy of this with the photo cut out, just know that was me.

Now the biography:

Because I'm known by a lot of media, my biography is going to be a bit more professional-looking. I don't want them to mock me for the rest of my life. I have enough problems already. Here's my bio and the rest:

————

LITERARY PUBLICITY: THE FINAL CHAPTER

by Joseph Marich Jr.

AUTHOR'S BIOGRAPHY

JOSEPH MARICH JR., PRESIDENT

Joseph Marich Jr. is founder and president of Marich Communications Inc. With an emphasis in literary, entertainment, and consumer publicity, Marich has worked in public relations for more than 10 years, planning and executing national and international campaigns for over 30 book launches; special events, fund-raisers, and openings in the theater, art, fashion, television, and film industries. He has worked with major publishing houses such as Knopf, Warner Books, Simon & Schuster, Henry Holt, Ballantine, HarperCollins and Delacorte Press.

Representing author-director-producer, Michael Crichton (*Disclosure, Jurassic Park*), Marich coordinates media tours (domestically and internationally), personal appearances, interviews, and press-kit production for Dr. Crichton, working closely with his publishers at Knopf and Ballantine in New York, as well as his international publishers throughout Europe. Marich continues his public relations duties for his top-rated television series, *ER,* with Warner Television, and for Crichton's latest business endeavor, Timeline Computer Entertainment, which is developing CD-ROM and Internet games.

Marich has also been involved in public affairs and crisis management for all the Warner Music Group labels and has provided counsel to Virgin Records, United Talent Agency, and Oracle Corporation, bringing special skills to the clients by preparing them in media training, special projects presentations, and developing and producing electronic media kits for satellite feeds.

Prior to starting his own company, Marich worked as a special events producer for The Donahue Group in Beverly Hills; as director of the Literary Division at Rachel McCallister & Associates Public Relations; and for Edelman Public Relations Worldwide in their entertainment division. At McCallister, Marich worked with such distinguished clients as Rock the Vote, DC/Marvel Comics, New Line Television, and Alliance Communications. Virgin Records, Oracle Corporation, and United Talent Agency were among his clients at Edelman Public Relations.

This is Marich's first (and probably last) foray into professional writing.

LITERARY PUBLICITY: THE FINAL CHAPTER

by Joseph Marich Jr.

SYNOPSIS

Literary Publicity: The Final Chapter is a fun, easy-to-read, step-by-step publicity guide specifically written for new authors. The book is divided into three parts. The first part gives a detailed account of the concepts underlying publicity. It explains the differences between advertising, marketing, and publicity, which are many. It also allows the author to decide who should actually create and execute the publicity for a book. Once they've decided to do it themselves, the first part helps them to learn about the different types of media and how to use these concepts in a practical and effective way.

The second part of the book puts these concepts into practice. This part is broken down into a step-by-step format, with several examples, allowing the author to see how this whole process works from a practical perspective. It shows authors how to create a media database, write a press release and the other collateral materials needed for a press kit, how to pitch the media effectively, and what to do once they book an interview—everything they will need to create their own publicity campaign.

The third part is a real-life case study in action. Readers can see how a professional publicist would create a publicity campaign for the very book they are reading! It also serves as an example of a publicity campaign for a nonfiction book.

LITERARY PUBLICITY: THE FINAL CHAPTER

by Joseph Marich Jr.

SAMPLE QUESTIONS FOR THE AUTHOR

1. How did you come up with the idea for this book?
2. What can new authors expect to learn from reading this book?
3. How successful do you think an author will be if he or she follows your plan?
4. Who did you write this book for?
5. What was the most surprising thing you learned from writing this book? With the shoe on the other foot, as it were?
6. What do you think will surprise an author the most after reading this book?
7. Why did you choose to include so much humor in this book? Why is it written in this tone?
8. What do you think is the most important idea to grasp in your book?
9. What is your best advice for a new author?
10. What is your next project?

LITERARY PUBLICITY: THE FINAL CHAPTER

by Joseph Marich Jr.

ADVANCE PRAISE

"Marich has a dry sense of humor that appeals to the reader and makes us believe he knows his stuff."

Wendy J. Lawrence, Publicity & Advertising Manager
Texas A&M University Press

"This is an excellent, essential desk reference for all those writers (both new and old) who want to make the most of publicizing their work."

John L. Flynn, Ph.D., Professor of English
Towson University

"As one who has written several books, I saw Marich's advice as practical, helpful, and best of all, realistic. He knows what he's talking about!"

Dean E. Nelson, Ph.D., Professor of Journalism and Writing
Point Loma Nazarene University

"Marich has written a guide to book publicity that manages to be useful, funny and surprisingly honest. He demystifies the entire process without making it seem too easy or too hard, and gives point-by-point tips that will help any author get the job done. The book has so much good advice that Marich might put both himself and other publicists out of business."

Stephen Randall, Executive Editor, Playboy Magazine
Author of "The Other Side of Mulholland" (LA Weekly Books)

LITERARY PUBLICITY: THE FINAL CHAPTER

by Joseph Marich Jr.

A STEP-BY-STEP GUIDE TO LITERARY PUBLICITY

After you have determined that you want to do this, that you have the right media-friendly book and that you can work within your budget, here are the practical steps to execute your publicity plan:

Reread your book

Jot down major plot points

List news tie-ins

Create a media shopping list

Create a media database

Create a headline for your press release

Write the lead for your press release

Write the body of your press release

Proofread and format your press release

Choose a photographer and get your picture taken

Write your one-page biography

Write a story synopsis for your book

Make a list of 10 sample questions

Make a list of potential "advance praise" writers

Gather related articles or past media clippings

Create your publicity timeline

Put your press kits together

Create mailing labels

Determine the correct postage

Mail out the press kit materials

Begin follow-up calls/pitching

Keep a running status report and mail log sheet

Do it all over again for round two

Be prepared for the unexpected

Stay on top of your plan.

Timeline for Literary Publicity: The Final Chapter

The timeline for this book is similar to the one outlined in Chapter 10. There are two exceptions. The first is that I am not planning on doing any book signings, so that will be taken off the timeline. And the months will, of course, be different. The exact date I will begin will depend on the exact date of publication. If the February 2001 date holds, I will begin my publicity plan in late October or very early November. I have to add extra weeks to execute this publicity plan because of the holidays in November and December. I will have to make up time for the two or three weeks the media will be focused on other things. The media also takes vacations during this time, too, just like us.

Other than these two alterations, the plan is the same as described Chapter 10.

A Sample Pitch Script

Remember always to speak in a very friendly, conversational voice. Speak clearly and *quickly!* Try not to make it sound like you're reading a script. Make it as conversational as possible. I like to have this typed out in a large font, just so I don't lose my place. You'll probably only need this for your first few calls. After that, you'll probably have it memorized and won't need it. You should keep it handy anyway, just in case you get distracted for a second. It'll help you get back on track.

———————

Hi, Bob, this is John Smith and I'm calling regarding materials I sent you on <u>DATE</u> regarding the book, Literary Publicity: The Final Chapter. *I wanted to make sure you received them and wanted to find out if you would like a review copy. I thought your (readers/listeners/viewers) would be interested in this book because it seems that everyone is writing a book these days and I thought it might be fun to give your (readers/listeners/viewers) a behind-the-scenes look at how publicity helps get books media coverage and on the best-seller lists. If you'd like more information, please feel free to contact me at <u>PHONE NUMBER</u>. Thanks, Bob, and I hope to hear from you soon.*

———————

Keep the main idea to one sentence, if possible. This is called a **slug line** in film scripts. Make sure you can boil your book down to one sentence.

You have only 15 to 20 seconds to get your point across. Any longer than that and they'll hit the delete button on their voice mail.

Practice this a bunch of times before doing the real thing.

Just adapt this for additional follow-up calls (e.g., *Hi, Bob, this is John Smith again. I was wondering if you've had time to look over the materials ...*).

A Media Alert

You may need to write a media alert if you are giving a lecture, making a public appearance, or doing a book signing. As you know, a media alert is a one-page notice sent to all local media to alert them to something you think they should cover on their television programs or in their newspapers. It is short and to the point. If they need more information, they'll call you, I promise. It includes the who, what, when, where, why, and how information they need to determine if they want to send out a reporter or camera crew.

A media alert should be clear and easy to understand. Don't get into too much detail. Also, make sure it's on your letterhead.

This is what is looks like:

LITERARY PUBLICITY: THE FINAL CHAPTER

by Joseph Marich Jr.

MEDIA ALERT!

FOR IMMEDIATE RELEASE   Contact: Name
February 14, 2001   310-555-1212

WHO: Joseph Marich Jr., author and internationally renowned professional publicist.

WHAT: Public appearance to celebrate the launch of his new book,
Literary Publicity: The Final Chapter.

WHEN: Saturday, September 15, 2001, from 7:00P.M.–9:00P.M.

WHERE: The Bookstore, 555 Main Street, Anytown, California

BACKGROUND:

Using his more than 10 years of professional public relations experience,
Joseph Marich Jr. shows new authors how to create their own "publicity
machine" and get media attention for their books in his new book, *Literary
Publicity: The Final Chapter* (Delmar, March 2001). In this easy-to-read, step-
by-step book, authors will learn how to target the right media, develop an
effective publicity plan, create an interesting and informative press kit—and
"do-it-yourself!" Marich works with world-renowned author/director/pro-
ducer, Michael Crichton, and has worked with many music industry giants as
well as many first-time authors.

ALL CAMERA CREWS ARE WELCOME!

#

Web Site Design

I've spent a day or two designing a Web site for this book. As I stated earlier, I'm going to add this directly to my company's existing Web site. Here's what I came up with. I want to make it very clear that I did not have any help with the design of this Web site—which may become glaringly obvious as we go through this. I'm no more skilled than you are with this stuff, and probably a lot less, in fact. That's why I usually hire someone else. What I can tell you is that I'm going to be much nicer to Web designers from now on. This was absolutely maddening, as well as very time-consuming! I hope you're better at this than I am or that you know someone who is.

The first thing I had to come up with was a header, kind of like the letter-head for the Web site. I tried to match the font style of the actual book. The one thing I didn't do is putz around with color choices, because this book is going to be printed only in black and white—why bother? For yours, you can pick from tons of different colors to make your Web site snazzy.

The header looks like this:

> **LITERARY PUBLICITY:**
> **THE FINAL CHAPTER**
>
> **by Joseph Marich, Jr.**

It's simple. It's contrasty and bold. It's divine.

Next, I had to develop the navigation bar. This took some preplanning. I needed to figure out how many Web pages I wanted and what they were going to say. I settled on six pages. (I couldn't fit a seventh across the top, either!) These six pretty much cover what I would want a consumer or media person to learn about the book online.

> **LITERARY PUBLICITY:**
> **THE FINAL CHAPTER**
>
> **by Joseph Marich, Jr.**

MAIN SYNOPSIS BIO PRESS RELEASES CONTACT PHOTOS

Since one can't have a bunch of blank pages, I had to come up with content for the main page. This is a short little ditty about the book. If they like what they read, they'll click around the Web site to find out more. To give you a timeframe, these first three steps and conceptualizing the whole thing took me about seven hours to develop and complete. The hardest part was creating the header. I tried a bunch of other designs that I absolutely hated before I came up with this. (Yes, this was the best of the bunch, if you can believe it. Scary, huh?)

LITERARY PUBLICITY: THE FINAL CHAPTER

by Joseph Marich, Jr.

MAIN SYNOPSIS BIO PRESS RELEASES CONTACT PHOTOS

If you're looking at this Web site, you're probably just finished writing a book and are wondering, *"Now what?"*

Literary Publicity: The Final Chapter, written by professional literary publicist, Joseph Marich Jr., takes the author through the entire publicity process, from concept to reality. Writing the most media-friendly book, the right targeting media, writing a press release, and contacting the media in the most effective manner are all discussed in great detail in this fun and informative book. There are no other books like this on the market. There are any great marketing books, but few (if any) publicity books specifically designed to show authors how to do their own publicity—step-by-step.

The next page is the synopsis page. It's exactly that: It gives a short synopsis of the book. Yours may be shorter or it may be longer. Just don't make it too detailed. You want them to buy the book (or write about it), not tell them the whole story and all of its subplots. Entice them!

LITERARY PUBLICITY: THE FINAL CHAPTER

by Joseph Marich, Jr.

MAIN SYNOPSIS BIO PRESS RELEASES CONTACT PHOTOS

Literary Publicity: The Final Chapter is a fun, easy-to-read, step-by-step publicity guide specifically written for new authors. The book is divided into three sections. The first section gives a detailed account of the concepts underlying publicity. It explains the differences between advertising, marketing, and publicity, which are many. It also allows authors to decide who should actually create and execute the publicity for their book. Once they've decided to do it themselves, the first section helps them to learn about the different types of media and how these concepts in a practical and effective way.

The second section of the book puts these concepts into practice. This section is broken down into a step-by-step format, with several examples, allowing the author to see how this whole process works, from a practical perspective. It shows authors how to create a media database, write a press release and the other collateral materials needed for a press kit, how to pitch the media effectively, and what to do once they book an interview—everything they will need to create their own publicity campaign.

The third section is a real-life case study in action. Readers can see how a professional publicist would create a publicity campaign for the very book they are reading! It also serves as an example of a publicity campaign for a nonfiction book.

Next, I thought I'd tell everyone about myself. As I started getting more confident with the design stuff, I came up with some jazzy ideas. Notice the navigation bar. I think it looks better in those little boxes. It took me forever to figure out how to do it, but I think it was worth the trouble. It also occurred to me that putting a title on each page wouldn't hurt either, so I added "Author's Biography" at the top. This way you can easily tell which page you're on without guessing. It's starting to look more balanced and clean, I think. If I knew how to do it, I would keep the header, navigation bar, and title stationary and have the text scroll up and down. I don't know how to do that, so I'll have to take my Web site designer friend, Laurie, out to dinner and beg for help.

| MAIN | SYNOPSIS | BIO | PRESS | RELEASES | CONTACT | PHOTOS |

AUTHOR'S BIOGRAPHY

Joseph Marich Jr. is founder and president of Marich Communications, Inc. With an emphasis in literary, entertainment, and consumer publicity, Marich has worked in public relations for more than 10 years, planning and executing national and international campaigns for more than 30 book launches; special events, fundraisers, and openings in the theater, art, fashion, television, and film industries. He has worked with major publishing houses such as Knopf, Warner Books, Simon & Schuster, Henry Holt, Ballantine, HarperCollins, and Delacorte Press.

Representing author-director-producer, Michael Crichton *(Disclosure, Jurassic Park)*, Marich coordinates media tours (domestically and internationally), personal appearances, interviews, and press kit production for Dr. Crichton, working closely with his publishers at Knopf and Ballantine in New York, as well as his international publishers throughout Europe. He continues his public relations duties for his top-rated television series, "ER," with Warner Television and for Crichton's latest business endeavor, Timeline Computer Entertainment, which is developing CD-ROM and Internet games.

Marich has also been involved in public affairs and crisis management for all the Warner Music Group labels and has provided counsel to Virgin Records, United Talent Agency, and Oracle Corporation, bringing special skills to the clients by preparing them in media training, special-projects presentations, and developing and producing electronic media kits for satellite feeds.

Before starting his own company, Marich worked as a special events producer for The Donahue Group in Beverly Hills, as director of the Literary Division at Rachel McCallister & Associates Public Relations, and for Edelman Public Relations Worldwide in their entertainment division. At McCallister, Marich worked with such distinguished clients as Rock the Vote, DC/Marvel Comics, New Line Television, and Alliance Communications. Virgin Records, Oracle Corporation, and United Talent Agency were among his clients at Edelman Public Relations.

This is Marich's first (and probably last) foray into professional writing.

I got one step fancier on the "Press Release" page. I decided to box the text in. I like how it looks, I don't know why. I also tried to recreate the exact press release in case the media want to download it as is. You should also notice that

the "contact name" line should be on the same line as "For Immediate Release."
Again, my skills are not that good. I'm told you have to create a ".gif" picture of
a blank box as a placeholder to push the text over on the same line. There is

LITERARY PUBLICITY: THE FINAL CHAPTER

by Joseph Marich, Jr.

| MAIN | SYNOPSIS | BIO | PRESS | RELEASES | CONTACT | PHOTOS |

PRESS RELEASE

<u>FOR IMMEDIATE RELEASE</u>
February XX, 2001

Contact: Name / 310-555-1212

**IF YOU WANT YOUR BOOK TO BE A BEST-SELLER, JOSEPH MARICH
JR., PUBLIC RELATIONS EXPERT, SHOWS YOU HOW IN *LITERARY
PUBLICITY: THE FINAL CHAPTER.***

You finally finished writing the final chapter of your book and you think
you're done, right? Wrong! You've really only just begun. You have one more
chapter and it is called: Literary Publicity. That is your final chapter. With
over 10 years of professional public relations experience, **Joseph Marich
Jr.**, shows new authors how to create their own "publicity machine" and
get media attention for their book in his new book, ***Literary Publicity:
The Final Chapter*** (Delmar, March 2001). In this easy-to-read, step-by-step
book, authors will learn how to target the right media, develop an effective
publicity plan, create an interesting and informative press kit—and "do-it-
yourself!"

"I wanted to create a book that would help aspiring authors, who may not
be able to afford a professional publicist, do their own publicity," says
Marich. "I wanted to give them a practical tool, like a dictionary, that they
can keep on their desk and refer to whenever the need arises." With the
thousands of books written every year, it is vital that authors understand
the publicity process—the media can make or break a book, no matter
how well-written it is. Understanding this process will give new authors an
edge.

(MORE)

(Literary Publicity, page 2)

The process of creating an effective publicity plan is no great secret. It just takes a basic understanding of some publicity principles, some writing skills, a lot of time, and an unlimited supply of determination. A little cash doesn't hurt, either. *Literary Publicity* is equally useful to novice and more established authors.

The process is the same—only the media changes. New authors may start by getting local media coverage for their book, while more established authors may move up to national coverage.

Literary Publicity: The Final Chapter takes the author through the entire publicity process, from concept to reality. It includes writing the most media-friendly book, targeting the right media, writing a press release, and contacting the media in the most effective manner. There are no other books like this on the market. There are many great marketing books, but few (if any) publicity books specifically designed for authors.

Marich has over 10 years' experience working for major public relations firms. His clients have included many corporations, product lines and services, film and television productions, and even more authors. Marich is the president of Marich Communications Inc., located in Beverly Hills, California, where his firm specializes in literary, entertainment, and consumer public relations.

If you would like more information or a review copy, or would like to arrange an interview, please contact NAME at 000-555-1212, or via e-mail at jmarich@pacbell.net.

# # #

no such thing as "tab" in HTML (the computer program used to create Web sites). I'm thinking about paying someone a lot of money to create this tab thing. I'd probably make more money on that than on writing this book. Laurie will be well-fed by the end of this.

And then we have more fancy-schmancy footwork. Check out the navigation bar on my "Contact Information" page. I think it looks *way* better with a black background and white letters, just like the header. FYI: I thought of this while I was eating lunch. Pizza was my muse.

Last, but not least, the "Photos" page. Here's where you have to include high-resolution photos of your jacket art and your headshot. You should thumbnail each of these pictures so the media can click on them to download a

LITERARY PUBLICITY: THE FINAL CHAPTER

by Joseph Marich, Jr.

MAIN | SYNOPSIS | BIO | PRESS | RELEASES | CONTACT | PHOTOS

CONTACT INFORMATION

Listed below is contact information for the author:

e-mail address

name@serviceprovidename.com

Snail Mail

NAME
ADDRESS
CITY, STATE, ZIP CODE

– OR –

NAME
C/O PUBLISHING HOUSE NAME
ADDRESS
CITY, STATE, ZIP CODE

---

bigger version of them. Make sure the bigger versions are 300 dots per inch (dpi), or it will look grainy when a magazine tries to reproduce it in print. This is a bit tricky, so you may want to ask someone to help you out for this page. Photos have to be scanned and embedded into the HTML program.

As my jacket art has not been designed as of this writing, I have used place-holders for the two pictures.

That's it! It only took me 14 hours, 2 packs of cigarettes, 4 pots of coffee, and a lot of hair-pulling.

I would rather have licked a couple hundred envelopes.

LITERARY PUBLICITY: THE FINAL CHAPTER

by Joseph Marich, Jr.

MAIN | SYNOPSIS | BIO | PRESS | RELEASES | CONTACT | PHOTOS

PHOTOS

Click on the thumbnail to download a high-resolution (300 dpi) version of the photo.

JACKET

ART

HERE

HEAD

SHOT

HERE

FINAL
THOUGHTS

Well, authors, we've come to the end of the book. I sincerely hope I've given you some useful pointers about publicity, the media, and what you can do to start promoting your book.

I hope I have included most of the practical information you'll need to do this on your own. I've tried to keep it clear and concise to allow you to follow the steps more easily. I've also tried to inject a little humor into this, in hopes that humor will anchor some of the more tedious, but necessary, concepts of literary publicity and a publicity campaign. If any of my humor has offended any of you readers, my sincere apologies—it was absolutely unintentional. In school, I always hated reading textbooks that could have been written by the British. I didn't want to write one of those. I hope you enjoyed reading some parts of this, at least.

Any errors and omissions are strictly accidental. The concepts and ideas that I have put down on paper here are the ones that I have found work best for me. If you ask another publicist, you will get slightly different answers. Each of us has our own way of doing things. One is not better than the other, they're just different. Use the system that makes the most sense to you.

To the best of my knowledge, nothing in here breaks any state or federal laws. Nor is any information contained herein copyrighted in any other publication. All of this came out of my own head (for better or worse), filtered through my own experiences.

Try not to absorb all of this at once. Read a section, think about it for a while and then go on to the next section. I've managed to cram a ton of information into this book. I am confident that the big picture will become clear as to how all these elements fit together, over time. Some of this stuff took me years to comprehend, so give yourself a break and just a little time. Take it one step at a time. And keep your sense of humor.

I hope you've enjoyed reading this as much as I've enjoyed preparing it for you. Again, I wish you good fortune and good luck on your project and your career.

GLOSSARY

Advertising: A controlled, for-pay, means of notifying the public about a product or service.

Bio: Written biography used by the media to get background information on the author.

Big-Mouth List: PR jargon meaning a list of well-connected people who will talk about your product or service.

Breaking News: Timely news that the media are bringing to the public with a sense of urgency or importance.

Bumper Card: A still image used by TV stations when cutting to or returning from commercial breaks.

Buzz: In publicity terms, the result of a successful publicity campaign—media and consumers talking about a product or service in positive terms.

Collateral Materials: The materials to include in a press kit, such as a bio, synopsis, photo, and so on.

Cover: PR jargon meaning that a media outlet has or will write or talk about a product or service.

Demographic Information: The set of characteristics that describe who is reading a newspaper or magazine, listening to a radio program, or watching a television program, such as age, sex, race, location, and salary range.

Electronic Media: Television and radio and sometimes the Internet.

Electronic Press Kit (EPK): A short pre-produced video created for a client and sent to television media outlets that explains, in video form, similar items covered in the print press kit.

Evergreen: Usually refers to a topic that can be reported on at any time of the year.

Fax Blast: The faxing of a media alert to all appropriate media during a short window of opportunity.

Glam Shot: A highly dramatic photo style (a.k.a. glamour shot).

Hit: PR jargon meaning that a media outlet has written or talked about a product or service.

In-House Publicist: A publicist who works directly for a publishing house.

Intangible Results: The results from a publicity plan that may not be immediately evident.

Jacket Artwork: The cover of a book.

Lead: The first paragraph of a press release containing all pertinent information: the who, what, where, when, why, and how.

Lead Time: Generally refers to the amount of advance time a media outlet needs to report on a story.

Local Media: Media that are read, seen, or heard throughout a city.

Market Classifications: The general "types" of media a publicist wants to contact by subject category. Similar to book genres.

Market Penetration: Getting into or reaching new stores or new consumers.

Marketing: The plan of action taken to get the product or service to market.

Media Alert: A one-page document typically faxed to the media as a reminder to cover a certain event.

Media Outlet: A specific newspaper, television, or radio program or magazine.

Media-Friendly: PR jargon meaning a product or service that the media is likely to cover.

Mediagenic: PR jargon coined a few years back based on the term *photogenic*. Similar to media-friendly.

National Media: Media that are read, seen, or heard throughout the country.

Outside Publicist: A publicist who is not a direct employee of the client.

Phoner: Industry lingo for a radio interview conducted by phone.

Print Media: Newspapers and magazines and sometimes newsletters.

Proof Sheet:A sheet of photo paper with rows of developed film printed on the page, used to select the promotional photo the author wants to use.

Public Relations: The managing, creating, and positioning of a client's reputation, visibility, and image.

Publicity: The means of generating interest and excitement about a product or service, usually through media or public appearances.Also a tactic or subsection of public relations.

Publicity Plan: A preconceived course of action that outlines the order in which the publicist will execute specific tasks to generate interest in his client's product or services by the media and the consumer.

Regional Media: Media that are read, seen, or heard throughout a small portion of the country.

Search Engine:Web sites used as a means of searching and sorting through the information available on the internet.

Sweeps: The three times a year when national and local television stations determine new rates for advertising on their programs, based upon viewership during a month-long period in November, February, and May.

Synopsis:A brief outline or overview of your book, usually one short page.

Talking Head: PR jargon meaning an expert appearing on television.

Tangible Results: The results from a publicity plan that can be linked directly to an action taken as prescribed by your publicity plan.

Target Market: The specific group of media or consumers thought to have interest in a product or service.

Target Media: The list of media a publicist feels is appropriate to contact on behalf of the client.

Trend: In media terms, a topic that is being covered by the majority of media outlets, usually for a short period of time.

Video News Release (VNR):The video version of a printed press release created for the client that contains a fully pre-packaged and tightly edited news story with the desired story angle, appropriate voice over and on-screen identifiers. It also contains 5-10 minutes of b-roll or raw footage that the news television stations can use to cut their own version of the story.

INDEX

NOTES